Terrorism and Peacekeeping

Terrorism and Peacekeeping

New Security Challenges

Edited by
Volker C. Franke

Foreword by General Joseph P. Hoar, USMC (Ret.)

PRAEGER

Westport, Connecticut
London

Library of Congress Cataloging-in-Publication Data

Terrorism and peacekeeping : new security challenges / edited by Volker Franke; foreword by Joseph P. Hoar.
    p. cm.
  Includes bibliographical references and index.
  ISBN 0–275–97645–9 (alk. paper)—ISBN 0–275–97646–7 (pbk. : alk. paper)—ISBN 0–275–98559–8 (instructor's manual)
    1. Terrorism—Government policy—United States. 2. War on Terrorism, 2001–
3. National security—United States. 4. Peacekeeping forces—United States.
I. Franke, Volker, 1963–
HV6432.T446   2005
355.3'57—dc22   2004017329

British Library Cataloguing in Publication Data is available.

Library of Congress Catalog Card Number: 2004017329
ISBN: 0–275–97645–9
    0–275–97646–7 (pbk.)
    0–275–98559–8 (instructor's manual)

First published in 2005

Praeger Publishers, 88 Post Road West, Westport, CT 06881
An imprint of Greenwood Publishing Group, Inc.
wwww.praeger.com

Printed in the United States of America

The paper used in this book complies with the
Permanent Paper Standard issued by the National
Information Standards Organization (Z39.48–1984).

10 9 8 7 6 5 4 3 2 1

Contents

Tables and Maps

Tables

Maps

Foreword

As a young Marine Corps officer, I was sent to Vietnam to fight in a war that was part of our nation's strategy to contain communism and eventually to win the Cold War. For nearly fifty years, American security policy centered on deterrence of a well-known enemy and the development of contingency responses to a possible Soviet attack against the United States or our European allies. Our involvement in Southeast Asia was considered part of this larger strategy that allowed for well-crafted and rehearsed foreign policy and military responses.

With the collapse of the Soviet Union, we have lost much of the predictability that had defined the international system and U.S. national security since World War II. But the end of the Cold War has also left the United States in a unique position to assert moral leadership, assure stability, and help shape an international order favoring democracy and prosperity. That has required prudence and care not to overstretch the boundaries of our superpower status.

Yet the tragic events of September 11, 2001, shattered notions of predictability and have thoroughly altered the way we will live our lives. They have also illustrated that America's global vision is not shared uniformly in all parts of the world. Today, we are faced with new challenges and a new war. Unfortunately, the "war on terrorism" obscures many of the underlying problems we face going forward. Terrorism is not an ideology comparable to communism, nor is it a political movement; it is a technique used to achieve various political or military results.

Consequently, we cannot simply assume that the tactics and strategies that served us well during the Cold War will also be appropriate to address new security realities. Our government failed to define correctly the nature of the war in Vietnam. A similar failure in the war on terrorism or in responding to the many emerging security challenges would very likely result in far more devastating consequences.

The threat of terrorism will likely persist for decades, as will accompanying uncertainties. September 11, 2001, was a wake-up call; it demonstrated the urgency to find new and innovative ways to respond to emerging problems and to protect and defend the United States from a growing range of threats. Iraq, Afghanistan, Bosnia, and the numerous other U.S. commitments have stretched the military painfully thin and make it difficult to respond adequately to crises in other hotspots around the globe. In addition to the heavy burden expanding operational commitments place on our troops—both active duty and reserve—and their families, they also divert economic resources from homeland security needs and the effort to combat terrorism and redirect money away from other important policy priorities.

The dangers we face today do not come from traditional adversaries of the past, such as Russia or China, but rather from failing states, such as North Korea, Somalia, Rwanda, Haiti, Bosnia, or Colombia. Other dangers arise from non-state actors such as terrorist groups or international crime cartels and are aggravated by global problems such as environmental degradation, scarce resources, proliferation of weapons of mass destruction, ethnic and civil conflicts, and humanitarian disasters.

In responding to these new realities, we must be careful not to overextend our military, neglect other policy priorities, or alienate our friends in the international community. Providing global leadership does not entail imposing our moral, political, and cultural values on others. Regardless of how long the war on terrorism lasts or the effort required to rebuild war-torn nations, America must demonstrate that its goal is not to be an imperial power or impress its will anywhere it chooses.

Indeed, the challenges are mounting and policymakers need to be prepared to confront them aggressively and wisely. In this volume, Volker Franke has compiled a series of case studies depicting the new realities that will aid this preparation. These cases place readers in the middle of the processes that lead to many of the decisions that have shaped American foreign and national security policy in recent years. They are invaluable instructive tools for both students of the national security decision-making process and practitioners who will be charged with making these security decisions in the future.

Responding to the security challenges of the twenty-first century requires creative thinking, new ideas, and adaptable strategies. Predetermined answers based on the rigid and automated containment strategies utilized during the Cold War no longer ensure peace and stability in a shrinking global world. The detailed analyses provided by Franke's book challenge readers to confront situations, consider their context and implications, and decide on courses of action with outcomes that have significant global implications.

These are challenging times that require our national leaders to readily adapt to rapidly changing decision demands and to develop creative solutions to emerging security needs. This book contributes innovatively to the training and preparation of these leaders and provides a valuable teaching tool for a variety of classroom settings.

General Joseph P. Hoar, USMC (Ret.)
Former Commander in Chief, U.S. Central Command (1991–1994)

Preface and Acknowledgments

Security during the Cold War meant deterring and containing a well-known enemy in order to prevent thermonuclear war. With the end of the Cold War security realities have changed. Today, U.S. forces are increasingly charged with asymmetric warfare and fighting terrorism or with humanitarian relief and peacekeeping missions. These new realities show the need for rethinking the strategies that have traditionally informed national security decision making. This book examines management, leadership, and accountability issues in the context of shifting global security requirements. Placed at the center of difficult decisions, each chapter challenges readers to develop strategies to satisfy future operational requirements most effectively and efficiently.

The purpose of *Terrorism and Peacekeeping*—and its compendium volume *Security in a Changing World: Case Studies in U.S. National Security Management* (Praeger, 2002)—is to aid the preparation of national security and foreign policy decision makers for facing a widening array of security challenges and, more generally, to improve the understanding of readers interested in national security–related policy issues. The case studies and exercises included in this volume were initially developed for National Security Studies (NSS), a partnership between Syracuse University's Maxwell School of Citizenship and Public Affairs and Johns Hopkins University's Paul H. Nitze School of Advanced International Studies (SAIS). Funded through a Department of Defense contract, National Security Studies provides executive education course offerings in national security management, leadership, and decision making to help prepare defense executives and senior military officers for the challenges of a changing global security context.

All cases compiled in this volume have been used successfully in a number of National Security Studies courses and in a variety of advanced undergraduate and graduate courses in international affairs, U.S. foreign policy, national security policy, journalism, public policy and administration, leadership, and management. In addition to traditional academic audiences, this book also should be of great interest to national security practitioners and to students in executive education or mid-career programs in public administration, leadership, and management. All case studies have been classroom tested—typically in a graduate seminar and in at least one of the National Security Studies executive education courses. Classroom testing ensures that cases achieve their pedagogical goals and learning objectives. Class participants provided extensive evaluations on the quality of each case and its effectiveness in outlining and discussing particular policy dilemmas. In addition to classroom tests, all case manuscripts were reviewed by specialists from academia and practitioners with considerable expertise in the area of national security.

Case development, testing and review, and ultimately, the realization of this book, would not have been possible without the enthusiasm, commitment, and dedication of the many individuals who contributed their time, resources, and efforts to this endeavor. Apart from the case authors, I am most grateful to Colonel F. William Smullen, III, the director of National Security Studies, whose commitment to excellence and dedication to expanding our horizons of strategic thinking have greatly influenced many of the cases included in this volume and will chart an exciting future for the NSS program. In addition, I would like to express my gratitude to The Honorable Sean O'Keefe who, as NSS director from 1996 until 2001, provided vision to the program and conceptualized and gave shape to its case studies component. Both the National Security Studies program and the case development component benefited invaluably from the services of Kathleen Millson, the program's senior administrator, without whose energy and devotion, professional dedication, organizational skills, and great sense of humor the program and this volume would be lacking in many ways. Finally, I would like to express my gratitude to Andrew Bacevich, William Banks, Mehrzad Boroujerdi, Steven David, L. Paul Dube, Tom Keaney, Melvin Levitsky, Mary Schumacher, and Jeffrey Straussman for their dedicated efforts in supplying countless reviews of case manuscripts.

Introduction

VOLKER C. FRANKE

In the fall of 1989, people all over the world celebrated the fall of the Berlin Wall and rejoiced over the newfound freedom of people all over Eastern Europe. It seemed to many as if the world had changed overnight. The historian John Lewis Gaddis, for instance, commented that the end of the Cold War was an earthquake-like event that "revealed deep and hitherto hidden sources of geopolitical strain."[1] Indeed, the collapse of the Soviet Union seemed to ring in a new era promising peace, cooperation, and prosperity. President George H. W. Bush, in an address to the United Nations General Assembly in October 1990, went so far as to predict "a very real prospect of a new world order." The United Nations, freed from the Cold War stalemate, he argued, was finally in a position to fulfill "the historic vision of its founders"[2] and "unite [its] strength to maintain international peace and security."[3]

But these exciting opportunities came at a price. Although the end of the Cold War has removed the threat of global thermonuclear holocaust, it has not left a world without dangers. In the last decade, we stood witness to natural disasters and famine, ethnic strife, civil wars, genocide, mass migration and floods of refugees, the spread of infectious diseases, and the proliferation of varying kinds of weapons of mass destruction. In addition, the nature of war itself is changing. Throughout the Cold War, much of America's national defense rested on the assumption that enemies would not attack the United States for fear of an overwhelming retaliatory response. Regrettably, asymmetric warfare and terrorism have now become prevalent threats to U.S. national security, as evidenced by the attacks against U.S. military installations in Saudi Arabia in the mid-1990s, the embassy bombings in Kenya and Tanzania in 1998, the attack on the USS *Cole* in the Aden harbor in October 2000, and, most tragically, the terrorist attacks on the World Trade Center and the Pentagon on September 11, 2001.

These new realities have fundamentally changed the global context within which America's military and its defense and security establishment must operate. With these new realities come new demands on the use of force. While military strength will unquestionably remain an essential instrument of American foreign policy, diplomacy and economic power become increasingly important for successful accomplishment of a widening range of functions, roles, and missions including disaster relief and humanitarian assistance, sometimes vaguely defined peacekeeping and peace enforcement missions, and, most recently, nation building efforts.

President Bush, in a speech before the U.S. Congress a few days after the September 11 attacks stated that the world, once again, had changed overnight.[4] The question of whether or not this change occurred overnight or whether the September 11 attacks reflect the culmination of a decade-long development is largely academic. What is clear, however, is the fact that the United States is faced with a series of emerging threats that require new ideas, strategies, and measures. It is in part the purpose of this book to assess the nature of some of these threats and present the dilemmas and challenges posed by them. The case studies presented here will not provide clear-cut answers, but rather they are intended to encourage readers to reflect on the current context of U.S. national security and to weigh the costs and benefits of various strategies and measures designed to complete missions successfully and effectively and to counter the growing array of emerging threats.

Given the events of September 11, 2001, and their still-unfolding aftermath, one may question the value of reading historical and projective case studies. The terrorist attacks are forever changing the nature of security and indeed of warfare itself, for the United States and the entire world. Did case studies enable analysts, security practitioners or policymakers to predict the terrorist attacks? Did they help prevent atrocities? Clearly, they did not. Understandably, one may wonder what relevance do cases, some of which reflect the pre-9/11 world, have for readers, be they students of international relations or national security practitioners who sooner or later may be tasked with making clear decisions in an increasingly complex and unclear environment? The answer is simple: the issues presented in the cases contained in this volume are as, or perhaps even more, relevant today than they were before the September 11 attacks. America and its partners face a future that is more uncertain and less predictable, and it is one where choices are no longer binary, informed by relative clear-cut options based on precise analysis.

Instead, national security decisions, today perhaps more than at any other time, demand decision making under terms of uncertainty. The issues presented in the following cases remain pertinent and are not amenable to simple prescriptions. They demonstrate that the value of planning lies not in how well we can predict the future, but how well it prepares us to succeed in a future that we cannot predict. Herein lies the great value of the cases and their utility for use in the classroom of the future.

In light of a rapidly changing international security context, one is likely to ask what is the future of U.S. national security? What strategies and policies will determine how resources are allocated and where and when force is used and troops are deployed? How do emerging security demands—from peacekeeping to countering terrorism—shape national security decisions? How best to manage an increasingly diverse, highly skilled, and more and more specialized force to take on ever more complex challenges? It is these questions, among others, that are at the heart of this book. Although this volume is not intended to provide conclusive answers to these types of questions, it seeks to contribute to the ongoing debate of and spark discussion on a variety of contentious policy issues—the answers to which will have a significant impact on U.S. national security management and leadership in the future.

THE PURPOSE OF THIS BOOK

The aim of this book is to aid the preparation of policymakers and students interested in learning more about pertinent management, leadership, and accountability issues related to U.S. national security. Although the cases collected in this volume revolve around national security–related policy questions, they also illustrate more general policy dilemmas and are designed to stimulate discussion of those issues inside and beyond the classroom. Cases highlight dilemmas at two levels: (1) pertaining specifically to the case (case dilemma) and (2) pertaining to the larger policy implications of the case (policy dilemma). Cases do not provide specific policy recommendations or definite answers for how to resolve these dilemmas. Quite the contrary, they present evidence in support of both (or more) sides of a policy argument and will often leave readers with some discomfort in terms of how dilemmas should be resolved. The absence of a one-sided argument, specific policy recommendations, or "logical" conclusions sets these case studies apart from typical academic publications. The purpose of the cases is for readers to recognize the importance of the issues at hand and their greater policy implications, to relate each case to other course materials, and to discern lessons that might apply to other areas of public policy, administration, and management.

ORGANIZATION OF THE BOOK

The book is divided into three separate parts, reflecting some of the most pertinent issues challenging U.S. national security in the twenty-first century. Case studies presented in Part I address issues emerging from the context of peacekeeping operations. Chapters 2 and 3 portray the difficulties associated with the UN peace operation in Bosnia and the Dayton Peace Accords. In Chapter 2 ("Peacekeeping in Bosnia"), William C. Banks and Jeffrey D. Straussman examine the merits of President Clinton's Balkan strategy. In 1995, within days of Congress voting with veto-proof majority to lift the arms embargo on Bosnia, the Croatian government launched an offensive against its dissident Serbian minority. Neither the Serb government in Belgrade nor Western nations responded, even though the Croatian operation was similar to the "ethnic cleansing" that the Serbs had earlier committed. When the Serbs continued to attack Muslim military positions in Sarajevo, President Clinton authorized air strikes against the Serbs. This blunted Congress's drive to override President Clinton's earlier veto on lifting the arms embargo and effectively brought the warring sides in Bosnia to the bargaining table. The U.S. commitment to a major peace operation in Bosnia serves to illustrate the evolving complexities of the executive/legislative relationship in national security. This chapter assesses the application of the Constitution's war powers to contemporary military operations and the effects of the multilateral operation on U.S. involvement.

In Chapter 3, Thomas A. Keaney and Scott Douglas retrace the steps that led to the Dayton Peace Accord which finally ended hostilities in Bosnia in November 1995. More specifically, "The Road to Dayton" examines the political and military actions taken in Bosnia by UN, NATO, and U.S. participants as they attempted to balance negotiations with the use of military force. It exemplifies the difficulties involved in managing peace operations, particularly those requiring coordination among multinational organizations. The chapter discusses the command-and-control difficulties involved in coalition operations, raises awareness of the complex relationship of force and diplomacy faced by military forces deployed in peace operations, and provides an understanding of the pitfalls endemic in such circumstances.

Chapter 4 moves readers back to peacekeeping in the Western Hemisphere. Theodore S. Wilkinson explores Latin America's oldest and most significant remaining border dispute between Peru and Ecuador. When the fighting erupted once again in 1995, the United States, along with Brazil, Argentina, and Chile, was asked to promise an observer force for the area of border hostilities. Wilkinson examines the policy pros and cons that had to be weighed in Washington in early 1995 before taking on any new peacekeeping adventure, bearing in mind recent American experience in Somalia and U.S. legislative resistance to the deployment of U.S. forces to Bosnia. Wilkinson reviews the guarantors' joint decision on the observer force and discusses the difficulties in getting Peru and Ecuador to negotiate and reach an agreement. The chapter illustrates several policy dilemmas faced by the United States: weighing the costs of sending an observer force against the risks of inaction; orchestrating the four guarantor nations to act in harmony so as to bring pressure on Peru and Ecuador to negotiate and settle; and finding the right mix of political and economic incentives to convince reluctant nationalists on both sides of the dispute to accept the compromise settlement that Presidents Fujimori and Mahuad finally signed in November 1998.

Part II of the book addresses the issue of terrorism and explores the merits of possible responses in the fight against terrorism. In Chapter 5, Andrew J. Bacevich takes readers back a decade in his discussion of the Clinton administration's 1993 response to Iraq's attempted assassination of former President Bush and explores the interaction between senior civilian and military officials that shaped the military options presented to the President. Questions raised by this chapter include: To what degree did the "right" factors receive the attention they deserved? Was the attack a success or a failure? Was the civil-military relationship effective? How should the concept of "proportionality" figure in considering the use of force in situations short of full-scale war?

Remaining in the region, Eliot A. Cohen examines the "Obligations of Leadership" (Chapter 6) resulting from a terrorist attack against a U.S. military installation in Saudi Arabia. On June 25, 1996, a truck bomb exploded at the Khobar Towers apartment complex in Dhahran, Saudi Arabia, leaving nineteen American military personnel dead and injuring hundreds of people from several nations. The bombing resulted in immediate finger-pointing between members of Congress, the Department of Defense (DOD), and the U.S. Air Force. Cohen illustrates the events and their aftermath and explores the nature of accountability and leadership in the United States military. By implication, the events described also raise questions about civil-military relations, the strategic challenges of the post-Cold War era, and the nature of service culture.

William C. Banks takes readers to Africa in Chapter 7 where he examines the effectiveness in "preventing and deterring international terrorism" of the U.S. retaliatory response to the August 1998 Kenya and Tanzania embassy bombings. On August 20, retaliatory strikes were launched at targets in Sudan and Afghanistan. The strikes were the product of a tightly controlled decision process, by a handful of officials. Although the United States acted quickly and firmly, questions and criticisms arose early on. What was the decision process? Was the decision to respond with military force effective? Were the strikes lawful? Will the strikes serve the purpose of deterring further acts of international terrorism? Banks' case raises a number of questions that are central to U.S. national security decision making options for the future: What are the domestic and international legal considerations in deciding whether and how to respond to acts of international terrorism? To what extent must the Congress be involved and what discretion does the Commander in Chief have to act on his own? Legal considerations aside, does the use of force as an instrument of counterterrorism policy pay off? Can the war against international terrorism be won through military means?

Banks revisits this last question in Chapter 8, which specifically examines U.S. military actions during the war in Afghanistan in October 2001. On the first night of the campaign, the United States nearly had a major success. Officials believed that they had pinpointed the location of the supreme leader of the Taliban, Mullah Muhammad Omar. While patrolling the roads near Kabul, an unmanned but armed CIA drone trained its crosshairs on Omar in a convoy of cars fleeing the capitol. Under the terms of an agreement, the CIA controllers did not have the authority to order a strike on the target and, while awaiting approval for the attack, Omar escaped. Proving more successful, on November 3, 2001, a missile-carrying Predator drone killed Mohammed Atef, Al Qaeda's chief of military operations, in a raid near Kabul. Then, in early May 2002 the CIA tried but failed to kill an Afghan factional leader, Gulbuddin Hekmatyar, an Islamic fundamentalist who had vowed to topple the government of Hamid Karzai and to attack U.S. forces. In this chapter, Banks explores a number of issues that are central to the present and likely future national security posture of the United States, ranging from host government co-operation, collateral damage, and the locus of decision authority, to tactical questions about the appropriate uses of technology and weaponry. Among other issues, the chapter reviews the emerging policies and procedures that permit targeting terrorists with lethal force, explores the evolving DOD/CIA relationship in this area, and assesses the legal authorities for and potential limits on targeted killing and the utility of targeted killing in the war on terrorism.

Part III of the book examines a number of other security challenges that have been emerging over the last decade, but that do not fit as easily under the broad categories of peacekeeping or terrorism. In Chapter 9, Laurence Pope discusses the history of and the ideas behind the Iraq Liberation Act (ILA) of 1998. In early 1998, the Clinton Administration was under pressure. Its covert support of mainly Kurdish Iraqi opposition groups based in northern Iraq under the banner of the Iraqi National Congress (INC) had collapsed in 1996 after an attempt by the INC to coordinate an offensive against the Iraqi army ended in a rout, and the imprisonment of hundreds, perhaps thousands, inside Saddam Hussein's gulag and torture machine. This chapter is the account of legislation adopted during this period that, despite opposition by the bureaucracy at State, Defense, CIA, and the NSC staff, was signed into law by President Clinton on October 31, 1998, at one of the weakest moments in his presidency. Without reference to UN Security Council Resolutions, which had been the underpinning of international efforts since the 1990 invasion of Kuwait, the ILA committed the United States to a policy of seeking the overthrow of the Iraqi regime. Pope examines the Clinton administration's (and to some extent the current Bush administration's) response to the Iraq Liberation Act of 1998. The ILA declared it to be U.S. policy to seek the removal of the regime of Saddam Hussein. Despite the fact that America's war against Iraq has ousted Saddam Hussein's regime, this case still proves valuable for its focus on a particular attempt to legislate foreign policy and for exploring the difficulties created by such legislative mandates for the women and men of the executive branch.

At a time when Americans are concerned about terrorism and the war in Iraq, Washington has quietly intensified its war on drugs. In Chapter 10, Volker Franke and Justin Reed examine America's "quiet war" in more detail. The prime target in America's war on drugs is Colombia, the world's leading producer and distributor of cocaine and a significant supplier of heroin to the United States. "Squeezing a Balloon" chronicles a half century of violence in Colombia, describes the nature and magnitude of U.S. involvement in its bloody civil war, and explores connections between America's war on drugs and its more recent war on terrorism. Franke and Reed focus specifically on the merits of Plan Colombia, the Clinton administration–initiated strategy of source-country drug eradication, and the effects and implications of the Bush administration's decision to intensify previous U.S. counter-drug efforts. Questions raised by this chapter include: What threats does Colombia's civil conflict pose to U.S. national security? How does Plan Colombia address those threats? Is Plan Colombia effective in achieving Washington's counter-drug objectives? Are drug interdiction and eradication legitimate national security concerns? How does the war on drugs affect the traditional roles and missions of the U.S. military? Finally, what is the connection between America's drug war and its war on terrorism?

It is becoming increasingly important for American forces deployed to peace operations to collaborate not only with forces from other countries but also with civilian, nongovernmental relief providers. In Chapter 11, Arthur Brooks studies the dilemma between philanthropy and national security based on the example of CARE International. In early 2001, CARE International decided to redesign its fundraising appeals particularly with respect to its longstanding policy of impartiality on political issues—such as the role of the U.S. military. Would an activist stance by CARE against American military activities have an impact on public opinion—perhaps lowering support for military activities—and consequently impact American national security? Brooks describes this dilemma and presents several sources of survey data on national security public opinion and fundraising, which are intended to help illuminate the situation.

In Chapters 12 and 13, W. Henry Lambright examines U.S. space policy since the end of the Cold War, specifically focusing on attempts by the Clinton and Bush administrations to cooperate with international partners, and particularly Russia, in building the International Space Station. As the Clinton administration took power in 1993, national security officials became aware that the Russians were about to transfer rocket technology to India, a move fraught with missile proliferation peril. However, instead of imposing trade sanctions to punish Russia, the Clinton administration decided to bring Russia aboard the International Space Station. This decision marked a turning point of historic significance for space policy. Born out of Cold War rivalry the Space Station now came to symbolize post–Cold War cooperation. Integrating Russia "securitized" the Space Station, linking post–Cold War foreign policy, Big Science, and geopolitics and aided NASA at a critical moment to gain funding to keep the program alive.

Chapter 12 illuminates the role of an agency head, NASA Administrator Daniel Goldin, seeking to move a large-scale technological program forward in the face of conflicting pressures, some of which were his own making. Lambright examines Goldin's ability to combine multiple values, especially international security and domestic budget cutting, while leading a huge and technically demanding project. What constitutes success in this case? Were Goldin's means effective? What did he do right or wrong? Did the very goal of combining security policy and space policy via the Space Station make sense? How was Goldin helped and hindered by President Clinton, the Congress, and the Russians in achieving his goals?

In Chapter 13, Lambright outlines the sequence of decisions that led to the development of the International Space Station which has emerged as a prime model for large-scale cooperation across nations in science and technology. Decision making constituted coalition building and it took much time to assemble a "winning" coalition. Whether successful in the end, the story of the International Space Station provides invaluable lessons about the dynamics of post–Cold War cooperation and the era of globalization. The chapter illustrates these lessons and the tension between U.S. control of a program and deference to other sovereign nations and their claims.

In Chapter 14, John Robinson explores the Department of Defense's struggle with vaccinating its personnel against the anthrax virus. Robinson details the story of Captain Clifton Volpe, a model pilot for the Air Force who consistently received high marks from his commanders. That all changed when Volpe refused a direct order to take a vaccination against anthrax in preparation for a deployment to the Persian Gulf. Although Volpe was only the second active duty pilot to be discharged from service for refusing the shot, his case represents an important flash point in a lingering problem for Department of Defense leaders. As of late 2001, DOD estimated only 350 personnel had been discharged for refusing to take the vaccine. However, some of those discharged, like Volpe, were pilots—a community that is a precious commodity in these days of far-flung deployments. Robinson highlights the unique challenge confronting the DOD for carrying out an effective plan to protect its forces against the threat of biological warfare without diminishing readiness. In addition, the anthrax vaccination plan has sparked an active resistance movement in the ranks, raising questions about the Pentagon's leadership and about the mistrust of the military leadership by rank and file personnel. An overriding concern, and perhaps much deeper challenge, however, is the open questioning of military orders—something that tears at the very fabric of the institution.

Unlike all the previous chapters, Chapter 15 presents a brief simulation exercise that James Blandin designed to explore the relationship between homeland security objectives, threats to homeland security, and the structuring of governmental programs and organizations necessary to achieve homeland security. Participants in the exercise will be challenged to work through this ends-means relationship in sequential fashion in the two parts of the chapter. In Part I, participants are tasked with defining homeland security objectives, identifying the major threats to homeland security and finally, developing a strategy for dealing with these threats. In Part II, participants will use the work developed in Part I as the basis for making recommendations on how to organize federal, state, and local government to provide an effective model for homeland security.

Notes

1. John Lewis Gaddis, "Living in Candlestick Park," *The Atlantic Monthly*, April 1999, p. 66.

2. Robert W. Gregg, *About Face?: The United States and the United Nations* (Boulder, CO and London: Lynne Rienner, 1993), p. 135.

3. Preamble of the United Nations Charter.

4. See http://www.whitehouse.gov/news/releases/2001/09/20010920-8.html.

Part I
PEACEKEEPING

Chapter 2

Peacekeeping in Bosnia

WILLIAM C. BANKS AND JEFFREY D. STRAUSSMAN

In December 1995 hearings before the Senate Appropriations Subcommittee on Defense regarding the U.S. commitment to Bosnia, Chairman Ted Stevens stated: "I oppose this deployment, but . . . it is [not] our prerogative here to debate . . . with the President . . . the President has ordered the deployment . . . we have no way to prevent that."[1] Senator Stevens had come to the view that Congress was powerless to prevent the U.S. commitment of military force to Bosnia, so much so that he seemed to conclude that it was fruitless to debate the wisdom of an operation he opposed. His lament reflects the ongoing evolution of executive/legislative relations in determining and implementing the nation's national security policy. This relationship faces new challenges in the less familiar terrain of the post–Cold War security environment. As regional conflicts, ethnic strife, and humanitarian emergencies have mushroomed in the 1990s, the United States has provided leadership and resources in these emergent conflict situations. The U.S. commitment to a major peace operation in Bosnia serves to illustrate the evolving complexities of the executive/legislative relationship in national security. This case study attempts to assess the critical aspects of this relationship.

There are two parts of the *Peacekeeping in Bosnia* case study. Part A, through the example of the commitment of U.S. military force to Bosnia, considers the application of the Constitution's war powers to many contemporary military operations. In particular, Part A provides some of the domestic historical context to Senator Stevens' opening statement. Part B considers the multilateral aspects of the Bosnia operation, and the effects of the multilateral operation on U.S. involvement.

PART A: THE WAR POWERS OF THE PRESIDENT
AND CONGRESS

In August 1995, events changed and President Clinton's Balkan strategy suddenly seemed vindicated. Within days of Congress voting with veto-proof majorities to lift the arms embargo on Bosnia, the Croatian government launched an offensive against its dissident Serbian minority. Neither the Serb government in Belgrade nor Western nations responded, even though the Croatian operation was similar to the "ethnic cleansing" that the Serbs had earlier committed. With the "clean" ethnic borders more or less in place, Serbia and Croatia appeared finally ready to move toward a settlement of the conflict that plagued the two countries since the breakup of Yugoslavia in 1991. However, when the Serbs continued to attack Muslim military positions in Sarajevo, Clinton was able to advance his alternative to lifting the arms embargo to the Western allies, namely, air strikes against the Serbs. This blunted Congress's drive to override President Clinton's earlier veto on lifting the arms embargo and effectively brought the warring sides in the Bosnian conflict to the bargaining table.

After several weeks of United States–sponsored negotiations at Wright-Patterson Air Force Base in Dayton, Ohio, the principals representing the three factions in Bosnia—Croats, Serbs, and Muslims—initialed a peace agreement on November 21, 1995. Asked whether he would seek congressional authorization before commencing what came to be called Operation Joint Endeavor, President Clinton responded that, while congressional "support" is "important and desirable," he would "reserve [his] constitutional prerogatives" and unilaterally order the operation if congressional "support" is not present.[2] The president was not specific as to which constitutional prerogatives he was referring. When he was asked earlier whether he would veto legislation requiring him to obtain congressional consent before sending ground troops to Bosnia, the president concluded: "[W]henever we are . . . making a decision which might lead to the use of force . . . the Constitution leaves the President . . . the ultimate decision making authority."[3] A few days after the formal signing of the Dayton Peace Accords (DPA) in Paris on December 14, President Clinton ordered the deployment of more than 20,000 U.S. troops as part of a NATO-led Implementation Force (IFOR) of 60,000, charged with patrolling and enforcing a cease-fire and a zone of separation for one year (until December 1996) between the newly created semi-autonomous entities in Bosnia—the Muslim–Croat Federation and the Serb Republic Srpska.

The United States has made a major commitment of military force to a multilateral peace operation. The decision to send troops to Bosnia once again brought to the forefront the continuing constitutional uncertainties concerning the balance of powers between the executive and legislative branches in matters of national security. The following sections review a brief history of how the United States has made decisions to commit the use of military force, describe the emergence of peace operations as a key development in U.S. national security affairs in the 1990s, summarize key developments in the Balkans war up to U.S. participation in a NATO-led force to enforce the Dayton accords, and assess the continuing U.S. role through involvement in a Stabilization Force (SFOR), the follow-on operation to IFOR.

From Muskets and Cannons to Humanitarian Relief Operations

In 1789, Jefferson wrote to Madison that "[w]e have already given . . . one effectual check to the Dog of war by transferring the power of letting him loose from the Executive to the Legislative body, from those who are to spend to those who are to pay."[4] Jefferson was referring, of course, to the framers' decision to vest the power to declare war in the Congress.[5] But he also was celebrating their strategy of cementing the congressional primacy over committing the nation to war through conferring on Congress the power of appropriating money for the exercises of the war power, in the Spending,[6] Army,[7] Navy,[8] and Necessary and Proper[9] Clauses of the Constitution. The package of controls was completed in the Appropriations Clause[10] by its prohibition on spending of public revenues without appropriation, and the Statement and Account Clause[11] by its requirement of a periodic accounting of how public money is spent. Thus, the system put into place by the framers separated the purse from the sword. The power of the purse supplemented the declaration power by allowing Congress to specify or restrict military spending *ex ante*. In the event that such controls failed, Congress was also given the power of supply, permitting Congress to determine through appropriations the magnitude and duration of U.S. involvement in a military engagement.

The framers clearly designed a complex and convoluted set of mechanisms for governing the use of force to make it difficult for the United States to engage in war. To be sure, it was not that the framers believed that the Congress would be more expert than the president in national security affairs. Rather, it was assumed that peace would more likely predominate if the Constitution placed obstacles in the path toward war. The Congress thus supplied a deliberative buffer to hasty action, while its role assured that the gravest decisions made by the nation would be made by those most accountable to the people. The process prescribed by the framers in the Constitution, stated simply, requires presidents to request from Congress authority to commit the United States to a military operation where the use of force is likely. The Commander in Chief may act without congressional authorization only in defense of sudden attack, to conduct a war commenced against us by an enemy, or to effect a time-urgent rescue, evacuation, and protection of American nationals and their property, and hot pursuit of their attackers.[12]

The history of how the United States made commitments to use military force abroad before 1950 was relatively consistent and mostly in keeping with this constitutional design. While there were occasional instances of arguably unconstitutional engagements by Commanders in Chief, most involved minor skirmishes, and none purported to usurp the congressional war power.[13] Indeed, even President Roosevelt's pre–World War II sympathies toward the plight of Europe and his predeclaration efforts to aid the allies were couched in the authorities Congress had granted. For example, Roosevelt answered the French appeal for military assistance this way: "Only the Congress can make such commitments."[14]

The constitutional design began to change with President Truman's unilateral commitment to send U.S. troops to fight a war in Korea. Commanders in Chief following Truman cited their independent constitutional authority (employing Korea as precedent), to deny the congressional primacy in initiating war (sometimes even denying that Congress is empowered to stop a president determined to act), by claiming that fast-breaking crises do not permit the luxury of congressional deliberation, and citing the United Nations and other treaty-based obligations as authorization for their military actions. In addition, changes in the technology and speed of modern warfare have compromised the ability and perhaps the will of Congress to exercise its power over war before the use of force abroad. In this respect, Congress has been relegated to the role of spectator in seminal national security decision making.

When President Bush was asked about his constitutional authority to order Operation Desert Storm without congressional approval, he observed that "history is replete with examples where the President has to take action."[15] One view is that customary law has developed to permit the president to use force without prior congressional approval. In defense of the Vietnam War, the State Department Legal Adviser invoked custom to claim a presidential power "to deploy American forces abroad and commit them to military operations when . . . [he] deems such action necessary to maintain the security and defense of the United States."[16] Thus, the decisions of Presidents Bush and Clinton not to seek congressional authorization before committing U.S. forces to peace operations in Somalia and Haiti may provide a legal precedent for a peace operation in Bosnia.

As the president's actual power over national security increased after the Korean War, and Congress increasingly ceded the initiative, the congressional role in deciding to commit the United States to war shifted from authorization to appropriations, from deciding in advance to grant the authority to act to ratifying or restricting *ex post*. The *ex ante* check on war making became an opportunity for *ex post* review and reaction. On occasion, Congress substantially influenced national security commitments after the fact. In the Southeast Asia War, for example, appropriations restrictions were employed, first to limit the scope of the war through area and use restrictions, and later to bring it to an end.[17]

In the waning years of the Vietnam War, Congress enacted, over Watergate-weary President Nixon's veto, the War Powers Resolution (WPR) of 1973. It was billed as a measure intended to restore congressional participation in national security decision making, through requirements that the president consult Congress before and report to them after deploying troops where hostilities may be imminent. But the political compromises that shaped the final bill resulted in a statute that arguably enhanced rather than reined in presidential power. The WPR unintentionally but apparently authorizes the president to initiate military operations for a period of days so long as the consulting and reporting requirements were followed.[18] Since President Nixon's resignation, presidents since have routinely disregarded or finessed its limited prescriptions without acknowledgment of the Act's constitutionality. Later attempts by Congress to curtail military operations through appropriations restrictions yielded mixed results. These included U.S. operations in Angola through the Clark-Tunney Amendment, in Nicaragua through the Boland Amendments, and in Somalia through a compromise measure arrived at with President Clinton. More often, some members of Congress tried but failed to muster the votes to curtail a military operation that they may not have authorized.

The Emergence of Peace Operations

The first challenge to the U.S. military after the end of the Cold War came in response to Iraq's invasion of Kuwait in 1990. While Operations Desert Shield and Desert Storm succeeded in driving Saddam Hussein from Kuwait, the Gulf War was an aberration among U.S. military engagements in the post-Vietnam era. Instead, the United States has increasingly found itself participating in various peace operations—in Iraq/Kuwait, Somalia, Western Sahara, Mozambique, Haiti, Rwanda, Yemen, and the former Yugoslavia.

Peacekeeping is a generic term to describe a variety of activities that the United States, the United Nations, and other international organizations engage in to encourage, maintain, enforce, or enhance the possibilities for peace. While the term *peacekeeping* gained currency in the 1950s, when the UN began to deploy "interpositional" forces to separate warring sides in a conflict and to supervise the keeping of a signed peace accord, today peacekeeping is used to describe a range of activities: the provision of election monitors, recreating police or civil defense forces for governments, organizing or providing humanitarian relief efforts, monitoring and enforcing cease-fire and other arrangements intended to separate parties in conflict.

Beginning in 1992, the UN began to describe operations where peacekeepers are allowed to use force as "peace enforcement."[19] At about the same time, DOD began to use the term *peace operations* to capture the range of peacekeeping activities, and to categorize peace operations as among its military "operations other than war" (OOTW). The definitional problem is more than mere semantics, however. As the United States learned in Somalia, the use of the term *peace* to describe this range of operations creates the potentially misleading impression that there is no risk of danger, that these operations do not present hostile situations that, to an observer, look a great deal like war. Operation Restore Hope in Somalia changed from the provision of humanitarian assistance to the pursuit of warlords and the eventual firefight that resulted in the death of eighteen U.S. special forces personnel. What had been a general willingness of Americans to participate in international peace operations changed markedly as a result of this episode.

After the Gulf War, where President Bush did seek and obtain Congress's authorization before sending U.S. troops into combat, U.S. forces participated in peace operations in Somalia and Haiti, in both instances without a prior congressional authorization. When President Bush deployed more than 20,000 American forces to Somalia in December 1992 in Operation Restore Hope to create a secure environment for delivering humanitarian relief, few in Congress argued that he should have sought authorization. But when the operation entered a more ambitious phase in March 1993, where a UN Security Council Resolution authorized UNI-SOM II to disarm Somali factions and to assist in economic rehabilitation and promote political reconciliation and help restore political institutions and civil administration throughout Somalia, President Clinton agreed to commit a 2,700-person logistical force and a quick reaction force of about 1,300, again without seeking congressional authorization. With Clinton's approval, command shifted to the UN, and after an ambush that resulted in the death of twenty-four Pakistani peacekeepers in June, UN forces were authorized to apprehend warlord Aideed. President Clinton then deployed Army rangers to Somalia, again without congressional approval, and the operational character changed and hostilities intensified, culminating in the October raid.

In the spring of 1994, and after the Somalia episode, President Clinton approved Presidential Decision Directive (PDD) 25 and, with it, a new set of criteria for governing the circumstances under which the United States would engage in peace operations. Purporting to reject the "assertive multilateralism" of the Bush and early Clinton administrations, in PDD 25 President Clinton sought to define a more limited and restrictive rule for U.S. involvement in peacekeeping. The primary criterion employed in PDD 25 for determining whether the United States will participate in peace operations is whether "there is a threat to or breach of international peace and security."[20] Listed examples of such situations include international aggression, a humanitarian calamity in a violent situation, the sudden interruption of an established democracy, or gross violations of human rights in a violent or potentially violent situation.

In determining whether to commit U.S. troops to a peace operation, PDD 25 asks that decision makers consider whether their presence is essential to an operation's success, that the risks to U.S. troops are acceptable, that resources are available, and that public and congressional support "exists or can be marshaled." Where combat situations may be encountered, the PDD asks whether there is "a determination to commit sufficient forces to achieve clearly defined objectives, a plan to achieve those objectives decisively, [and] a commitment to reassess and adjust"[21] the size, composition, and use of forces as necessary.

While some critics claimed that national security policy guided by the

PDD 25 directive represented a dangerous statement of "assertive multilateralism" that could result in the subordination of U.S. forces and foreign policy prerogatives to the UN, others asserted that the PDD guidelines were either too vague or too restrictive. Still others have maintained that the guidelines will simply encourage U.S. involvement in operations that appear manageable but end up costing more lives and money than U.S. interests merit. Through the period of reassessing the U.S. policies regarding peace operations in 1993 and 1994, several central issues emerged.

Of overriding concern was the suitability of the operation for the U.S. military. This might be characterized as the "does this make sense?" criterion. In addition, involvement in peace operations rephrased the traditional constitutional questions concerning consultation with and authorization from the Congress. In addition to congressional authorization or consultation, PDD 25 was viewed as critical in assessing the U.S. role in peace operations to determine how an operation would be funded— by Congress, or through the UN or other multilateral arrangements. Finally, several operational issues drifted to the forefront of any discussion of peace operations, including the effects of such U.S. participation on the readiness of the military for other operations, the questions of foreign versus U.S. command relationships, the operational tempo effects of peace operations, and the rules of engagement appropriate to these operations.

Fresh from the Somalia experience, Congress began to focus on Haiti long before the president had an operational plan. Still, the president indicated his intention to send troops to Haiti to enforce the Governors Island accord and his unwillingness to seek prior congressional authorization. When last-minute diplomacy against the backdrop of an imminent invasion transformed planned combat operations into an agreed occupation, the crisis was eclipsed.

The recent cases in Somalia and Haiti were in the minds of decision makers as the United States moved toward participation in a peace operation in the former Yugoslavia. How should we interpret the Constitution's allocation of war powers between Congress and the president in the context of this diverse spectrum of military operations? Would the eventual operation in the former Yugoslavia clarify or further complicate the war powers picture?

From Yugoslavia to IFOR

The collapse of the socialist regimes in Eastern Europe and the former Soviet Union between 1989 and 1991 eventually reached Yugoslavia. Yugoslavia dissolved into five republics: Slovenia, Croatia, Bosnia-Herzegovina, Serbia and Montenegro, and Macedonia. Attempts by the Yugoslav federal army to prevent the breaking away of Slovenia and Croatia precipitated the first hostilities in the region after the end of the Cold War. Then, in December 1991, the Muslim Bosnian president asked the European Community to recognize Bosnia-Herzegovina as an independent state, an event that many expected to lead to civil war, given the religious and ethnic makeup of the region—44 percent Muslim, 31 percent Serb, and 17 percent Croat. In April 1992, shortly before formal recognition of the new state by the European Community and the United States, Serb and Yugoslav army forces seized over 70 percent of Bosnia's territory. Serb leaders stated that their goal was for all Serbs to live in either a small Serb-led Yugoslavia, or in a larger, independent Serbia. Serb attacks in the region were thus characterized as "ethnic cleansing" and atrocities against civilian Muslims and Croats were reported in the international press. While Muslims and Croats also fought each other in the early rounds of the conflict, by March 1994, the Bosnian Croats and Muslims agreed to form a federation in Bosnia.

The response to Serbian aggression was set in 1991, temporarily at least, when NATO decided not to intervene in what it regarded as a Bosnian civil war. Instead, the allies defaulted the initiative to the United Nations and in 1992 the UN imposed an arms embargo and insisted on remaining impartial in the face of Serbian atrocities. A UN force deployed to deliver humanitarian aid was charged with the protection of six cities as "safe areas." In March 1993 a "no-fly" zone was enforced over Bosnia-Herzegovina by the UN and NATO, including U.S. forces. The U.S. forces initially assigned F-15 and F-18A fighter aircraft, equipped for combat and ready to fire in self defense. President Clinton reported to Congress on these flights. The U.S. response to the events in Bosnia evolved slowly and unevenly.

In 1993, pursuant to UN and NATO authorization, President Clinton ordered U.S. participation in relief operations, and enforcement of a no-fly zone and an arms embargo. His actions were modest and they did not carry a significant risk to U.S. personnel. The United States acted only as part of a multilateral force, ground forces were not used, and the United States did not take sides in the conflict. Although the president talked of seeking congressional "support," he sought no authorization or appropriation for these actions.

Later in 1993 Congress considered but failed to enact restrictions on military initiatives in Bosnia. President Clinton responded to the proposed restrictions by announcing that he would fight or ignore any attempts to interfere with his foreign policy prerogatives. Then, congressional leaders and the administration compromised on nonbinding "sense of the Congress" statements expressing concern about placing U.S. forces under foreign command. Congress's strongest "sense of the Congress" statement in 1993 was one that maintained that defense appropriations should not be expended for a deployment in support of a peace settlement in Bosnia-Herzegovina "unless previously authorized by the Congress."[22]

NATO leaders contemplated and then initiated additional air strikes in 1994. In February, U.S. fighters shot down four Serbian bombers over Bosnia. In April, U.S. planes bombed Bosnian Serb forces involved in laying siege around the Muslim-held city of Gorazde. In August, U.S. jets again hit Serbian positions, and in November thirty NATO jets, including American planes, bombed Serbian antiaircraft weapons and a Serbian airfield. President Clinton made no effort to seek congressional authorization for these operations. Instead he simply noted in a report to Congress that U.S. forces "participate in these actions pursuant to my constitutional authority to conduct U.S. foreign relations and as Commander in Chief."[23] He further noted that the air strikes were "to support NATO's enforcement of the no-fly zone . . . as authorized by the UN Security Council."[24] As such, the UN and NATO made the policy, and the president, not Congress, made the decision to commit the United States to the operation. The U.S. participation in air strikes and bombing raids on Serbian positions continued through the first half of 1995.

Meanwhile, after considerable Western media attention and public revulsion at the scenes of genocide and stories of rape and barbaric prison camps wrought by Serbian aggression, Congress voted in 1994 in "sense of the Congress" resolutions to lift the arms embargo on Bosnia to permit the Muslim government to defend itself more effectively. In 1995, when Congress eventually required that the embargo be lifted, President Clinton vetoed the bill, asserting that a U.S. decision to lift the embargo would cause the European allies to withdraw their forces from the conflict and, thus, actually make conditions more difficult for the Bosnian Muslims. In his veto message, the president berated Congress for attempting "to regulate by statute matters for which the President is responsible under the Constitution."[25] As the Defense Department appropriation and authorization bills were passed in the fall of 1994, the most that Congress could distill from its debates on the role of the United States in Bosnia was another nonbinding provision, stating the "sense of Congress" that no U.S. funds should be spent on implementation of a peace settlement in Bosnia "unless previously authorized by the Congress."[26]

As the negotiations toward a peace accord proceeded in Dayton in the late summer and fall of 1995, President Clinton indicated to Senate Majority Leader Dole that he would welcome a "strong expression of support"[27] from Congress before committing U.S. forces to the implementation of an accord. While at first he phrased his request as one for "authorization," it was soon modulated to a request for "support" or "approval," all the while maintaining his "constitutional prerogatives in this area."[28] In the weeks before and after the signing of the Dayton Accords and leading up to the actual deployment of U.S. forces on December 20, 1995, both Houses debated whether to support the introduction of U.S. ground forces in Bosnia. On September 29, the Senate passed an amendment to an annual appropriations bill expressing the sense of the Senate that funds provided by the bill should not be used to deploy U.S. combat troops to Bosnia unless Congress first authorized the deployment or the deployment was necessary to evacuate endangered UN peacekeepers.[29] The House passed two measures: a nonbinding resolution stating that such forces should not be deployed without congressional approval, then a flat-out prohibition on the deployment.[30] In the Senate, the debate was heavily influenced by Majority Leader and presidential candidate Dole's statements that "the President has the authority . . . to send these forces. The Congress cannot stop the troop deployment from happening."[31] After the Dayton Accords were made, the Senate declined to approve the House prohibition,[32] and it narrowly defeated a resolution expressing opposition to sending troops to Bosnia. As the peace agreement was being readied for signature in Paris, the Senate passed a resolution supporting the troops but doubting whether it was wise to send them.[33] Similarly, the House passed a nonbinding resolution expressing "serious concerns and opposition to the President's policy,"[34] although it also expressed confidence that the U.S. forces would excel at their task. These disparate resolutions were never reconciled.

On December 15, 1995, the day after the peace agreement was signed in Paris; the UN Security Council authorized the multilateral NATO-led Implementation Force (IFOR) under Chapter VII of the UN Charter. President Clinton promptly ordered the deployment of 22,000 U.S. ground troops to Bosnia, a decision he explained in a letter to Congress on December 21 as being based on his "constitutional authority to conduct the foreign relations of the United States and as Commander in Chief and Chief Executive."[35] The fiscal 1996 Defense Authorization Act, which contained limitations on the President's use of ground forces in Bosnia and on his discretion to secure funds from operational accounts to pay for unbudgeted contingency operations (such as Bosnia), was presented to the President a few days later. In part because of the Bosnia restrictions, President Clinton vetoed the bill and thus caused the objectionable provisions to be dropped from the version that he signed in January 1996.

A Deadline Passes

The Dayton Accords called for IFOR to enforce the peace and to provide a secure environment for other parts of the peace plan to take place. The United States was the major force provider to IFOR, and Americans held the key military leadership positions that conducted the operation. The principal military tasks for IFOR were to mark and monitor a four-kilometer-wide zone of separation between the three factions, patrol the zone of separation, and oversee the withdrawal of forces and weapons away from the zone and to containment areas. When the deployment was begun, DOD listed among "[m]ajor threats to IFOR":

- Indirect fire against unprotected forces
- Land mines, civil disorder, snipers, non-combat losses
- Extremist elements
- Hostage taking for political goals
- Undisciplined local factions

Defense Secretary William J. Perry and Joint Chiefs Chair General John M. Shalikashvili testified that we "must be prepared for casualties."[36] Based on the prior deployment of UN Protective Force (UNPROFOR) personnel in Bosnia, DOD estimated that there would be about fifty casualties in a year's deployment. Among the risks encountered by the troops were problems in identifying friends and foes, land mines (which claimed a U.S. casualty in February 1996), snipers, checkpoint control, and area and perimeter surveillance and protection. Military personnel deployed to Bosnia in IFOR were eligible to receive imminent danger pay. While no U.S. military were killed in combat in Bosnia during IFOR, the risk of casualties remained throughout the operation.

As the one-year anniversary of the deployment approached it became increasingly clear that it was not realistic to expect that the U.S. ground troops' presence in Bosnia would end in a year's time. The decision to delay municipal elections in Bosnia, an integral part of the Dayton Accords and the movement toward a sustained peace, reflected that little progress had been made in transforming the war zone into some form of nation. Most of the political or economic structures necessary for nation building were not yet in place in Bosnia, and the enmity and initiation of violence continued among the three factions. In November 1996, the bloodiest postwar clash between Serbs and Muslims left at least one dead and ten people wounded, when a group of 600 Muslim villagers attempted to return to their prewar homes, located on what is now Serb land. NATO officials opined that Bosnian army officers forced the Muslims to return to the Serb-held village in an effort to provoke the Serbs. In an effort at peace enforcement, U.S. troops raided a Muslim army brigade and a Serb police station and seized weapons and armored personnel carriers.

A report by the independent International Crisis Group concluded in November 1996 that the civilian provisions of the Dayton Accords "are in crisis."[37] Their report noted that indicted war criminals remained at large; leaders earlier held responsible for the outbreak of war had gained new mandates to govern after fraudulent elections; and repatriation of refugees has failed. The IFOR troops were not charged with resolving these problems, only promoting the stability thought necessary to make solutions possible. As the problems persisted, however, the stability forced by armed forces was itself tenuous.

Although no firm commitments were made prior to the November 1996 election day, it seemed likely that only a continuing, probably long-term international ground force, would be able to prevent the rekindling of war. In a November 15, 1996, speech, President Clinton announced that, in place of IFOR, an 8,500-strong Stabilization Force (SFOR) would "in principle" remain in Bosnia until mid-1998. Although Defense Secretary Perry admitted that he erred one year ago in recommending to the president that the objectives of the Dayton Accords could be met in one year, he expressed confidence that the mid-1998 withdrawal target could be met.

Less than a month after the reelection of President Clinton, the administration officially announced the extension of U.S. military involvement in Bosnia. In a letter to congressional leaders President Clinton wrote

In order to contribute further to a secure environment necessary for the consolidation of peace throughout Bosnia and Herzegovina, NATO has approved, and I have authorized U.S. participation in, an IFOR follow-on force to be known as the Stabilization Force (SFOR). SFOR's tasks are to deter or prevent a resumption of hostilities or new threats to peace, to consolidate IFOR's achievements, to promote a climate in which the civilian-led peace process could go forward. Subject to this primary mission, SFOR will provide selective support, within its capabilities, to civilian organizations implementing the Dayton Peace Agreement.[38]

The president indicated that he was reporting "consistent with the War Powers Resolution" and that he ordered U.S. participation in SFOR "pursuant to . . . constitutional authority to conduct U.S. foreign relations and as Commander in Chief and Chief Executive."[39] The new NATO force included 8,500 U.S. troops. It was scheduled to stay until June 1998.

Postscript

On December 18, 1997, President Clinton announced that American troops would stay beyond the June 1998 deadline. When pressed for a new pull-out date, the president said, "I wasn't right, which is why I don't want to make that error again."[40]

PART B: ASSERTIVE MULTILATERALISM AND KEEPING THE PEACE IN BOSNIA

Beginning with President Truman in Korea, to President Bush in Iraq and Somalia, and President Clinton in Somalia, Haiti, and Bosnia, presidents have sought authority for use of military force, not from Congress, but from international and regional organizations, particularly the UN and North Atlantic Council. Even after President Bush decided to seek the support of Congress before taking military action against Iraq, he persisted in the view that he did not need "permission from some old goat in the United States Congress to kick Saddam Hussein out of Kuwait."[41] This part of the case summarizes the legal and political bases for the transformation from congressional to international and multilateral approval for the use of military force, with specific application to the Bosnia campaign.

During the waning days of the 1992 presidential campaign, candidate Bill Clinton praised President Bush's Somalia initiative but criticized him for not acting "urgen[tly] to end the bloodshed" in the Balkans.[42] While neither candidate could then foresee the more complex and difficult path that the Somalia operation would follow in 1993, both men were certainly aware that the prospects for U.S. intervention in Bosnia—in terms of terrain and the military situation on the ground—could make Somalia in comparison seem like a cakewalk.

After the election, when Operation Restore Hope was launched, the media began to speculate and editorialize that either exiting President Bush or President-elect Clinton would take "firm action on that other human and political disaster, Bosnia."[43] President Bush was counseled against any large-scale American involvement on the ground in the former Yugoslavia by General Colin Powell of the Joint Chiefs of Staff and Defense Secretary Dick Cheney. General Powell expressed his caution this way: "What I saw from my perch at the Pentagon was America sticking its hand into a thousand-year-old hornet's nest with the expectation that our mere presence might pacify the hornets. When ancient ethnic hatreds re-ignited in the former Yugoslavia in 1991 and well-meaning Americans thought we should 'do something' in Bosnia, the shattered bodies of Marines at the Beirut airport were never far from my mind in arguing for caution."[44]

As Clinton's inauguration drew near, he certainly did not lack for advice on the subject of Bosnia. Congressional delegations toured the Balkans and came back recommending U.S. participation in enforcement of a no-fly zone over Bosnia, air strikes against Serbian strongholds, and lifting the arms embargo on the Muslim government. More aggressive options were suggested by former State Department Yugoslavia specialist George Kenney and former Air Force Chief of Staff Gen. Michael J. Dugan. In a *New York Times* op-ed, they urged that a U.S.-led coalition of nations arm and train Bosnian Muslim forces in preparation for Operation Balkan Storm.[45]

Although no formal policy was formulated in the first weeks of his presidency, President Clinton announced through Secretary of State Warren Christopher that U.S. support for the continuing UN and European Community efforts at a diplomatic solution to the crisis would include participation in a multilateral military operation to enforce a peace deal. The multilateral ground force idea was thus placed on the table in early 1993. Meanwhile, as diplomacy continued to stall, and the atrocities in the Balkans continued unabated, members of Congress were staking out polar positions. For example, the Democratic chairman of the Senate Foreign Relations European Affairs Subcommittee, Joseph R. Biden, Jr., called for much tougher steps to counter Serbian aggression in Bosnia, including lifting the arms embargo on the Muslims.[46] Democratic Representative Frank McCloskey accused the United States and its allies of sending a "message to the people of Bosnia . . . to stay where you are and reach some compromise with the thugs who are slaughtering you and raping you and starving you."[47] At the other end of the spectrum, as U.S. cargo planes parachuted relief supplies into eastern Bosnia, senior Republican House Armed Services Committee member Floyd Spence expressed concern about putting American lives at risk and argued: "Why should we get involved? Who appointed us as designated hitter?"[48] According to Spence, the administration had embarked upon a policy of open-ended incrementalism: "Are we putting ourselves in a position where we will have little alternative but escalation if the conflict widens?"[49]

As the crisis worsened in the Balkans, some in the U.S. administration believed that someone had to "do something" in Bosnia. From the earliest commitment of relief supplies and their delivery with U.S. cargo planes, to enforcement of the no-fly zone, to air strikes targeted at Serbian militias in Bosnia, to supplying ground troops in IFOR and SFOR, a consideration of overriding importance in determining U.S. policy had been its international legal, political, and strategic dimensions.

The Legal Regime for Multilateral Military Operations

In 1945, the drafters of the UN Charter responded to the devastation of World War II by attempting to circumscribe the unilateral use of force as a means for resolving international disputes, and by fashioning a mechanism to resolve disputes peacefully. Realizing that threats to peace could nonetheless occur, the drafters determined that the UN Security Council could recommend or decide to take collective action, including the authorization to "take such action by air, sea, or land forces as may be necessary to maintain or restore international peace and security."[50] Thus, in Article 43 of the Charter, members agreed "to make available to the Security Council, on its call and in accordance with a special agreement or agreements, armed forces . . . necessary for the purpose of maintaining international peace and security."[51] These special agreements would be negotiated "as soon as possible" and would be ratified by member states "in accordance with their respective constitutional processes."[52] Once concluded, the special agreements would permit the Security Council to deploy earmarked national military contingents, assisted by a UN Military Staff Committee comprised of the Chiefs of Staff of the five permanent Security Council members.

While Cold War tensions effectively eviscerated efforts toward any special agreements and prevented Security Council authorization of any collective military action in response to acts of aggression until the Gulf War—with the exception of Korea, when the Soviets were absent from the Security Council session where military action was authorized—the UN was able only to develop the more limited deployment of lightly-armed "peacekeeping" forces, who, with the consent of the parties, could monitor cease-fires and observe demobilization of opposing forces.

The expectations for a greater UN role in maintaining international peace increased since the Gulf War. This expanded role has challenged legal interpretations of the constitutional allocation of the war powers. The Bosnia situation has raised the issue of the application and meaning of Congress' war declaration power when the UN requests U.S. participation in a multilateral peace operation. One interpretation, for example, is that UN authorization supplies the president with sufficient legal authority to commit U.S. forces to armed conflict without the prior consent of Congress.

When the Senate provided its advice and consent to ratification of the UN Charter, the Senators understood that the Charter gave sweeping powers to the Security Council. To protect their constitutional war powers, the Senators were satisfied with the provision for a special agreement in Article 43, which would permit the U.S. government to determine in advance just what sort of commitment should be made to UN operations. In the UN Participation Act,[53] codified soon after ratification of the Charter in 1945, U.S. forces could be made available to the Security Council through an Article 43 agreement that would in turn specify the number, type, degree of readiness, and general location of forces. Congress would have to approve such an agreement; the President could not conclude an agreement unilaterally. In addition, if the president wished to commit forces beyond those provided for in an agreement, he would be required to return to Congress for authorization. At the time, this compromise seemed satisfactory: The United States could contribute to the needs of the Security Council to respond quickly and flexibly to small-scale crises, but Congress's prerogatives would be preserved for more significant military commitments.

These expectations quickly vanished with the onset of the Cold War. When North Korean forces attacked the Republic of Korea in June 1950, President Truman ordered U.S. air and naval forces to combat in support of the Republic of Korea even before the Security Council authorized member states to use force to "repel the armed attack"[54] on June 27. There was wide bipartisan support for the president's actions, despite the fact that the deployment took place without prior authorization from Congress. When a handful of Senators challenged the president's legal authority to make the Korea commitments, Truman argued that, because the UN Charter is a treaty that he must faithfully execute, he had the authority to commit the troops to combat once the Security Council voted for the operation. He also maintained that the Commander in Chief has customary power to take military action to protect "the broad interests of American foreign policy," and that UN-authorized use of force is an international "police action,"[55] not a war, so that Congress' power was not triggered.

A more recent example of the president's reliance on UN authorization to launch a large-scale military operation occurred in the Gulf War. In response to Iraq's invasion of Kuwait in 1990, the Security Council voted on November 29 to authorize the use of force to expel Iraqi forces from Kuwait unless they were removed by January 15, 1991. Although President Bush successfully sought congressional authorization for Operation Desert Storm, he maintained throughout and since that he did not require congressional approval to act.

Like the UN Charter, the NATO treaty of 1949 provides that an armed attack against one or more of the parties "shall be considered an attack against them all."[56] In response to such an attack, the treaty provides that any signatory country agrees to take "such action as it deems necessary, including the use of armed force, to restore and maintain the security. . . ."[57] However, the treaty also states that it shall be ratified and carried out "in accordance with [the parties'] respective constitutional processes."[58] During hearings on the treaty in 1949, Secretary of State Acheson told the Senate Foreign Relations Committee that the treaty "does not mean that the United States would automatically be at war if one of the other signatory nations were the victim of an armed attack. Under our Constitution, the Congress alone has the power to declare war."[59] This position was reinforced by Congress in the War Powers Resolution in 1973, in its admonition that authority to introduce U.S. forces in hostilities shall not be inferred "from any treaty heretofore or hereafter ratified unless such treaty is implemented by legislation specifically authorizing"[60] the introduction of U.S. troops.

Nonetheless, Presidents Bush and Clinton in Somalia, and Clinton in Haiti and Bosnia have relied on UN and/or NATO authorization as a sufficient legal basis for their actions. Although there was virtually no opposition to President Bush's unilateral determination to support a humanitarian relief effort in Somalia in Operation Restore Hope, the UN resolution authorized "all necessary means" to establish "a secure environment for humanitarian relief operations,"[61] which later was relied upon by President Clinton to justify the more controversial decision to seek out the Somali warlords. In July 1994, the Security Council adopted a resolution "inviting" all states to use "all necessary means"[62] to remove the military leadership from Haiti. When President Clinton announced that he was prepared to launch a military invasion of Haiti, he referred to the UN resolution in support of his determination not to seek congressional authorization for the operation.

Similarly, when the president decided to participate in humanitarian relief flights into Sarajevo and to enforce a no-fly zone over Bosnia, and then later to join air strikes against Serb positions in Bosnia, he maintained that "the authority . . . requires the common agreement of our NATO allies."[63]

Political, Strategic, and Operations Considerations

In contemplating U.S. involvement in peace operations, decision makers take into account the political dynamics, domestically and internationally. Apart from legal requirements, the President must determine whether and to what extent he should seek support from Congress and the public and what operational configurations the members and their constituents will likely tolerate before they move to stop the administration.

Following the signing of the Bosnian Peace Agreement in Paris on December 14, 1995, NATO was given a mandate by UN Security Resolution 1031 to implement the military aspects of the Dayton Accords. This was NATO's first ever ground force operation, its first ever deployment "out of area," and its first ever operation with non-NATO countries. The multilateral implementation force (IFOR) was charged with conducting Operation Joint Endeavour. The role of IFOR was to help the parties implement their Accord, in an even-handed manner. IFOR was not to fight a war or impose a settlement. Its tasks were to ensure compliance with the cease-fire; ensure withdrawal of forces from the agreed cease-fire zone of separation, back to their respective territories, and to ensure the separation of forces; ensure the collection of heavy weapons into containment sites and barracks and the demobilization of remaining forces; create conditions for the safe, orderly, and speedy withdrawal of UN forces that have not transferred to IFOR; and control the airspace over Bosnia-Herzegovina. In addition, "within its capabilities and limits," IFOR was also charged with creating secure conditions for free and fair elections; assisting in the observation and prevention of interference with the movement of civilian populations, including refugees; and assisting in the monitoring and clearance of mine fields and other obstacles.

The IFOR command was unified, NATO-led, under the Alliance's North Atlantic Council. Overall military authority was in the hands of NATO's Supreme Allied Commander Europe (SACEUR). Theater command was placed in NATO's Commander in Chief Southern Command (CINC-SOUTH) as the first Commander in Theater of IFOR (COMIFOR). Operating under Chapter VII of the UN Charter,[64] IFOR had robust rules of engagement, providing for the use of "necessary force"[65] to ensure compliance with the terms of the Accords, and to ensure IFOR's own protection. IFOR also was obligated to observe the international legal principles of proportionality, minimum use of force and the requirement to minimize the potential for collateral damage.

The mandate for IFOR expired on December 29, 1996. On December 10, NATO announced that it was prepared to lead a stabilization force (SFOR), at about one-half the size of IFOR, authorized by another UN Security Council Resolution under Chapter VII, to succeed IFOR for a planned period of eighteen months. The general contours of the SFOR mission remained to deter hostilities and to stabilize the conditions for peace.

Beyond SFOR: A Postscript

In commenting on the evolution of the multilateral operation in Bosnia, Deputy Secretary John Hamre said: "Bosnia saved NATO."[66] At about the same time, chief peace administrator for Bosnia, Carl Bildt, asked NATO to consider keeping troops in Bosnia longer than the currently planned pullout date of SFOR in June 1998. Indeed, the persistent and unchecked influence of leaders like indicted war criminal Rodovan Karadzic and others wanted for war crimes, but who still called the shots in the Serbian portion of Bosnia, caused ongoing consternation within the Clinton administration still committed to withdrawing SFOR American forces by mid-1998. The fear, of course, is that U.S. withdrawal will simply re-ignite the Balkans war. Along with the war crimes issue, the failure to seal the fate of more than a million refugees is evidence that, notwithstanding the relative success of the military objectives of the Dayton Accords, hardly any of the political and economic components of Dayton have been implemented. The Dayton signatories have simply refused to carry out most of its provisions. A recent GAO report concludes that some international peacekeeper force will be needed in Bosnia "for many years."[67] Defense Secretary William Cohen told reporters during his early 1997 European trip that if Bosnians want to "go back to slaughtering each other," that will be "up to them."[68]

Some in the State Department have publicly lamented that the military has missed several easy opportunities to arrest indicted Bosnian Serbs. To one Bosnian negotiator, Karadzic has "become a walking symbol to the rest of the region that you can defy NATO and get away with it."[69]

Notes

1. Bosnia Costs and Funding Requirements, Hearing Before a Subcommittee of the Committee on Appropriations, United States Senate, S. Hrg. 104–286, pp. 34–35 (December 1, 1995).

2. Letter to Rep. Gingrich, 141 Cong. Rec. H13228 (daily ed. November 17, 1995).

3. 29 Weekly Comp. Pres. Doc. 2097, 2101 (October 18, 1993).

4. Letter from Thomas Jefferson to James Madison (September 6, 1789), in Julian P. Boyd, ed., *The Papers of Thomas Jefferson* (Princeton, NJ: Princeton University Press, 1958), pp. 392, 397.

5. U.S. Const. Art. I, § 8, cl. 11 (granting Congress the power "[t]o declare War [and] grant Letters of Marque and Reprisal.").

6. U.S. Const. Art. I, § 8, cl. 1 (granting Congress the power "to pay the Debts and provide for the Common Defence.").

7. U.S. Const. art. I, § 8, cl. 12 (granting Congress the power "[t]o raise and support Armies.").

8. U.S. Const. art. I, § 8, cl. 13 (granting Congress the power "[t]o provide and maintain a Navy.").

9. U.S. Const. art. I, § 8, cl. 18 (granting Congress the power "[to make all Laws which shall be necessary and proper for carrying into Execution the foregoing powers.").

10. U.S. Const. art. I, § 9, cl. 7 ("No money shall be drawn from the Treasury, but in Consequence of Appropriations made by Law . . .").

11. Ibid. ("[A] regular Statement and Account of the Receipts and Expenditures of all public Money shall be published from time to time.").

12. Although the original understanding of the Constitution is often obscure, the power to commit the nation to war, big or little, declared or undeclared, was clearly given to Congress. Only defensive actions where time does not permit deliberation by Congress may be lawfully conducted by the Executive without congressional authorization. See Stephen Dycus, Arthur L. Berney, William C. Banks, and Peter Raven-Hansen, *National Security Law* (2nd ed., Boston: Little, Brown

and Co., 1997), pp. 9–27. See also Peter Raven-Hansen, "Constitutional Constraints: The War Clause," in Gary M. Stern and Morton H. Halperin, eds., *The U.S. Constitution and the Power to Go to War: Historical and Current Perspectives* (Westport, CT: Greenwood Press, 1994), pp. 29–54.

13. A Senate report stated: "[T]he practice of American Presidents for over a century after independence showed scrupulous respect for the authority of Congress except in a few instances." S. Rep. No. 797, 90th Cong., 1st Sess. 23 (1967). While proponents of broad presidential power have developed various lists purporting to show instances in which the President has ordered military action without congressional authorization, these lists tend to mislabel an operation authorized by Congress, or the actions listed involve minor skirmishes with pirates, or operations to rescue Americans abroad. See Francis Wormuth and Edwin Firmage, *To Chain the Dog of War: The Power of Congress in History and Law* (2nd ed., Urbana: University of Illinois Press, 1989), pp. 135–151; Dycus et al., *National Security Law*, pp. 334–341.

14. Public Papers and Addresses of Franklin D. Roosevelt (1940), p. 267.

15. *New York Times*, Nov. 15, 1990, p. A18.

16. Leonard C. Meeker, "The Legality of United States Participation in the Defense of Vietnam," 54 Dept. State Bull. (1966), p. 474.

17. For an analysis of the force and effect and constitutionality of restrictive national security appropriations, see Peter Raven-Hansen and William C. Banks, "Pulling the Purse Strings of the Commander in Chief," 80 *U. Va. L. Rev.* 1994, p. 833.

18. The WPR states that "[t]he President in every possible instance shall consult with Congress before introducing United States Armed Forces into hostilities or into situations where imminent involvement in hostilities is clearly indicated by the circumstances . . ." 50 U.S.C. § 1542. The reporting provisions of the WPR state that "in any case in which United States Armed Forces are introduced—(1) into hostilities or into situations where imminent involvement in hostilities is clearly indicated by the circumstances," 50 U.S.C. § 1543(a)(1), "[w]ithin sixty calendar days after a report is submitted or is required to be submitted . . . the President shall terminate any use of United States Armed Forces with respect to which such report was submitted (or required to be submitted), unless" Congress authorizes or extends the operation or is unable to meet because of an armed attack upon the United States. 50 U.S.C. § 1544. The sixty-day period may be extended by thirty days "if the President determines and certifies to the Congress in writing that unavoidable military necessity respecting the safety of United States Armed Forces" requires their continued use toward the end of removal. Ibid.

19. This shift derives from the text and structure of the UN Charter. Peace-

keeping may be viewed as a reasonable extension of Chapter VI's provisions, "Pacific Settlement of Disputes." Chapter VII gave a more substantial power to the Security Council to determine whether "any threat to peace, breach of the peace, or act of aggression" existed, and to recommend or decide what action to take in response, including military action. UN Charter art. 39. Because peacekeeping transcends the literal provisions of Chapter VI, a UN publication opined that "it is almost necessary to imagine a new 'Chapter Six and a Half.'" United Nations Department of Public Information, *The Blue Helmets: A Review of United Nations Peace-Keeping* (2nd ed., New York: United Nations Publications, 1990), p. 5.

20. Mark M. Lowenthal, "Peacekeeping and U.S. Foreign Policy: Implementing PDD-25," *Cong. Rsrch. Serv.*, Issue Brief, Dec. 7, 1994.

21. Ibid.

22. 107 Stat. 1476, § 8146 (1993).

23. Public Papers of the Presidents, 1994, I, p. 355.

24. Ibid., p. 354.

25. 31 Weekly Comp. Pres. Doc. 1439 (1995).

26. Pub. L. No. 103–335, § 8100 (1994).

27. 141 Cong. Rec. S14637 (daily ed. September 29, 1995).

28. 141 Cong. Rec. H13228 (daily ed. November 17, 1995).

29. Richard F. Grimmett, "The War Powers Resolution: Twenty-Two Years of Experience" (*Cong. Rsrch. Serv.* No. 96–476 F, May 24, 1996), p. 37.

30. H.R. Res. 247, 104th Cong. (1995); H.R. 2606, 104th Cong. § 1 (1995).

31. 141 Cong. Rec. S17, p. 862 (daily ed. November 30, 1995).

32. 141 Cong. Rec. S18, p. 470 (daily ed. December 12, 1995).

33. S.J. Res. 44, 104th Cong. (1995). The Resolution also called for detailed reports, every sixty days, on the civilian and military aspects of enforcing the Dayton Accords. Ibid.

34. H.R. Res. 302, 104th Cong. § 2 (1995); 141 Cong. Rec. H14, p. 849 (daily ed. December 13, 1995).

35. 31 Weekly Comp. Pres. Doc. 2144 (December 6, 1995).

36. Bosnia Costs and Funding Requirements, Hearing Before a Subcommittee of the Committee on Appropriations, United States Senate, S. Hrg. 104–286, p. 49 (December 1, 1995).

37. Quoted in Elaine Sciolino, "Loosening the Timetable for Bringing G.I.s Home," *New York Times*, November 17, 1996, p. E4.

38. 32 Weekly Comp. Pres. Doc. 2535–2536 (December 27, 1996).

39. Ibid.

40. Quoted in James Bennet, "Clinton Calls for Keeping Troops in Bosnia With No New Exit Date," *New York Times*, December 19, 1996, p. A1.

41. Public Papers of the Presidents, 1992–93, p. 995.

42. "Statement by Governor Bill Clinton on the crisis in the Balkans," National Campaign Headquarters, July 26, 1992, p. 1.

43. David C. Morrison, "U.S. Troops in Somalia: Where Next?", *National Journal*, December 12, 1992, p. 2842.

44. Colin Powell, *My American Journey* (New York: Random House, 1995), p. 291.

45. *New York Times*, November 29, 1992, noted in Morrison, "U.S. Troops in Somalia: Where Next?"

46. 138 Cong. Rec. S15, 950–15, p. 951 (daily ed. October 1, 1992).

47. Carroll J. Doherty, "Diplomatic Strategy on Bosnia Leaves Many Still Skeptical," 51 *Cong. Qtly. Wkly.*, p. 394 (February 20, 1993).

48. Pat Towell, "GOP Critics Begin to Question Clinton's Handling of War," 51 *Cong. Qtly. Wkly.*, p. 539 (March 6, 1993).

49. Ibid.

50. UN Charter, art. 42.

51. Ibid., art. 43.

52. Ibid.

53. Pub. L. No. 264, §§ 1–7, 59 Stat. 619 (1945).

54. S.C. Res. 83, UN SCOR, 5th Sess., 474th mtg., p. 5 (1950).

55. Public Papers of the Presidents, 1950, pp. 503–504, 522.

56. 63 Stat. 2244, art. 5. The treaty also provides that, in the event of an attack, the member states may exercise the right of individual or collective self-defense recognized by Article 51 of the UN Charter.

57. Ibid.

58. Ibid., art. 11.

59. U.S. Senate Hearings on The North Atlantic Treaty Before The Senate Committee On Foreign Relations, 81st Cong., 1st Sess., pt. 1, p. 11 (1949).

60. War Powers Resolution, 50 U.S.C. § 1547(a) (2) (1994).

61. S.C. Res. 794, UN Doc. S/RES/794 (1992).

62. S.C. Res. 940, UN Doc. S/RES 940 (1994), p. 993.

63. Public Papers of the Presidents, 1994, I, p. 186.

64. In general, "peace enforcement" operations fall into a middle category between major combat operations and consensual peacekeeping. While peacekeeping is authorized pursuant to Chapter VI of the UN Charter, peace enforcement is authorized under Chapter VII, on the theory that military action is both authorized and anticipated in the authorizing Resolution, albeit on a smaller and more limited scale than in major operations.

65. Operation Joint Endeavour (IFOR), "The General Framework Agreement," Annex 1A, "Agreement on the Military Aspects of the Peace Settlement," Art. I, § 2.b., http://www.nato.int/ifor/gfa/gfa-an1a.htm.

66. Interview with the authors, Washington, D.C., May 6, 1997.

67. Quoted in Michael Dobbs, "In Bosnia, a Dubious Peace Process," *Washington Post*, May 2, 1997, p. A1.

68. Ibid.

69. Ibid.

Chapter 3

The Road to Dayton: Diplomatic and Military Interaction in Bosnia

THOMAS A. KEANEY AND SCOTT DOUGLAS

In November 1994, Lieutenant General Michael Ryan, NATO air commander in Southern Europe, organized what was at the time the largest bombing raid in Europe since the end of World War II. The target, an airfield in the Krajina region of Croatia, served as a launching base for Serb aircraft conducting bombing raids into Bosnia. Ryan's task, however, was not to make war on Croatia or on the Serbs, but to support United Nations (UN) peacekeeping forces in Bosnia. As a result, he had to limit the effects of his attack so as not to hinder diplomatic efforts then underway or compromise the neutrality of the UN forces on the ground.

Further complicating Ryan's task were the command structures in place. Ryan himself reported through NATO channels, ultimately to political authorities in Brussels, Belgium. The UN forces he supported traced their command channels back to UN headquarters in New York. Ryan, an American, commanded mainly U.S. air forces, but the UN peacekeeping force he supported had no Americans—the United States had refused to take part in this peacekeeping effort.

Tangled command arrangements notwithstanding, it had taken more than two years to reach a point whereby the NATO and UN forces could act in coordination to enforce the UN resolutions, and the attack on the airfield at Udbina represented a test of the partnership. General Ryan favored a comprehensive attack of the airfield, with strikes against the aircraft, runways and taxiways, as well as the air defense system and weapons in the area.[1] And, with the full support of Admiral Leighton Smith, USN, the theater commander for NATO forces in Southern Europe, Ryan sought the necessary UN approval for the strike plan.

The approval process itself reflected the differing opinions of NATO and

UN officials about the role and extent of military force necessary. These disagreements dated to the beginning of the NATO-UN partnership in 1992 and would continue for the next ten months. Both organizations agreed that a punishing raid was in order, but on little else. UN Secretary General Boutros Boutros-Ghali, in an effort to avoid provoking either the Croatians or Bosnian Serbs, or showing a lack of proportional restraint consistent with the UN mission, approved attacks against only the runway and taxiways at the airfield, specifically excluding strikes against aircraft or air-defense systems. Smith and Ryan, however, argued that such measures would put NATO aircrews in greater jeopardy and would have little impact, either as symbolic punishment or on the airfield's operational capability. Boutros-Ghali compromised by approving attacks against defense systems of immediate threat to NATO aircraft only, but not against Serb aircraft.

On November 21, 1994, thirty-nine NATO aircraft cratered the runway and struck several antiaircraft artillery and surface-to-air missile sites in the immediate vicinity. The next day NATO released photographs of large holes the strikes had made in the runway at Udbina. It was immediately obvious, however, that the strikes, labeled "pinpricks" by the press, had accomplished little damage; the runway could be and was repaired in a day or two.[2] Immediately after the air strikes, Ambassador Yasushi Akashi (the UN Secretary General's Special Representative for the former Yugoslavia) assured the Bosnian Serb leadership that the United Nations, and the NATO forces acting on its behalf, remained neutral in the Bosnian conflict and "were neither the enemy or ally of any party."[3]

BOMBING WHILE PEACEKEEPING

Authorizing the bombing of an airfield while proclaiming neutrality typified the curious position of the multinational peacekeeping forces, and the frustrations felt by many of them, who were trying to bring order to Bosnia as the conflict in that country edged toward its fourth year. Along the way, the difficulties of conducting peacekeeping operations to separate and control the contending parties had brought increasing acrimony to relations between the UN, the major European powers, and United States.

All were bitterly divided over how best to use force to improve the situation in Bosnia. The differences were often exacerbated by the fact that one's preferred strategy for achieving order often depended heavily on how one interpreted the war in Bosnia. At one level the war appeared to be a three-way struggle in which Bosnian Croats, Bosnian Serbs, and Bosnian Muslims competed to carve out their own ethnic territories within Bosnia. At the same time the United States and others regarded the war as an attempt by Serbia and Croatia to seize and annex portions of a sovereign state—Bosnia. The United Nations' force on the ground trod the difficult path of attempting to assist the local populations, keep the warring parties apart, not appear to take sides, and all the while defend themselves from attack.

The UN's position was aptly summarized in a comment made by British Lieutenant General Sir Michael Rose (UN operational commander in Bosnia at the time): "Patience, persistence, and pressure is how you conduct a peacekeeping mission. Bombing is a last resort because then you cross the Mogadishu line," referring to the international operation in Somalia and a notional crossover point when neutral intervention becomes partisan participation in a conflict.[4] By 1995, however, peacekeeping in Bosnia had exacted a toll: 167 UN peacekeepers killed, with another 1,420 wounded.

A new team of UN military commanders had taken over in 1995 as part of a restructured command. The UN established in Zagreb, Croatia, the United Nations Peace Forces (UNPF) with Ambassador Yasushi Akashi as the head of this mission and French Lieutenant General Bernard Janvier as the military commander. They oversaw the UN operations in Croatia, Macedonia, and Bosnia. In Bosnia, British Lieutenant General Rupert Smith took command of the United Nations Protective Force (UNPRO-FOR), subordinate to General Janvier's overall military command. Both generals had great familiarity with United States military operations.

During the Gulf War, Janvier commanded the French ground forces deployed to the region; Smith commanded the British 1st Armoured Division attached to U.S. VII Corps. Though these men differed in their opinions of when and how to use force, they agreed that present conditions could not continue. As an internal UN memo admitted, "UNPRO-FOR is, in many areas, unable to supply itself, unable to protect the delivery of humanitarian aid, unable to deter attacks, unable to fight for itself and unable to withdraw."[5] Janvier and Smith sought to find a way to revise the political agreement that kept UNPROFOR in such a precarious position, but the difficulty of securing the original compromise position with the principal actors in the Security Council argued against reopening the debate.

Similar divisions existed within NATO. NATO had agreed to serve as the UN peacekeepers' primary source of protection from direct attack, but the UN rules for providing this aid threatened NATO's credibility as a military organization. The United Kingdom and France, who had a large number of troops serving on the ground, took a cautious approach, while the United States, with no peacekeepers at risk, took the lead in urging broader and more decisive action. For both organizations, the inability to arrive at a workable solution confounded the efforts of the United Nations and NATO and threatened the United States' leadership role in both. Not without reason had U.S. Secretary of State Warren Christopher called the situation in Bosnia "the problem from hell."

BOSNIA REAPPEARS ON THE WORLD STAGE

This latest strife in Bosnia had begun with the secession of several of Yugoslavia's republics in 1991 and 1992.[6] When Slovenia declared its independence in June 1991, followed shortly thereafter by Croatia, the Yugoslav army attempted to reclaim these territories. That army found itself overwhelmed in Slovenia, but, after heavy fighting in Croatia, managed to control Serbian enclaves within Croatia, most notably in the Krajina region. In January 1992, the Yugoslav army turned these enclaves over to a United Nations force, the UN Protective Force (UNPROFOR), whose mission it was to disarm the Serb militia and protect the inhabitants from reprisals by the Croatians.

The UN force was barely in place before conflict began among the Croats, Serbs, and Muslims in Bosnia. A referendum for independence sponsored by Muslim and Croat parties, boycotted by the Serbs, showed overwhelming approval for independence, and Bosnia-Herzegovina[7] declared its independence on March 3, 1992. The U.S. and the European Union recognized Bosnia as an independent state a little over a month later. Bosnia contained a more complex intermixture of ethnic groups than any of the other Yugoslav republics, and when the parties drew up the tentative ethnic regions, thirteen of them, there was little agreement on the borders of each region. Armed conflict to enforce ethnic claims throughout the newly declared country started almost immediately, and UNPROFOR was called on for help.

Initially, the UN sent 1,100 members of UNPROFOR from Croatia to the city of Sarajevo to open the airport and deliver humanitarian assistance to the city. As UNPROFOR's mandate expanded, the UN turned to NATO for help in protecting its convoys. NATO's response set the context for what full intervention would entail: securing a route from the Adriatic Coast to Sarajevo and forcibly guaranteeing the unimpeded flow of hu-

Map 3.1
Bosnia-Herzegovina and Surrounding Region after Dayton Accords Division

manitarian aid was estimated to require a heavy corps, or a total of 100,000 troops. Since NATO was not prepared to assemble a force of such size, it was obvious that UNPROFOR could operate in the country only if each of the warring parties perceived it as neutral. UNPROFOR grew in size to 6,000 troops, but did so as a benign presence among the three factions, subject to their checkpoints and toleration, and depending on success based on negotiation, not force.[8]

As violence escalated and created increasing hardships for the civilian populations, a number of humanitarian and international organizations attempted to intercede through various measures. Over the next three years, the major powers worked through the UN and other organizations to enforce embargoes, establish a war crimes tribunal, and create no-fly zones and safe areas in hopes of limiting the fighting and at least containing the combatants. Since the major powers had no wish to become actively involved in the fighting and no common vision for a settlement, the various efforts at intercession were largely limited to maintaining a peacekeeping neutrality while attempting to lead the contending parties to some sort of agreement.

Over time, the peacekeeping efforts became a complex mixture in which more aggressive postures and roles co-existed with increasingly compromised freedom of movement. Successive UN resolutions expanded UNPROFOR's rules from monitoring, to using force in reply to bombardment, and finally to permit NATO to conduct close air support missions in direct defense of UN peacekeepers under attack.[9]

THE U.S. LIMITS ITS ROLE

While active in the negotiations for ending the conflict in Bosnia, the United States refused to provide ground forces in the country, either for full-scale intervention or for the peacekeeping role of UNPROFOR. The U.S. Joint Chiefs of Staff opposed large-scale commitments of troops for any purpose. Lieutenant General Barry McCaffrey of the Joint Staff stated operations in Bosnia would involve the "tremendous challenge" of controlling "the most mountainous and inaccessible fortresslike" heartland against an enemy strategy that "borrows more from Giap than from classical Western military thinking."[10] Although in 1992 presidential candidate Bill Clinton advocated a more active role for the United States in Bosnia, the U.S. experience in Somalia in 1993 further soured American attitudes toward taking part in peacekeeping operations, or for any operations which placed U.S. forces under UN command. The United States was more willing to assume a role in air operations over Bosnia as part of a NATO force, and as the scope of those operations intensified, so too did U.S. involvement.

THE CHAIN OF COMMAND

While authorizing NATO to undertake air strikes in support of UN peacekeepers, the UN retained the right to veto the action. Using a security system for launching nuclear weapons as a model, NATO commanders could "turn their key" and give consent for air strikes, but air strikes could not be executed without a second "key" being turned by the UN authorities. UN Secretary General Boutros-Ghali kept a tight rein on the UN key. Only he could authorize offensive air strikes, while his special representative in the region, Ambassador Yasushi Akashi, could authorize close air support missions. Akashi was a diplomat with an accomplished record with the UN mission to Cambodia and was widely perceived as someone with a preference for diplomatic compromise over military action. Akashi, for instance, insisted on giving advance warning to the party about to be bombed. Because UNPROFOR counted on the cooperation of all sides, Akashi argued "the man you bomb today is the same man whose cooperation you may require tomorrow for the passage of a humanitarian convoy."[11]

In the NATO organizational framework, responsibility for the Bosnian area air operations belonged to NATO's 5th Allied Tactical Air Force (ATAF) at Vicenza, Italy. An Italian general commanded 5th ATAF, and the line of command passed upward to the Commander, Allied Air Forces Southern Europe (COMAIRSOUTH—a U.S. Air Force general, at the time Lieutenant General Michael Ryan) and through him to the Commander in Chief of Allied Forces Southern Europe (CINCSOUTH—a U.S. Navy admiral, at the time Admiral Leighton Smith) and ultimately to the Supreme Allied Commander Europe (SACEUR—a U.S. four-star general, at the time General George Joulwan).

Since the 5th ATAF headquarters operations center was not equipped with the latest communications equipment necessary to control the expanded operations, new equipment, largely of US-origin, began arriving in Vicenza. The personnel arriving to operate the equipment were mainly U.S. personnel, and as the operations increased in tempo and breadth, the command authority of the Italian general diminished. For operational purposes, the U.S. commander of the operations center at Vicenza reported directly to the U.S. general at AIRSOUTH (Ryan), and since the bulk of the support and strike aircraft were also American, the chain of command became heavily "Americanized" from the tactical level through the top NATO commander (SACEUR).

Significantly, SACEUR, despite being an American, was not under the direct command of the U.S. government, but rather received instructions from the North Atlantic Council and the NATO Secretary General. Thus, it was quite logical that the chief U.S. representative involved in diplomatic negotiations in Bosnia in 1995, Richard Holbrooke, could be working to achieve somewhat different goals than the top U.S. military commanders in Europe.

IDENTIFYING VICTIMS AND AGGRESSORS

A number of developments in 1994 had special significance for the UN peacekeeping forces. First, in March, the United States helped effect a reconciliation between the Bosnian Croats and the Bosnian Muslims. Establishing a common Muslim-Croat effort reduced the fighting between those two factions, aided somewhat UNPROFOR's peacekeeping efforts in that part of the country, and lent renewed credibility to the Bosnian government's claim to multi-ethnic legitimacy. At the same time, U.S. diplomacy increasingly sided with the Muslim-led Bosnian government and reserved the bulk of its condemnation for the actions of the Bosnian Serbs. Russia, meanwhile, became the most visible supporter of the Bosnian Serbs, leading to Russian-NATO tension at a time when NATO generally sought to improve its relationship with Russia. One bridge of this gap was the creation of the five-nation Contact Group, comprised of the United States, Germany, France, Great Britain, and Russia. It was hoped that the Contact Group would reduce tensions among these major powers and help create a common platform that would be difficult for the warring parties to reject.

The UN-NATO relationship also suffered continued stress. In April 1994 NATO responded to the first UNPROFOR close air support request to stop a Bosnian Serb attack on the Bosnian Muslim enclave in Gorazde in eastern Bosnia. NATO conducted a number of air strikes against Bosnian Serb heavy artillery positions, ammunition depots, air defense sites and troops threatening UN observers. The Bosnian Serb Army responded by taking 150 UN personnel hostage. In a subsequent air strike, a NATO aircraft was brought down by a Serb antiaircraft missile while attempting to engage Serb tanks.

NATO-United Nations relations suffered from this event. NATO commanders expressed concern that UNPROFOR had asked the pilot to make several passes over the target to confirm that the targeted tank was indeed attacking, thus exposing the aircraft to danger. The Commander in Chief of NATO's Southern Command informed the Commander of United Nations forces in Bosnia that, due to the risk to his aircraft, he would not approve any further attacks on tactical-level targets, but only on strategic-level ones. The impasse was not resolved, since that same day the

Serbs had agreed to a cease-fire and the release of the UN peacekeepers,[12] but the incident created a sharp dispute between NATO and the UN that still persisted when action over Udbina (described earlier) became an issue seven months later.

THE UN AND NATO ESCALATE

Under increasing international and domestic pressures to bring the conflict to some sort of resolution, the UN, NATO, and the United States all attempted new approaches. As European and then Contact Group efforts seemed to flounder over the winter of 1994–1995, the United States took a stronger role. Although the multinational Contact Group continued to be the official locus of international diplomatic efforts, the United States directed Assistant Secretary of State Ambassador Richard Holbrooke to act as special negotiator in attempts to broker an agreement among the three combatants.

Frustrated by continued inability to keep apart the warring factions or to enforce the UN resolutions, in the wake of the Udbina attacks the United Nations leadership began making arrangements to either change the UN mandate or, failing that, withdraw their forces from Bosnia.

During the same period, NATO's military commanders attempted to repair some of the defects they perceived in the previous air strikes—or at least to present the political authorities with a more extensive set of options. Shortly after the Udbina raid, General Ryan changed OPLAN 40101, NATO's basic planning document for any involvement in the Bosnian theater, to allow for more extensive attacks on the Suppression of Enemy Air Defense (SEAD) targets. Unlike the other missions NATO had previously drafted in support of UN mandates, the new planning assumptions did not confine attacks to a particular geographic area immediately surrounding a violation, but instead permitted strikes against SEAD targets all across Bosnian Serb-held territory.[13] Still, NATO plans openly "admonished NATO airmen to ensure that their strikes . . . were 'proportional' " and included three successively larger tiers of prospective targets for all NATO air strikes. However, requests by U.S. commanders for senior non-U.S. officers to be a part of the planning and operational headquarters at AIRSOUTH were largely unsuccessful, leaving the NATO staff at all levels in the Bosnian air effort almost exclusively American.[14]

Before the Security Council or the Contact Group members could agree on any changes based on the new UNPROFOR and NATO options, events came to a head in Bosnia over heavy weapons violations. On May 22, the Bosnian Serb Army seized two artillery pieces from a UN weapons collection depot, and fighting intensified dramatically between Bosnian Serbs and Muslims around Sarajevo. In some instances the Bosnian Serbs had opened fire from artillery pieces inside UN weapons collection compounds. UNPROFOR's General Smith issued an ultimatum on May 24 for the return of the seized artillery pieces within twenty-four hours and for both sides to respect the heavy weapons exclusion zone.

As the deadline passed on May 25, NATO aircraft bombed two Bosnian Serb ammunition dumps outside of Pale. The Bosnian Serbs responded by seizing some UN military observers and chaining them to strategic targets around Pale in full view of Western news cameras. On May 26, the Bosnian Serb Army shelled Tuzla, striking a cafe in the city center and killing more than seventy people. With the Bosnian Serbs still defiantly refusing to hand over either the heavy weapons in question or release the UNPROFOR hostages, NATO launched a second series of air strikes against the remaining ammunition bunkers near Pale. In response the Bosnian Serbs Army seized more than 350 UNPROFOR hostages in the next few days. No further air strikes were launched.

Western reaction was mixed, and the debate over the options presented to the Security Council intensified. To meet what had become a crisis in NATO relations, NATO defense ministers met in Paris on June 3. At this meeting NATO developed two plans: one to create a rapid reaction force to protect and support the peacekeepers; another to support a withdrawal operation of the peacekeepers, if necessary. Planning for either of these eventualities resulted in the creation of a new heavily armed European Rapid Reaction Force (RRF), 15,000 troops, for Bosnia operations. Unlike their fellow countrymen already serving in UNPROFOR, the new troops had no blue berets and white-painted vehicles; instead they were heavily armed and wore full battle camouflage when they took up positions on Mount Igman near Sarajevo. The RRF mission remained ambiguous, however, since even after deployment there remained controversy of how to employ the force.

As the RRF was being organized, the UN Security Council debated the advisability of taking more aggressive action in Bosnia, essentially of moving from the neutrality of peacekeeping to peace enforcement operations. Secretary General Boutros-Ghali opposed the change, summing up his argument as:

The logic of peacekeeping flows from political and military premises that are quite distinct from those of enforcement; and the dynamics of the latter are incompatible with the political process that peacekeeping is intended to facilitate. To blur the distinction between the two can undermine the viability of the peacekeeping operation and endanger its personnel.[15]

As an alternative to peace enforcement, Boutros-Ghali proposed to the Security Council that they revise the UN mandate to include only those tasks that the peacekeeping operations could reasonably expect to perform, in effect reducing the threat of force, particularly air power, only to instances of self-defense. Facing these alternatives, the Security Council remained divided and took no action.[16]

Trapped between two visions of its mission, the RRF deployed to Bosnia in the midst of conflicting opinions, even between the military commanders. General Janvier, the overall commander, declared that the RRF (he called it the "theater reserve") would operate under peacekeeping rules of engagement. General Smith, commander of UNPROFOR, to which the RRF was assigned, argued that if the force could not be used for fighting he would prefer not to have it at all. After several weeks of discussion by the UN leadership in Bosnia and New York, on July 6, the UN reemphasized to all parties that the RRF would remain under peacekeeping rules.[17]

During these discussions, the United States readied forces to deal with a possible withdrawal of the UN forces. While again reaffirming its refusal to commit ground troops to Bosnia, the United States did agree to support a withdrawal plan and other associated movements. Specifically, the United States agreed to use ground troops to aid in an emergency extraction of UNPROFOR or to assist in the emergency movement of UNPROFOR within Bosnia.[18]

The UN and NATO's resolution was tested on July 6, when the Bosnian Serbs launched a barrage of missiles at Srebrenica, followed by an attack on the eastern end of the enclave. Bosnian Serb soldiers bloodlessly seized the southernmost Dutch observation post atop a strategic hilltop. When the Bosnian Serb Army continued to advance over the next few days and began capturing more outposts and taking more Dutch soldiers as prisoners, the Dutch commander requested close air support. Because of difficulties in the UN-NATO approval process, the requested air strikes did not take place for another thirty-six hours.

Accounts of the attack vary, with the most optimistic claiming two Dutch F-16s destroyed a Bosnian Serb tank and heavily damaged another. At that point one of the captured Dutch soldiers radioed the Dutch headquarters in Srebrenica to inform them that if the air strikes persisted all

Dutch prisoners would be executed and the city and its inhabitants shelled. Subsequently, the Dutch Defense Minister called the UN command requesting a halt to the bombing, and the UN complied.

The fall of the enclave meant that the Bosnian Muslims there fell into the hands of the Bosnian Serbs, with tragic results. Investigations since have revealed that several thousand Bosnian Muslim males were summarily executed.[19] Even at the time, there were sufficient horror stories on the fate of its inhabitants to produce public outrage in the West, prompting Prime Minister John Major to call an ad hoc international conference for July 21. At this London Conference, attended by foreign or defense ministers from fifteen countries (contributors of troops to UNPROFOR, members of the Security Council, and NATO countries), the attendees agreed to a series of changes in UN and NATO procedures. All had agreed to extend the threat of NATO air strikes in the event of Bosnian Serb attacks, even if UNPROFOR troops were not directly targeted. At the UN, the Secretary General agreed that the UN's "keys" would officially devolve to General Janvier. Meanwhile, the NATO Secretary General announced "that such operations, once they are launched will not lightly be discontinued." That statement signified perhaps the most important change of all: once the bombing began, it would require the concurrence of both the UN and NATO to *cease* the operations. Three NATO generals were sent to personally convey NATO's determination to the Bosnian Serbs.[20]

NATO divided its target list into three levels, or options, by their perceived importance with the first option "direct" targets, local military forces engaged in attacks, and extending to the third option, the most wide ranging—including facilities such as oil refineries or power stations. A few days later, Janvier informally agreed that option two targets (the air defense system, ammunition bunkers, etc.) would be a better way to coerce the Bosnian Serbs in defense of a safe area rather than simply attacking "smoking guns." A short while later, NATO and the UN extended the deterrent of air power to cover all of the remaining safe areas: Bihac, Tuzla, and Sarajevo. In short, not only were the array of targets expanded, but also the allowable geographic extent of the strikes. Bosnian Serb aggression in one area would invite retaliation against their forces throughout Bosnia.

THREE OFFENSIVES

While the London Conference met, another escalation of the conflict took place when the Croatian Army launched a surprise offensive, which

Map 3.2
Bosnia-Herzegovina Ethnic Divisions in May 1995

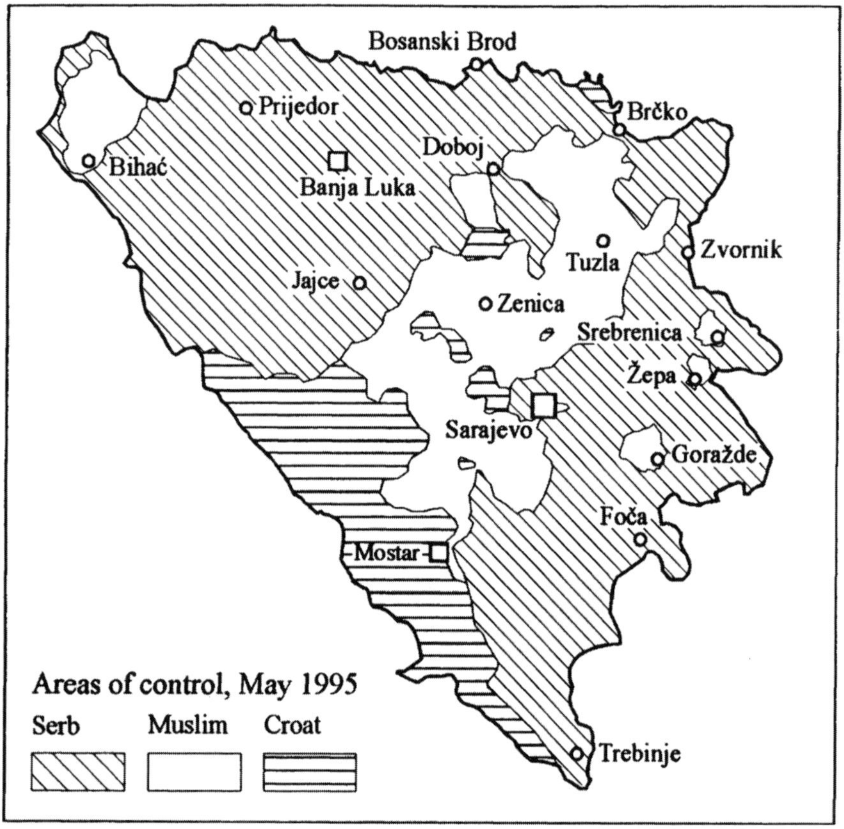

Information from U.S. Central Intelligence Agency Map 735935.

resulted in the collapse of Serb resistance in the Krajina region of Croatia and the loss of almost all of this region within four days. Amidst reports of atrocities and intimidation of UN troops, some 200,000 Croatian Serb civilians fled eastward into Bosnia and the Serb-held territory around Bihac. Ironically, the first post–London Conference NATO air action took place against Croatian forces that were firing on UN observers.[21] Coincident with the Croatian Army attack, Bosnian Government's V Corps broke out of their enclave and began pushing eastward toward Bihac.

As Bosnian and Croatian forces continued to gain ground, the new latitude in NATO operations had become formalized to the point that the operational NATO commanders, Admiral Smith and General Ryan, and UNPROFOR's Generals Janvier and Smith signed a memorandum of understanding for a joint operational plan. In addition, General Ryan brought in U.S. manpower and equipment to expand the Vicenza air operations center's capabilities. Several hundred temporary duty augmentees began flowing in from U.S. bases, along with a flood of state-of-the-art communications, intelligence, and automated planning systems.[22]

New diplomatic activities also got underway as President Clinton and his advisors agreed on a "Seven Point Initiative." Immediately, a U.S. negotiating team lead by Ambassador Richard Holbrooke left to begin a shuttle diplomacy mission between Zagreb, Sarajevo, and Belgrade. On the way to Sarajevo on August 19, the mission was cut short when a UN armored personnel carrier in the convoy slid off the Mt. Igman road. Among the dead were three members of the American negotiating team, including Ambassador Frasure who had led the previous Contact Group talks with Slobodan Milosevic.[23]

On August 27, Holbrooke appeared on NBC's "Meet the Press" before leaving to restart the shuttle diplomacy process. In response to a question about leverage with the Serbs, Holbrooke remarked "if the Serbs don't want to negotiate, then the game will basically just be to wait for the trigger for air strikes" which, he implied, could last as long as six months or more and would "level the playing field." Such objectives, however, "of leveling the playing field, or of bombing the Bosnian Serbs to the bargaining table," were not NATO's goals, which had remained limited to securing the safe areas from Bosnian Serb attacks.[24]

The next morning (August 28, 1995), a mortar shell struck the same Sarajevo marketplace hit the previous year, this time killing thirty-eight people and wounding more than eighty. In contrast to previous mortar attack, however, it took less than twenty-four hours for UNPROFOR forces to determine that the Bosnian Serb Army had fired the shells. NATO began preparations for an air campaign. General Ryan and his staff began planning what became known as Operation DELIBERATE FORCE. At 2:00 AM on the morning of August 29, General Rupert Smith informed his NATO counterparts that he was calling for air strikes against the Bosnian Serbs, but requested a twenty-four-hour pause to allow UNPROFOR to withdraw its most vulnerable personnel.[25]

At NATO headquarters, Secretary General Willy Claes further simplified the process for taking military action: "Instead of calling for another formal meeting of the NATO Council to make a decision, Claes simply informed the other members of NATO that he authorized . . . [General Joulwan (SACEUR) and Admiral Smith] to take military action if it was deemed appropriate."[26]

Almost precisely twenty-four hours after UNPROFOR's request, the first NATO jets released their bombs on Bosnian Serb targets. In addition, the Rapid Reaction Force began shelling Bosnian Serb positions around Sarajevo. Air attacks took place across northern and western Bosnia, in areas that had nothing to do with the mortar attack, but were aimed at Bosnian Serb air defense assets and other targets of value across the country. Since Ryan believed that collateral damage would be a pivotal issue, he personally reviewed the profile of each mission, to include its flight time, composition, weapons load, and target. Afterwards, Ryan also reviewed the bomb damage assessment.

COORDINATING FORCE AND DIPLOMACY

At this point, General Mladic (Commander of the Bosnian Serb Army) contacted General Janvier to press for talks. Janvier agreed and, with the concurrence of Admiral Smith, announced a suspension of bombing operations for at least ninety-six hours, after only two days of bombing. When informed of the bombing pause, NATO Secretary General Claes and General Joulwan were furious; Joulwan called it "snatching defeat from the jaws of victory."[27] They directed their anger both at the UN commander General Janvier and the NATO operational commander, Admiral Smith. Involved too, was the American envoy Richard Holbrooke, who argued by phone with Admiral Smith about the necessity of resuming bombing. After relating the conversation, which Holbrooke says, left Smith "fuming," Holbrooke relates:

> In my view, Smith was edging into an area of political judgements that should have been reserved for civilian leaders. But Smith saw it differently: he told me he was "solely responsible" for the safety and well-being of his forces, and would make his decision, under authority delegated to him by the NATO council, based on his own judgement. In fact, he pointed out, he did not even work for the United States; as a NATO commander he took orders from Brussels.[28]

Admiral Smith, who also blocked any contact between Holbrooke and General Ryan, argued that he "did not want either of them [Holbrooke or his military deputy U.S. Army General Wesley Clark] to even think they had an avenue by which they could influence me." The U.S. ambassador to NATO at the time, Christopher Hill, agreed that the division of efforts was correct and that any " 'tactical' cooperation between [Smith and Holbrooke] would have been a 'very big mistake.' " Holbrooke later related that he was "fully aware of his exclusion from NATO and UN command channels . . . [and] never based his pre-DELIBERATE FORCE negotiating plans on a bombing campaign, even though he believed that one would facilitate their successful outcome greatly."[29]

The NATO senior command prevailed on Janvier and Smith to end the bombing pause after four days, and when NATO's ultimatum to General Mladic to withdraw his forces drew only partial compliance, the bombing resumed with even greater intensity. On September 10, as part of the bombing campaign, thirteen Tomahawk cruise missiles, fired from U.S. Naval vessels in the Adriatic, struck a series of communications and radar facilities outside of Banja Luka.[30] The decision to use the weapons was made by NATO planners simply out of operational considerations and a desire to minimize the risk to NATO aircrews in an area believed to have significant air defense capability.[31] However, as Holbrooke relates, the use of the Tomahawks was widely perceived as an escalation in political circles. In addition to the expected complaints from the Bosnian Serbs, the Russians expressed grave concern and threatened to withdraw from the Contact Group. At the North Atlantic Council the next day, France, Canada, Spain, and Greece complained that launching cruise missiles represented an unauthorized escalation.[32] Additionally, the Italian government refused basing rights to six F-117 "stealth" aircraft that the United States intended to employ in the campaign.[33]

Diplomatic efforts, NATO operations, and the Croat and Bosnian ground offensives all continued to operate parallel to one another but without any formal links, and some disconnects began to emerge. Ambassador Holbrooke was told during a National Security Council meeting on September 11 by Admiral William Owens, the Vice Chairman of the JCS, that NATO was running out of authorized (options one and two) targets. Option three targets had not yet been struck, but everyone understood that in the present circumstances there was no chance of getting approval from the NATO allies to attack them.[34] As a result, Holbrooke concluded that NATO would halt its bombing shortly thereafter, and thus accelerated the pace of his negotiations by a week "to get what he could from the Serbs before the bombing ended."[35]

A very different assessment of the situation emerged from the air operations center in Vicenza, Italy. There, the staff planners even discussed slowing down the pace of the air campaign because of signs of aircrew fatigue. They rejected the idea, however, believing that "the diplomatic vulnerability of the operation required maximum effort to ensure that it had a decisive effect before it was shut down for political reasons." In other words, "the military planners pressed their operations to get their full diplomatic effect before the *diplomats* arbitrarily cut off the bombing, even as the diplomats scrambled to get what diplomatic effect they could before the *commanders* arbitrarily cut off the bombing."[36]

Negotiations took place on two levels: between Bosnian Serb forces under General Mladic and UNPROFOR under General Janvier; and between Serb, Croatian, and Bosnian government leaders and Ambassador Holbrooke. The latter effort brought results. On September 8, the Bosnian, Croatian, and Serbian Foreign Ministers all met in Geneva and initialed the framework arranged earlier that officially recognized Bosnia, its borders, and a basic federal structure. Four days later, Holbrooke had won agreement in the Bosnian Serbs name to a withdrawal of forces and a host of other items. Holbrooke's odd diplomatic position became apparent when he had to explain to the Bosnian Serbs that only they would sign the document and that he would give no signature or guarantees as he "had no formal authority to reach any agreement concerning the activities of NATO or the UN."[37]

Meanwhile, the Bosnian and Croatian armies were scoring significant victories as their offensives continued in Bosnia, driving the Bosnian Serbs from approximately 1,300 square miles in Western Bosnia. International pressure mounted to halt these offensives, however, when the Croat Army threatened to take Banja Luka, the largest Serb-populated city in Bosnia. Such an event would have seriously threatened the Bosnian Serb position in the country and led to a second mass exodus of Serb refugees to the east. NATO Secretary General Claes and UN Secretary General Boutros-Ghali issued a joint statement of "deep concern" over the military offensive, recognizing that the Bosnians and Croats were taking advantage of the NATO bombing campaign.[38] Confused by U.S. pressure to halt the attacks, Croatian President Franjo Tudjman asked Holbrooke for clarification and his personal views. Citing the value of the offensives for the eventual map negotiations, Holbrooke responded, "Mr. President, I urge you to go as far as you can, but not to take Banja Luka."[39]

The following morning Holbrooke delivered the unilateral Serb agreement to Janvier. Both Janvier and Admiral Smith agreed to suspend the bombing campaign for seventy-two hours starting at 10:00 AM that day. On September 20, six days later, Operation Deliberate Force officially

Map 3.3
Bosnia-Herzegovina, Changes in Ethnic Divisions between May and October, 1995

Information from U.S. Central Intelligence Agency Map 737414.

ended. In total, Deliberate Force included 3,515 aircraft sorties, two-thirds of them by U.S. aircraft, and 1,026 weapons expended against 48 targets, plus 13 Tomahawk cruise strikes and a two-day artillery barrage.[40]

The war in Bosnia began to come to a close after an official country-wide cease-fire was announced on October 5. Part of the cease-fire agreement included a provision that the presidents of Croatia, Bosnia, and Serbia meet for full negotiations at an as-of-yet undisclosed location in the United States. The negotiations began on November 1, with all three presidents arriving at a U.S. Air Force base in Dayton, Ohio, and concluded on November 21, 1995, leading to an agreement that would become popularly known as the Dayton Accords.

The Accords defined the Republic of Bosnia and Herzegovina as composed of two entities: the Muslim-Croat Federation and the Bosnian Serb Republic. The Bosnian Serbs were to control 49 percent of the territory (they had control of 70 percent of the country in July, 1995, before the Croat-Muslim offensive), with the Muslim and Croat regions constituting the other 51 percent. A constitution was established recognizing the partition, and an Implementation Force authorized. The Implementation Force (IFOR) consisted of 60,000 troops, principally from NATO countries, with the mission of enforcing the cease-fire and other terms of the Accords. The UN Security Council turned over implementation control to NATO. The United States committed ground forces as part of IFOR and agreed to take part in the equipping and training of the forces of the Muslim-Croat Federation.

PRINCIPAL PLAYERS

Ambassador Yasushi Akashi (Japan), Special Representative of the UN Secretary General for the Former Yugoslavia

Dr. Boutros Boutros-Ghali (Egypt), Secretary General of the United Nations

Willy Claes (Belgium), Secretary General of NATO

Lieutenant General Bernard Janvier (France), Commander of Theater Forces, United Nations Protective Forces (UNPF)

General George Joulwan (U.S.), NATO, Supreme Allied Commander Europe (SACEUR)

Ambassador Richard Holbrooke (U.S.), U.S. Assistant Secretary of State and Chief U.S. negotiator for the Former Yugoslavia

General Radko Mladic, Commander-in-Chief, Bosnian Serb Army

Lieutenant General Michael Rose (UK), Military Commanders of United Nations Forces in Bosnia and Herzegovina (UNPROFOR), January 1994 to January 1995

Lieutenant Michael Ryan (U.S.), Commander of NATO Allied Air Forces Southern Europe

Admiral Leighton Smith (U.S.), Commander of NATO Allied Forces Southern Europe

Lieutenant General Rupert Smith (UK), Commander of UNPROFOR in Bosnia-Herzegovina, March to December 1995

PARTIAL CHRONOLOGY OF EVENTS RELEVANT TO THE BOSNIAN WAR (1992–95)

1991

June—Croatia and Slovenia declare independence; The European Community (EC) takes the lead in mediating conflict.

July—Yugoslav Army enters Croatia; EC offers recognition if states will hold national referendum and respect minority rights.

1992

Feb—Under UN Security Council Resolution 743, UNPROFOR peace-keepers enter Croatia.

April—EC and U.S. recognize Bosnia-Herzegovina.

June—UNPROFOR mandate expanded to include Bosnia-Herzegovina.

October—UNSCR 781 prohibits unauthorized flights in Bosnia (Operation Sky Watch).

1993

April—UNSCR 816 authorizes countries to take a more active role in enforcing no-fly zone; NATO Operation Deny Flight begins.

May—UN declares enclaves "safe areas."

June 4—Under UNSCR 836, NATO provides close air support for UN-PROFOR and possible wider strikes in support of safe areas mandate; dual-key system established.

1994

February 28—Four Croatian Serb fighters from Udbina shot down.

April—Bosnian Serb Army attacks Gorazde; first NATO air strikes take place; UNPROFOR personnel taken hostage.

November—UN extends no-fly zone to cover Croatia; Croatian Serb aircraft violate flight ban; NATO launches attack on Udbina airfield.

December—Bosnian Serb Army takes UNPROFOR prisoners to avert further air strikes.

December 2—UN and NATO jointly agree to suspend air strikes over Bosnia and resume talks with Bosnian Serbs. Former U.S. President Carter brokers a four-month cease-fire.

1995

May 1—Croat army begins offensive operations against Serbs within Croatia.

May—Bosnian Serbs seize heavy weapons in safe areas; NATO conducts air strikes on May 25 and 26; video broadcasts of UNPROFOR hostages seen worldwide.

June 2—USAF Captain O'Grady shot down; Bosnian Serbs release 121 hostages.

July 11—Srebrenica overrun, with widespread executions of Bosnian Muslims.

July 21—London Conference takes place; RRF occupies Mt. Igman near Sarajevo.

August 4—Croatia begins attack on Serb-held Krajina in Croatia, driving refugees into Bosnia.

August 28—Sarajevo marketplace bombing.

August 30—Deliberate Force air strikes begin.

September 1—General Janvier, with Admiral Smith's agreement, suspends air strikes.

September 5—Air strikes resume.

September 10—TLAM attacks on Bosnian Serb air defense system.

September 14—Offensive air operations suspended based on negotiated agreement.

November 21—Agreement on the Dayton Accords.

GLOSSARY OF TERMS (DEPARTMENT OF DEFENSE DEFINITIONS)

Peace Building Post-conflict actions, predominately diplomatic and economic, that strengthen and rebuild governmental infrastructure and institutions in order to avoid a relapse into conflict.

Peace Enforcement Application of military force, or the threat of its use, normally pursuant to international authorization, to compel compliance with resolutions or sanctions designed to maintain or restore peace and order. Also called PE.

Peacekeeping Military operations undertaken with the consent of all major parties to a dispute, designed to monitor and facilitate implementation of an agreement (cease-fire, truce, or other such agreement) and support diplomatic efforts to reach a long-term political settlement. Also called PK.

Peacemaking The process of diplomacy, mediation, negotiation, or other forms of peaceful settlements that arranges an end to a dispute, and resolves issues that led to it.

Peace Operations A broad term that encompasses peacekeeping operations and peace enforcement operations conducted in support of diplomatic efforts to establish and maintain peace. Also called PO.

Notes

1. Robert Owen, "Summary of the Air University Balkans Air Campaign Study," November 1997 Draft (Maxwell AFB: USAF School of Advanced Airpower Studies, November 1997) Unclassified Draft, p. 9. Hereafter referred to as BACS.

2. Richard Holbrooke, *To End a War* (New York: Random House, 1998), p. 61.

3. BACS, p. 9.

4. Michael Beale, *Bombs Over Bosnia: The Role of Airpower in Bosnia-Hercegovina* (Montgomery, AL: Air University Press, 1997), p. 27.

5. Jan Honig and Norbert Both, *Srebrenica: Diary of a War Crime* (New York: Penguin Books, 1996), p. 150.

6. The brief history of the Bosnian conflict presented here serves only to place the actions by the international organizations involved in context. For an excellent history of the conflict, particularly of the time period described here, see Steven L. Burg and Paul S. Shoup. *The War in Bosnia Herzegovina: Ethnic Conflict and International Intervention* (Armonk, NY: M.E. Sharpe, Inc., 1999).

7. The official name; the shortened and more familiar name, Bosnia, is used throughout this account.

8. Adolf Carlson, "No Balm in Gilead: The Employment of Military Force in the War in Former Yugoslavia and Prospects for a Lasting Peace," in Stephen J. Blank (ed.), *Yugoslavia's Wars: The Problem from Hell* (Carlisle, PA: U.S. Army War College Strategic Studies Institute, 1995), pp. 97–8.

9. UN Security Council Resolution 836, June 4, 1993.

10. Ibid, as quoted from Sean Taylor, "A Shot in the Dark," *Army Times*, August 24, 1992.

11. Yasushi Akashi, "The Limits of UN Diplomacy and the Future of Conflict

Mediation," *Survival*, Vol. 37, No. 4 (Winter 1995–6), p. 96, as cited in Honig and Both, *Srebrenica*, p. 186.

12. United Nations, "Report of the Secretary General Pursuant to General Assembly Resolution 53/35 (1998), Sebrenica Report" (New York: 1999), Para. 138.

13. BACS, p. 11.

14. Ibid., p. 10.

15. United Nations Security Council document S/1995/444, Para. 62.

16. Ibid., Paras. 206–209.

17. Ibid., Paras. 214–220.

18. Defense Link, Defense Issues, Vol. 10, No. 60, "U.S. Policy on Bosnia Remains Consistent," prepared statement by Secretary of Defense William J. Perry to the Senate Armed Services Committee, June 7, 1995. Though not acknowledged at the time, the RRF could also serve as a covering force for a withdrawal of UN forces.

19. United Nations, "Report of the Secretary General Pursuant to General Assembly Resolution 53/35 (1998), Sebrenica Report" (New York: 1999), Paras. 318–390.

20. BACS, pp. 11–12.

21. To complete the confusion, the Serb air defense forces, misinterpreting the NATO aircraft's intent, locked on with their radars, and made themselves the target of HARM missiles from the NATO aircraft. See BACS, Chp. 2, footnote #82.

22. BACS, pp. 12–13.

23. Holbrooke, *To End a War*, pp. 3–18, 73–4.

24. BACS, pp. 25, 26.

25. Ibid., p. 13.

26. Holbrooke, *To End a War*, p. 99.

27. Rick Atkinson, "In Almost Losing Its Resolve, NATO Alliance Found Itself," *Washington Post*, November 16, 1995.

28. Holbrooke, *To End a War*, p. 118.

29. BACS, p. 21.

30. Rick Atkinson, "Put to the Test NATO, Shows Its Mettle" *International Herald Tribune*, November 20, 1995.

31. BACS, p. 17.

32. Holbrooke, *To End a War*, pp. 143–4.

33. Atkinson, "In Almost Losing Its Resolve, NATO Alliance Found Itself."

34. Holbrooke received confirmation from Admiral Smith the next day that an estimated three days of new targets remained. Holbrooke, *To End a War*, p. 146.

35. BACS, p. 22.

36. Ibid., pp. 22–3.

37. Holbrooke, *To End a War*, pp. 151–52.

38. Rick Atkinson, "NATO Suspends Bombing in Bosnia," *Washington Post*, September 15, 1995.

39. Holbrooke, *To End a War*, pp. 158–60.

40. BACS, p. 14.

"Guaranteeing" Peace Agreements: The Peru-Ecuador Border Dispute

THEODORE S. WILKINSON

The outbreak of border conflict between Peru and Ecuador at the beginning of 1995 came as a surprise. Most Latin American countries had solved or shelved their post-colonial border disputes. The Peru-Ecuador dispute had simmered on for years, but there was no apparent reason for it to boil over at that particular time.

As guarantors of a 1942 framework peace agreement between the two Andean countries, Argentina, Brazil, Chile, and the United States were called into action to stop the conflict and monitor a cease-fire. U.S. men and materiel would be needed. But how much to invest in peace? Decisions on how to respond to calls for the United States to step in had to consider factors unique to the Latin American context—the nature of the conflict, U.S. interests in the region, and U.S. obligations as a guarantor. These decisions also had to take into account the global context, where the proliferation of dangerous U.S. peacekeeping missions had become a politically charged issue. The arguments for participating fully had to be weighed against the risks of sending U.S. forces into harm's way. Once the decision to go ahead with an observer mission had been made, U.S. policy officials still faced challenges in minimizing the risks and coordinating an exit strategy to end the mission.

Coping with these issues fell heavily on Assistant Secretary of State Alexander Watson in Washington and on U.S. special envoy Luigi Einaudi, who divided his time between interagency coordination in Washington and dealing with Peru, Ecuador, and the other guarantors in their capitals. This case study assesses competing U.S. interests that Watson, Einaudi, and other policy-level officials had to take into account in responding to the challenges of the Peru-Ecuador dispute. A list of principal players and a brief chronology are given at the end of the chapter.

THE NATURE OF THE CONFLICT

The focus of fighting was the virtually uninhabited Andean valley of the upper Cenepa River, where repeated earlier efforts to resolve a lingering dispute about the frontier had failed. As of December 1994, Ecuadorian army chiefs had sent troops to construct camps in the disputed territory, very likely without the knowledge of their own president. Peruvian patrols that frequently combed the area encountered them, challenged them at first, and soon began skirmishing. Sporadic exchanges of fire produced casualties. By mid-January there was a sort of mountain jungle battle line. Reinforcements arrived from both sides, close air support was called in, and by late January 1995 the threat loomed of wider hostilities between the two countries, including in the heavily populated coastal area, or even at sea.

To the outside observer, it was hard to imagine why Peru and Ecuador could be on the verge of war over this remote and inhospitable territory without any proven resources, but the roots of the dispute ran deep, perhaps even back to the last days of the Inca empire, when rival pretenders ruled in Quito and Cuzco. Both countries naturally sought to control the headwaters of the Amazon River, which rises in the Andes, but Ecuador's Amazonian ambitions had suffered in the last two centuries. In 1802, before the end of the Spanish colonial empire, administration of much of the territory adjoining the Marañón River—the westernmost of the Amazon's principal tributaries—had been reassigned from Bogota and Quito to Lima. In negotiations in the 1820s to settle post-colonial boundaries, the issue arose again. The Caracas-born Simon Bolívar, liberator of the northern half of the continent from Spain, thought that the newly independent union of Gran Colombia (present-day Venezuela, Colombia, and Ecuador) should extend to the Marañón in the south and meet Peru there, but the issue outlived Bolívar.

Gran Colombia split apart in 1830, still without an agreed southern frontier, and one after another effort to settle the issue foundered in the ensuing century. One difficulty was the Ecuadorian people's traditional, emotion-laden self-image as an Amazonian nation. Ecuadorian maps showed the country extending as far east as Brazil. To overcome weaknesses in Ecuador's legal case, its negotiators demanded that history and equity as well as law be taken into account, and insisted that any border agreement include at least an ample stretch along the Marañón. A proposed arbitral award by the King of Spain in 1910 would in fact have given Ecuador some fifty miles of frontage on the Marañón, but reports of the agreement sparked opposition demonstrations in Ecuador and retaliatory fervor in Peru. Both sides began mobilizing forces, and the King abandoned the effort.

Mediation efforts were picked up by the United States, Brazil, and Argentina through the next three decades, but Peru's legal arguments gained force as Lima continued to consolidate effective control over both sides of the Marañón. A 1936 Peruvian map showing the *de facto* border along the Andes *cordillera* north of the Marañón was never directly rebutted by Ecuador. As World War II began in Europe mediation efforts had reached a virtual standstill. Heightened tensions led to a border war in mid-1941, with Peru occupying parts of southern Ecuador.

Once more the United States, Argentina, and Brazil—soon joined by Chile—sought to act collectively to restore the peace. The entry of the United States into World War II added new urgency. The realities of the situation—continued Peruvian occupation of southern Ecuador and the importance of restoring hemispheric solidarity in the face of the Axis challenge—dictated a quick and pragmatic solution. The result was the Protocol of Rio de Janeiro (the "Rio Protocol") negotiated during a January 1942 meeting of hemispheric foreign ministers. Laying down a series of points and lines to delimit the frontier, the Protocol broadly codified the status quo, and identified the four sponsors as guarantors. Ecuadorian Foreign Minister Julio Tobar sought to delay adoption of the document, but was subjected to heavy collective pressure from his colleagues. In the end he concluded that Ecuador had no real choice and reluctantly signed it on January 29. The Ecuadorian Congress accepted his decision at the time and ratified the agreement a month later, as did the Peruvian Congress.

The agreement contains more than just territorial commitments. Significantly, it also committed the two countries to negotiate a treaty of commerce and navigation, so that Ecuador could at least have legally recognized use of the Marañón River for trade. It gave Ecuador the additional assurance that the four guarantor countries would remain involved until Peru withdrew its troops from occupied Ecuador, until the frontier was fully demarcated, and until any other problems of implementation had been worked out.

The Protocol's points and lines were clear and simple, but disputes soon arose on how to interpret several geographic features that were supposed to be used to demarcate the frontier. Even Brazilian arbitration failed to resolve them entirely in the Andes and at one key juncture near the tri-point with Colombia (see Map 4.1).[1] In the most sensitive central Andean sector, the United States compounded the problem while trying to help. At considerable cost (including two lost aircraft and crews), the U.S. Army Air Force surveyed and mapped the upper Cenepa Valley, which had not been thoroughly mapped before. The survey showed that the Cenepa River and its drainage basin extend northwards along most of the Andean Cordillera del Condor, separating two other watersheds that are mentioned specifically in the Protocol—the Santiago and the Zamora. Because the Protocol implied that these two watersheds were adjacent, the U.S. survey cast new doubt on the language of the Protocol itself.

These new doubts enabled Ecuadorians to begin distancing themselves from commitments that they had accepted only with the greatest reluctance in the first place. Ecuador seized on the study to call the 1942 treaty "inexecutable" in that part of the Andes, and to stop work on approximately 100 miles of the border along the Cordillera del Condor that had not yet been demarcated. Later, in 1960, Ecuadorian President Velasco denounced the agreement entirely. Neither Peru nor the guarantors accepted the validity of the Ecuadorian denunciation.

Despite the guarantors' firmness in support of the Protocol, Ecuadorians continued to look for outside support for adjustments based on equity. They had found sympathizers in the United States from time to time—principally among diplomats seeking new ways to arrange the elements of a possible compromise settlement. They found new hope when at the 1977 Panama Canal Treaty signing ceremonies in Washington President Carter referred publicly to the meetings he had just had with the parties' presidents, and to the possibility of discussions of Ecuadorian "access" to the Marañón.[2] It soon became evident, however, that Carter was simply trying to build bridges, and that Peru was not willing to discuss territorial "access."

The long, uneasy standoff that followed Ecuador's denunciation of the Protocol broke down in 1981, when Ecuador stationed small detachments in the disputed upper Cenepa Valley and resisted Peruvian attempts to dislodge them. The guarantors were called into action. They insisted on a pull-back by both sides and sent their military attaches to observe it, but the United States lost yet another aircraft—a helicopter and three crewmen—during the mission. The loss was attributable to bad weather rather than to hostile action, but the incident established beyond any doubt just how hazardous Andean observer operations could be for U.S. forces.

Hostilities were narrowly averted again in 1991, when Peru and Ecuador

Map 4.1
Peru-Ecuador Conflict, Areas of Dispute

Maps provided by www.worldatlas.com.

accepted a "gentlemen's agreement" to pull back overlapping military outposts in another disputed portion of the Andes frontier fifty miles northeast of the Cenepa (near the border marker "Cusumaza Bumbuiza," in the area subsequently designated "Zone Alfa" by observers).

Bilateral relations improved after the 1991 disengagement, and in January 1992 Peruvian President Alberto Fujimori became the first incumbent Peruvian president to visit Ecuador. Fujimori used the occasion to present a detailed package of bilateral settlement proposals, including an offer to negotiate the treaty of commerce and navigation that had been foreseen in 1942, with a free port for Ecuador on the Marañón. Fujimori's conditions were that Ecuador must once again accept the full validity of the Rio Protocol, including arbitral decisions about it, drop claims to a southern frontier on the Marañón, and agree to finish the process of demarcation. The Ecuadorian government avoided a direct answer to these specific proposals, but in general did not appear ill-disposed to Fujimori, who was coming under sharp criticism elsewhere in the hemisphere in 1992–94, including in the United States, for autocratic domestic policies. The stage scarcely seemed set for the outbreak of hostilities on the frontier at the midpoint of the 1990s.

HOW MUCH TO INVEST IN PEACE

The Guarantors Organize

As in many similar situations, decisions on how the guarantors should respond to this sudden new crisis had to be made on the basis of partial and uncertain information. After the initial clashes, Ecuador and Peru had massed more troops in the Cenepa Valley and put forces elsewhere on a war footing. The situation was chaotic in the steamy, remote Cenepa area, with Ecuador once again seeking to hold disputed territory and being challenged by Peru. More than 5,000 troops were intermingled in the jungle, and not even local commanders could say with any certainty who held what territory. Both sides were claiming control of outposts with names like "Tiwintza" that did not appear on any existing maps, located somewhere near the source of the Cenepa. Even without the enemy, troops on patrol had to cope with trailless jungle, heat, torrential rains, snakes, insects, knee-deep mud, and mines. Scouting the area for the U.S. Southern Command (CINCSouth) in Panama immediately on the heels of a cease-fire in late February 1995, U.S. Marine Major John Legters observed: "On a hardship scale of one to ten for fighting terrain, this is a twelve."[3] Whatever the actual situation on the ground, it was clear that both sides generally wanted a way to avoid escalation, a fig leaf behind which they could disengage without losing face.

Using the best information that they could gather from the parties, the press, CINCSouth, and their own diplomatic channels, the guarantor ambassadors in Brasilia began meetings in the third week of January with the Brazilian deputy foreign minister, but their joint public calls for mutual restraint by the parties failed to stop the fighting. As a next step, the deputy foreign ministers of Peru and Ecuador were summoned to Rio de Janeiro, where they were met by senior officials from all four guarantor capitals. Assistant Secretary of State Alexander Watson joined U.S. Ambassador to Brazil Melvyn Levitsky to lead the U.S. team. Watson, an engaging and unflappable career diplomat, had served from 1986 to 1989 as American Ambassador to Peru and knew President Fujimori well. With extensive prior experience in other Latin American posts, Watson was Secretary of State Warren Christopher's "point man" for problems in the hemisphere. In fact, Secretary of State Christopher had assigned him to work full-time on the "tequila crisis"—the late 1994 to early 1995 collapse of the Mexican peso—and was reluctant to let him leave Washington at all at the time. Watson argued that the United States had to be represented in Rio at least at his level, and that if he could not go, someone higher in the hierarchy such as Under Secretary for Political Affairs Peter Tarnoff would have to. Christopher relented by allowing him an initial twenty-four hours to make a firefighting trip to Rio.[4]

Watson's twenty-four-hour pass was scarcely a realistic time frame. The guarantors' meetings with Peru and Ecuador dragged on day and night for a week in Rio in the old palace of Itamaraty, only one room of which was air-conditioned. The effort left the diplomats drained, but there was still no general agreement on the terms for a cease-fire. Levitsky needed to get back to Brasilia to resume his regular bilateral U.S.-Brazil work. Watson had gotten an extension from Christopher to stay for a week but could scarcely go on focusing exclusively on Peru and Ecuador, even when the issue was one of war or peace. Watson decided to turn to Luigi Einaudi, who at that time was serving as deputy director of the State Department's policy planning staff, to join the talks as a special U.S. envoy.

Grandson of the first Italian president after Mussolini, Einaudi was a Harvard-educated civil servant who had advised assistant secretaries of state for Latin America for two decades. Named Ambassador to the Organization of American States (OAS) during the Bush administration, Einaudi was equally articulate in English and Spanish, and had honed his crisis management skills in the OAS, dealing among other matters with Latin American reactions to the U.S. anti-Noriega police action in Panama (1989). He had studied Peru and knew the issues and many of the players well, and was adept at keeping the influential media both informed and interested.

Watson recalls picking Einaudi to take on the assignment not just because of his background and ambassadorial rank, but also because he was widely respected in the hemisphere and because of his patient personal style. "He listens, he thinks, he is creative, and he is not overbearing." Watson asked Einaudi to look at the task as a long-term undertaking, in which he would work towards a "permanent solution, so the conflict wouldn't just break out once again later."[5] Einaudi agreed, but asked to be authorized to maintain close liaison with the military—in particular with CINC-South, General Barry McCaffrey, whose support he considered essential for any peacekeeping efforts.[6] McCaffrey could not only provide the essential men and materiel for the mission; he could also exercise considerable influence with both Peruvian and Ecuadorian militaries to make a settlement stick.

In the weeks that followed until a cease-fire and the years of peace-building thereafter, Einaudi's three guarantor counterparts were the political deputy foreign ministers of Brazil, Argentina, and Chile—in effect, the third-ranking officers of their foreign ministries. The guarantors customarily deferred to Brazil as host and the acknowledged coordinator of the four, but much of the informal, behind-the-scenes persuasion was actually done on the telephone or in private meetings by Einaudi. In public the four senior diplomats followed the "one for all: all for one" rule of Dumas's musketeers: they made no pronouncements unless all four had met and agreed on them.[7]

The U.S. Responds

How much should the United States and the other guarantor governments invest once more in bandaging a wound that never seemed to heal? The parties wanted the guarantors to provide a truce supervisory force to police a disengagement in the upper Cenepa Valley. The burden of putting together an observer force would clearly fall most heavily on the United States, since only General McCaffrey's CINCSouth command was in a position to provide the helicopters, communications, and most of the necessary logistics for such a force in a timely way. Thus the United States had to start its review of how to respond by asking how large a drain on Southern Command resources would be involved. To help focus the answer, discussions among the guarantors in Brasilia in early February 1995 began projecting forty observers, four Blackhawk helicopters, and a minimum package of logistic support.

Assuming that the Southern Command could accommodate supporting an observer mission at this level without undue strain, the United States still had to consider what interests would be served. Few, if any, global military security interests were involved. There was no longer any danger of Soviet exploitation of a regional conflict. Moreover, no American citizens were threatened; no counter-narcotics efforts would be advanced, at least in any direct way. Nor was there any precedent for the deployment of U.S. military truce supervisors anywhere on the South American continent.

As for legal considerations, nothing in the Rio Protocol promised any kind of military intervention by the guarantors. Even if it had, the Protocol did not have the force of a treaty for the United States Unlike Peru and Ecuador which had ratified it as parties, the United States and the other guarantors had only signed the document, in effect as witnesses, and had not submitted it to their legislatures for ratification.[8]

GET IN OR STAY OUT? REGIONAL CONSIDERATIONS

Despite these negatives, the regional pros and cons weighed heavily in favor of a positive response. The U.S. image in the hemisphere was a major factor. After two years in office, President Clinton was already being accused, as had many presidents before him, of concentrating on Europe, the Middle East, and East Asia, and ignoring Latin America. To counter this perception and to advance a hemispheric agenda, including a Free Trade Area of the Americas (FTAA), the president had called together a regional summit meeting in Miami in mid-December 1994. This initiative led even such Clinton critics as Henry Kissinger to admit: "As far as Latin America is concerned, he [Clinton] has got it right."[9] Previously, the Bush administration had used a kind of task force approach to Latin American problem solving: one group of nations to expand trade (NAFTA); another to counter narcotics trafficking (summit meetings with the Andean cocaine producers plus Mexico); other groups and forums to promote law enforcement cooperation, restrict money laundering, etc. In contrast, the Clinton administration approach was to bring all the hemispheric presidents together and to seek a common regional agenda, in the hope of achieving more long-term results and reviving Simon Bolívar's appealing concept of common purpose in the Western Hemisphere.

Only days after a highly successful Miami summit, however, the "tequila crisis" had broken out, substantially offsetting the positive impact of the meeting. To limit the damage Secretary Christopher told Watson to work out a package of political steps that Mexico itself could take to help persuade the U.S. Congress to approve a major financial bailout, and Watson began conferring daily with Mexican Foreign Minister Angel Gurría. In the midst of this, Watson recalls: "The last thing I needed was to have to deal with a Peru-Ecuador crisis at the other end of the continent!"[10]

Yet for Watson at first, and later for Einaudi, there was no way to ignore or sidestep the possibility that hostilities between Peru and Ecuador might continue or even escalate. For the time being, the fighting was localized in a remote area some 100 miles east of the heavily settled coastal corridor. But casualties were already in the hundreds, national passions were inflamed, and there was ample precedent for wider hostilities. Tank-led Peruvian forces had advanced into populated southern Ecuador in 1941 and were poised to take Guayaquil when a cease-fire was achieved. This time there could be parallel air and sea battles.

In the face of such dangers, the risks to the peace of *not* providing the framework for disengagement were too high. Moreover, Watson's State Department bureau had worked hard to get consensus on an ambitious hemispheric agenda at Miami, including projected joint measures towards democratization, law enforcement and counter-narcotics cooperation. War between Peru and Ecuador would be a serious setback to the joint action program. If the guarantors declined to act, one or the other of the parties was almost certain to look further afield for outside support and to take the matter back to the OAS (which had delegated action to the guarantors) or even to the United Nations, with the likelihood of weeks of debate that would be long on rhetoric and short on remedies.

In contrast, if they did respond positively, the guarantors could use the situation to try to force an end to the protracted dispute. "We had a one-time opportunity to solve this permanently," Watson recalls. Moreover, the U.S. promise to serve as a guarantor might not be airtight legally, but Watson considered it "a solemn commitment" which the United States had been respecting in practice for fifty years.[11]

These were paramount considerations for regional policymakers. For Watson and Einaudi, the balance of regional political and economic interests was clearly in favor of sending military observers. McCaffrey agreed from the military standpoint, and felt that the mission was readily "manageable." In fact, he preferred having the U.S. Southern Command provide the entire logistics support package, rather than the alternate possibilities of splitting it up among the guarantors or having the parties seek private contracts for helicopters and observers.[12]

GET IN OR STAY OUT? GLOBAL CONSIDERATIONS

In the White House, however, the balance taking global interests into account was not quite so clear. U.S. military peacekeeping and related duties abroad were political mine fields. The 1993 humiliation of U.S. ground forces in a UN operation in Somalia was still fresh in public memory. Even within the hemisphere, U.S. and UN efforts to buttress democratization in Haiti with military forces had gotten off to a poor start just a few months earlier. Despite the record, the administration was in the process of seeking congressional approval and funding for yet another deployment of U.S. forces into a charged atmosphere, in Bosnia. Most legislators were skeptical or opposed. The U.S. administration could scarcely afford bad news from any military deployment abroad, even a lost helicopter in South America, for fear of losing key votes in support of funding a key peace-keeping initiative in the Balkans.

Confronted with such misgivings, Watson argued that the Western Hemisphere as opposed to other continents was predominantly at peace; that no country had gone to war to solve a territorial issue since the Honduras-El Salvador "soccer war" of 1973; and that the idea of solving disputes with violence must not be permitted to prevail now. Therefore the guarantors must act. Nevertheless, he found the Latin America staff at the National Security Council (NSC) "scared as hell" about the possibility of casualties.[13] In view of the legislative sensitivities, there was even resistance in the White House to using the word "peacekeeping" in connection with the proposed Peru-Ecuador operation.[14]

Despite General McCaffrey's readiness to send forces, the Pentagon was similarly cautious. Watson and his deputies found Defense as worried as the NSC about the possibility of casualties, and concerned about making "open-ended commitments." If the United States was to participate, Pentagon spokesmen echoed McCaffrey's reservations about any operation that would involve shared logistic support, on the grounds that a U.S.-only support package would be far safer for all concerned, because it would have better equipment, training, and command, control and communications.[15]

While Watson was fighting these battles in Washington, Einaudi stayed in daily contact with him and kept the parties and the other guarantors sensitized to the White House's cold feet. It was clear that he would have to bend over backwards with the other guarantors to keep the White House and the Defense Department on board.[16] Since restricting U.S. participation in the guarantor observer force to a token element was unrealistic, it would be necessary to avoid an open-ended commitment in another way—by limiting the duration of the mission. Einaudi was instructed to insist that the initial guarantor deployment be for no more than ninety days. This would constitute part of an "exit strategy" that would allow the United States to withdraw if necessary. Most other participants felt that such a short time frame was impractical, but went along with the U.S. imperative on the understanding that extensions could and almost certainly would be sought.

There was no disagreement among the guarantors about the need for one other element in the agreement to send observers. Whether it proved necessary to extend the observer force or not, there must also be a commitment by the parties to seek an end to the dispute and to terminate the guarantors' responsibilities under the Rio Protocol, which had already lasted a half century more than originally contemplated. As Einaudi had been instructed to insist, the parties must agree to sit down and work out a final solution if they wanted the guarantors to monitor a cease-fire in the interim. In effect, the commitment by the parties to address their dispute would become a second pillar of an exit strategy. If the parties failed to live up to this promise, the U.S. commitment to provide truce observers would also end. The United States at least was unwilling to go through the front door of sending observers until assured that it could get out through an unlocked and unobstructed back door. The other guarantors were less concerned, but went along with U.S. insistence on an exit strategy.

With all these elements in play, a general agreement among the six governments meeting in Brasilia still took several more weeks to work out. The time and effort that went into it was not lost. The Declaration of Itamaraty that emerged on February 17, 1995, set the framework for both the guarantor Military Observer Mission, Peru-Ecuador (which came to be known as MOMEP) and for efforts to resolve the dispute. To meet the guarantors' essential condition for acting, the parties agreed to enter into "talks" (*conversaciones*)—so designated because Peru continued to insist that there was nothing new to "negotiate" about. The subject of the talks was to be the "underlying impasses," a formulation designed to avoid taking sides on the merits of the Rio Protocol. Prospects for the "talks" were substantially improved by Ecuadorian President Sixto Duran Ballen's public radio acknowledgment on the same date, February 17, that the Rio Protocol, even if flawed, could the basis for a settlement.

On the ground, the Declaration of Itamaraty stipulated that MOMEP was to separate the combat forces in the upper Cenepa Valley and recommend a zone around the confrontation area that would be demilitarized. In further deference to U.S. reservations about participation, Peru and Ecuador were put on notice that they would have to bear the costs of deploying MOMEP, although regular salaries and equipment costs would continue to be borne by the guarantors for their own forces. (This was later made explicit in agreed rules of procedure for the observers.) As in the case of the exit strategy, the other guarantors were less insistent on dunning the parties for the bill, but of course their expenses at the outset would be minimal in comparison with those of CINCSouth.

RECOUPING THE INVESTMENT AND IMPLEMENTING THE EXIT STRATEGY

Problems on the Ground

High-level U.S. concerns about political exposure and about the safety of U.S. forces continued during the formation and deployment of MOMEP and caused continuing frictions with the other guarantors. The first issue was how to structure command. Washington wariness about the mission was heightened by the prospect of putting U.S. forces under foreign command. It was agreed that each guarantor would provide ten observers and that the commander and his staff would rotate between border command headquarters in Patuca, Ecuador, and Bagua, Peru, but General McCaffrey had reservations about handing over complete control of the helicopters and the bulk of the logistics, which the United States was providing. Yet in Peru-Ecuador guarantor matters, 50-plus years of practice had established that Brazil was the lead partner. One way or another, the United States would almost certainly have to pay lip service to Brazil's primary responsibility here in the heartland of South America.

The command enigma was finally solved as MOMEP was deploying in early March by giving the Brazilian general assigned to MOMEP overall "coordination" and operational control over observer missions, but leaving operational control over the helicopters and support elements in the hands of the senior U.S. officer present. In the view of Colonel Glenn A. Weidner, the initial U.S. contingent commander, the compromise "was reassuring to U.S. military and political authorities, but it implicitly challenged the authority of the Brazilian coordinator and would become a serious issue at the outset of the mission."[17]

There were further strains when the observers actually arrived at Patuca from Brazil on March 12. The U.S. Blackhawk helicopters had arrived concurrently from Panama. The four teams of guarantor military officers thought it was urgent to deploy to the Cenepa Valley some thirty miles away and begin separating forces. Peruvian and Ecuadorian forces were still skirmishing and suffering casualties despite the cease-fire. However, permission for U.S. helicopters and personnel to proceed was held up by CINCSouth pending a complete agreement among the guarantors on a concept of operations. Impatient with U.S. firmness, the observers of the other three guarantor countries went ahead to begin operations on their own, using Peruvian and Ecuadorian helicopters.[18]

At the core of disagreements over the concept of operations was what should come first—the separation of forces or fixing the limits of a demilitarized zone (DMZ). Once again, concern about the safety of the observers dictated the U.S. position. Establishing a DMZ first would provide greater security; since observers in an empty DMZ would run little risk of exposure to hostile fire. On instructions from Panama, Weidner insisted on getting an agreed DMZ first. In contrast, Brazilian General Candido Freire, the first MOMEP commander, thought that this would lead to "endless haggling" between the parties, who were both fearful that a DMZ decree could somehow prejudge an ultimate territorial settlement, and would delay further the most pressing task of getting the troops apart and turning the cease-fire into a reality. It took Einaudi's intercession with Mc-Caffrey to overcome the DMZ/separation impasse with a compromise. A temporary "security" zone would be established first. All troops in the combat area would have to be withdrawn except for one 50-man outpost on each side. This temporary measure would be followed later with an agreement on the precise limits of the DMZ.[19]

By August 1995 MOMEP's initial military tasks had been done, but interguarantor strains continued with each 90- or 180-day renewal of the on-site observer force for the next two years. The United States pressed for progress towards a solution and more burden-sharing by others. With less at stake, the other guarantors demanded less of the parties. But in late 1997 the problem was largely resolved for the United States through a scheme devised jointly by the Brazilian military and the U.S. Embassy in Brazil. The Brazilian military wanted Blackhawk helicopters but couldn't get their civilian chiefs to authorize funding. Levitsky helped them make their case by pressing Brazilian President Cardoso and his Strategic Affairs Secretary Sardenberg to set aside funds for the helicopters and to assume a posture fitting for Brazil as lead guarantor, taking over helicopter and other primary MOMEP logistic support functions from the United States. The process was painfully slow, but the Brazilian government finally acquiesced. When the change was accomplished, White House concerns about U.S. vulnerability in MOMEP eased considerably. "We heaved a sigh of relief," recalls NSC Staff Deputy for Latin America Ted Piccone.[20]

Apart from logistics support, Einaudi had pressed from the outset for another eventual evolutionary change in MOMEP—including Peruvian and Ecuadorian observers in MOMEP, along with those of the guarantors. The idea was to increase the transparency of MOMEP operations for both parties and at the same time to reduce progressively the size of the guarantors' own observer contingents. The parties accepted the idea, and over the ensuing two years more than half of the guarantor observers were replaced with Peruvians and Ecuadorians.

As a result of these changes, by the end of 1997 the United States had in effect substantially implemented the military part of the "exit strategy." Exposure of U.S. forces to danger had been reduced to a minimum. What remained to complete the strategy was to get Peru and Ecuador to negotiate a final settlement.

At the Negotiating Table

On the diplomatic side, the problem for Einaudi and the State Department after mid-1995 was getting the negotiations underway and bringing them to closure. The United States wanted the dispute settled so that important regional policy efforts could thrive. Moreover, with the United States now committed to participation in peace-making, there was no longer an issue of policy choices. The dilemma was to find ways to achieve the goal. In the abstract this should not have been difficult for the United States, which now exercised "uncontested hegemony" in the hemisphere as a result of ". . . the implosion of the Soviet Union, the withdrawal of extrahemispheric powers, and the triumph of neoliberal ideology."[21] Beyond that, the United States was working with the largest and second largest powers in South America (Brazil and Argentina) as co-guarantors. If they had seen fit to threaten the parties, the guarantors could surely have induced them to settle rapidly. But short of that, even working collectively the guarantors had great difficulty finding the persuasive tools to bring two smaller countries to bend and reach an agreement. The only tangible "stick" was a threat to terminate and withdraw MOMEP. The "carrots" were hard to find.

Moreover, there was no shortage of hurdles to be overcome. First of all, the parties had to agree on procedures for the talks and on the role that the guarantors would play. Then they had to be coaxed through talks and finally prodded to accept a reasonable solution. The first effort consumed 1996, the second 1997, and the third much of 1998. Apart from stalemates along the way over such standard issues as agenda and procedure, other major complications arose. Peruvian Foreign Minister Francisco Tudela (who had designed the strategy for Peruvian participation in the talks) was taken hostage by the Tupac Amaru in the Japanese Embassy for four months beginning in December 1996. Soon thereafter, in February 1997, Ecuadorian President Bucaram was found incompetent by the Congress and replaced with a new president and cabinet.

Shepherding the parties promptly through the necessary steps and facilitating a settlement might still have appeared manageable for U.S. diplomacy, given clear U.S. goals and economic and military preeminence in the hemisphere, but it wasn't. Efforts to set deadlines fell by the wayside. Beginning in 1997, Einaudi sought to use the forthcoming second Summit of the Americas meeting, which was to be held in Santiago in April 1998, as an "action-forcing event." The United States in particular hoped to embellish the summit with an important peace agreement, but the parties and the other guarantors dismissed an April target date as unrealistic. Einaudi lamented that the other guarantors found the effort "typical American impatience," the Peruvians thought it was "unwanted pressure," and the Ecuadorians were "reminded of 1942."[22] A compromise target date of May 30, designed to reach an agreement before Ecuadorian national elections, also proved too optimistic and ended up being set aside without any new deadline.

Another potential avenue to accelerate the peace talks was joint political pressure from all four guarantors, but the United States had difficulty mobilizing joint action. Einaudi's senior diplomatic counterparts were all busy with broad commitments in their ministries and often difficult to assemble for meetings. Even when they could be brought together, they tended to view the dispute as a centuries-old irritant that was unlikely to disappear overnight. In the end in 1998, Brazil at least became much more active along with the United States in exerting pressure on the parties to come to an agreement, taking into account the burden of its own new responsibilities in MOMEP substituting for the United States, and no doubt also Brazilian President Cardoso's personal interest in having an agreement signed in Brasilia during his autumn 1998 campaign for reelection.

As an additional inducement, U.S. officials dangled the prospect of increased U.S. economic aid before the parties' leaders during bilateral visits. In the later stages of the talks in 1998 a commission of prominent Peruvians and Ecuadorians was set up in Washington to look at economic stimuli for the frontier region of Peru and Ecuador after a settlement, with the World Bank, the Interamerican Development Bank, and the Andean

Development Corporation each pledging to earmark $500 million for border integration projects. In parallel, potential donor countries were to be invited to buy one or more shares at $5 million each in a peace fund to finance frontier development projects. The private sector was invited to match these governmental contributions, for a total of $3 billion in projected frontier development funding. The commission produced an impressive border integration plan with a panoply of worthwhile projects and prospective sponsors, but the document was no more than a declaration of intent, which would depend on eventual specific government appropriations for actual funding.

The final possibility was using military assistance to coax reluctant Ecuadorians into a peace agreement. In the aftermath of the 1995 conflict Ecuador had upgraded its aircraft inventory by acquiring four used Israeli KFIR aircraft. By 1997 Peru had raised the ante by acquiring several squadrons of MIG-29 and Sukhoi-25 aircraft from Belarus. Ecuador's generals were pressing the president to buy a similar package of modern fighter aircraft. Should the U.S. sell F-16 aircraft in return for Ecuadorian military support for a peace agreement? The possibility was considered internally, but the policy counterarguments were overwhelming. Apart from the obvious irony of supplying arms to promote peace, the United States had been maintaining an embargo on F-16 sales to Latin America for over a decade and had been leaning heavily on other governments to discourage arms sales to Peru and Ecuador since early 1995.

Closing the Loop

In the end, implementing an exit strategy to terminate MOMEP and to allow the guarantors to retire for good had to rely on diplomacy. By late 1997 the preliminary formalities were over. With Peru's consent, the "talks" were finally to become "negotiations" and to be accelerated by splitting them up into four separate topical commissions, one in each of the guarantor capitals (including the Washington commission mentioned above).[23] Press and public optimism about the possibilities of a settlement were rising. Leaders on both sides had made clear to Einaudi that the time was at hand for a settlement, "but both knew they would need help."[24] In Ecuador in particular, Deputy Foreign Minister Francisco Carrion said that polls taken by the government showed that "75 percent of the people opposed an agreement without territorial adjustments favoring Ecuador's case."[25] Yet independent experts in May 1998 produced a report for both parties that largely favored Peruvian legal and technical positions in the talks. Negotiators might be able to modify the experts' findings in some way to make them more palatable, but they could scarcely simply set them aside or override them. The task called for both imagination and tough decisions.

It also called ultimately for firm leadership by the two presidents, Peru's Fujimori and the newly elected Jamil Mahuad of Ecuador, who had been inaugurated on August 10, 1998. The two first had to overcome a new crisis brought on by renewed Ecuadorian military deployments and Peruvian challenges outside the DMZ but in a disputed part of the Cenepa Valley. Once again the guarantors induced the two sides to pull back under MOMEP supervision, but the confrontation left raw nerves and brought home to both presidents that the frontier would continue to be a tinder box until they personally pulled together the threads of a full settlement and tied them up. Mahuad in particular was faced with challenging domestic economic problems (which ultimately contributed to his downfall in January 2000). With considerable prescience he reckoned that he needed to clear the decks for a storm. Both presidents were motivated to move quickly to finish an agreement, but they needed ideas to help them sell concessions to nationalistic home audiences.

TYING THE KNOT

The ideas came collectively from Einaudi's negotiating group of guarantors plus the foreign ministers of Peru and Ecuador and their assistants. A long foreseen compromise solution was quickly firmed up to overcome Ecuador's interest in free navigation of the Marañón River and Peru's resistance. Ecuador was to be allowed to establish two bonded depots on the Marañón near Iquitos.

There were still raw nerves, however, about the Andes frontier. For the Andes issue two substantive ideas and one procedural one emerged in the last stages of high-level negotiations. Since Peru seemed unlikely to budge in its determination that the frontier must be demarcated in accordance with the opinion of independent legal and technical experts, the negotiators adopted the idea of setting up two adjoining "peace parks" on each side of the Andes divide in the Cenepa area. For presentational purposes the two parks would be environmental sanctuaries, but they would also be demilitarized and thus serve as buffers between the military deployments of the parties. To make it easier for Ecuador to give up long-standing claims, the additional idea surfaced of granting Ecuador ownership of a square kilometer of territory at the Tiwintza outpost in the Cenepa Valley, where the two sides had fought for control in 1995. Peru would remain legally sovereign over all the Cenepa basin, including Tiwintza, but it would be understood that Ecuador could establish a war memorial at Tiwintza for "commemorative acts" and that Peru would build a road to provide Ecuador with access to it.

Even with these modifications an overall agreement would have been hard for either president, in particular Mahuad, to sell to fractious congresses. Accordingly, the guarantors further undertook to present the supplementary measures as their own proposals in a package, on the condition that both congresses would agree beforehand to accept guarantor recommendations.

Spared of the political consequences of having to vote on specific concessions to the other party made by their own negotiators, the congresses agreed in mid-October 1998. Signature by the executive branches of the detailed set of resulting agreements was the final, formal step. The package of frontier dispute settlement agreements was signed by Mahuad and Fujimori at a formal ceremony in Brasilia on October 26, in the presence of a number of Latin American presidents.

EPILOGUE

Just how artificial the Peru-Ecuador dispute had been was nowhere more evident than in the speed with which it seems to have become ancient history. Implementation of the agreements during the first year was smooth and impressive on both sides. The newly agreed frontier was demined and demarcated, bilateral cooperative commissions were set up, and the functions of the guarantors under the Rio Protocol were finally completely fulfilled.

To implement the promises of frontier region development on which the agreements had been sold to suspicious congresses, the two countries set ten-year planning goals intended to benefit the 4.5 million people broadly deemed to be living in the border area. A network of intergovernmental working groups was set up to pursue the planning goals, together with private sector liaison organizations, and both sides now publish bimonthly newsletters on their progress.

At the time of this writing, only five years have now passed since the agreements were signed, but both nationalistic animosities and border tensions seem to be well on the road to oblivion. Peru's and Ecuador's new presidents now meet frequently, and bilateral trade has tripled. Peruvian labor has been filtering northward to earn Ecuador's newly dollarized currency, and to fill jobs left open by Ecuadorian emigration.

Among possible disruptive factors, there are still a few radical Peruvian dissidents in Iquitos who continue to oppose an Ecuadorian presence, but they have no national following. On the Ecuadorian side, army leaders who probably feared losing their *raisons d'être* and budgets without a Peruvian threat have now been assigned a new mission protecting the northern frontier against the real danger of a spillover from the civil war in Colombia.

At the end of 2003, the United States, Japan, and Europe had come through with about half of the $500 million in aid foreseen from them, but the international financial institutions (IFIs) that were being counted on for $1.5 billion in assistance have so far contributed only some $60 million. In fact, the IFIs' weak performance to date may have contributed to bringing Peru and Ecuador closer together, in cooperative efforts to convince them to open their purses.

PRINCIPAL PLAYERS

Fernando Henrique Cardoso, President of Brazil, 1994–2002

Warren Christopher, U.S. Secretary of State, 1993–97

Sixto Duran Ballen, President of Ecuador, 1992–96

Luigi Einaudi, U.S. Special Envoy for Peru-Ecuador Talks, 1995–98

Lt. General Candido Vargas de Freire, Brazilian Army, first "coordinator" of Military Observer Mission, Peru-Ecuador (MOMEP), 1995

Alberto Fujimori, President of Peru, 1991–

Melvin Levitsky, U.S. Ambassador to Brazil, 1994–98

Jamil Mahuad, President of Ecuador, 1998–2000

General Barry McCaffrey, U.S. Army, Commander in Chief, U.S. Southern Command, 1994–97

Francisco Tudela, Peruvian Foreign Minister, 1995–97

Colonel Glenn A. Weidner, U.S. Army, first commander of U.S. forces in MOMEP, 1995

Alexander Watson, U.S. Assistant Secretary of State for Inter-American Affairs, 1993–96

CHRONOLOGY OF EVENTS

1941

July—War between Peru and Ecuador breaks out over centuries-old border dispute. Peru occupies parts of southern Ecuador.

1942

January 29—Foreign Ministers of Peru and Ecuador sign broad border agreement in Protocol of Rio de Janeiro, with United States, Brazil, Argentina, and Chile, to serve as guarantors.

1943–45

Brazilian arbitration resolves some but not all issues of interpreting Rio Protocol.

1947

U.S. aerial survey modifies understandings of border geography, and stimulates Ecuador to challenge parts of Rio Protocol and stop joint work on demarcation.

1960

August—Ecuadorian President Velasco denounces Rio Protocol.

1981

January—Armed forces clash briefly in disputed Upper Cenepa Valley, but forces are separated at insistence of guarantors.

1991

August—Forces clash in another area fifty miles east of the Cenepa, and are separated by a "gentlemen's agreement" along disputed frontier.

1994

December—Peruvian patrols find Ecuadorian camps in Upper Cenepa and challenge them.

1995

January—Clashes in Cenepa Valley intensify, leading to reinforcements and localized hostilities. Guarantors begin intensive talks with parties in Rio and Brasilia.

February 17—Peru and Ecuador sign Declaration of Itamaraty in Brasilia, which calls for a cease-fire and steps towards a permanent settlement.

March 12—Guarantor observer force (MOMEP) arrives at base in Patuca Ecuador, to begin separation of forces in the Cenepa.

1996

October 29—Foreign Ministers of Peru and Ecuador together with guarantors agree on framework for border talks to end dispute.

1997

April–September—Formal first round of talks is held in Brasilia.

1998

January 19—Work plan is agreed for further negotiations, to be split into four commissions, one in each of the guarantor capitals.

August 10—Jamil Mahuad takes office as elected President of Ecuador.

mid-August—Peru challenges new Ecuadorian deployments in disputed territory and guarantors must act again to hold off armed clashes. Negotiations to conclude remaining issues are moved up to the presidential level.

October 26—Presidents Mahuad and Fujimori, in presence of other Latin American presidents, sign package of border agreements in Brasilia.

Notes

1. Map 4.1, showing the entire frontier, indicates six areas of dispute. Except for the circle at Rio Lagartococha and the large rectangle at the Cordillera del Condor, these disputes were technical or administrative in nature, and were dealt with relatively easily in early negotiations.

2. William Krieg, *Ecuadorian-Peruvian Rivalry in the Upper Amazon*, 2nd ed. (Washington, DC: Department of State, Office of External Research Study, 1986), p. 222.

3. Remark made to the author at Ecuadorian Coangos base on Andes *cordillera* above the Cenepa River, February 25, 1995.

4. Interview with former Assistant Secretary of State Alexander Watson, September 29, 1999.

5. Ibid.

6. Luigi Einaudi, "The Ecuador-Peru Peace Process," in Chester A. Crocker, Fen Osler Hampson, and Pamela Asli (eds.), *Herding Cats:Multiparty Mediation in a Complex World* (Washington, DC: United States Institute for Peace Press, 1999), p. 410.

7. Ibid, p. 417.

8. T. Michael Peay, "Rio Protocol Guarantors: Legal Considerations," State Department Memorandum to Ambassador Einaudi and the Peru-Ecuador Interagency Working Group, February 12, 1996.

9. Meeting with former Secretary of State Kissinger in Brasilia, October 1995.

10. Interview with Watson, September 29, 1999.

11. Ibid.

12. Ibid. When the observer mission was actually deployed, the United States did provide nearly all the logistics at the outset, including not only the helicopters for transportation, but also such essentials as communications, intelligence, and mess personnel. According to Colonel Weidner in a conversation with the author on April 12, 2000, the United States provided 92 personnel out of the initial total guarantor observer force complement of 132.

13. Ibid.

14. Conversation with former Deputy Assistant Secretary of State Edward Casey, November 10, 1999.

15. Ibid.

16. Interview with Ambassador Einaudi, March 15, 1999.

17. Glenn A. Weidner, "Peacekeeping in the Upper Cenepa Valley," in Gabriella Marcella and Richard Downes (eds.), *Security Cooperation in the Western Hemisphere: Resolving the Peru-Ecuador Conflict* (North South Center, Miami: University of Miami Press, 1999).

18. Ibid.

19. Glenn A. Weidner, "Operation Safe Border: The Ecuador-Peru Crisis," *Joint Forces Quarterly,* Spring 1996, p. 55.

20. Office meeting with former NSC Assistant for Latin America Ted Piccone, June 25, 1999.

21. Peter Smith, *Talons of the Eagle: Dynamics of U.S.-Latin American Relations* (New York: Oxford University Press, 1996), p. 334.

22. Einaudi, "The Ecuador-Peru Peace Process," p. 422.

23. As noted above, border integration economic development was to be discussed in Washington. Frontier demarcation issues were to continue in Brasilia,

but the treaty on navigation and commerce was to be completed in Buenos Aires, and military security issues were henceforth to be handled in Santiago.

24. Einaudi, "The Ecuador-Peru Peace Process," p. 415.

25. Conversation in Quito with Ecuadorian Deputy Foreign Minister Francisco Carrion, March 23, 1998. Carrion said these adverse findings were reversed to about 75 percent in favor, 25 percent opposed, after the final agreement was signed and publicized in the fall on 1998, largely as the result of effective educational groundwork with opinion leaders carried out over the preceding two years by Ecuadorian Foreign Minister Jose Ayala.

Part II

THE WAR
AGAINST TERRORISM

— Chapter 5 ———————————————————————

"A Firm and Commensurate Response": U.S. Retaliation for the Bush Assassination Attempt

ANDREW J. BACEVICH

Late on the night of April 13, 1993, two vehicles, one a Mercedes Benz sedan, the other a Toyota Land Cruiser, their headlights darkened, crossed undetected from Iraq into Kuwait. The two vehicles carried a total of ten passengers, all Iraqi citizens. They also carried a cargo that included illicit whisky, handguns, an AK47 assault rifle, ammunition, and eighty kilograms of explosives built into the frame of the Land Cruiser. Their mission was a deadly serious one: to exact a modicum of revenge for the humiliation that Iraq had suffered two years earlier at the hands of the United States and its coalition partners during the Persian Gulf War. More specifically, their mission was to assassinate former U.S. President George Bush on his forthcoming visit to Kuwait.

Arriving at the outskirts of Kuwait City, the would-be assassins hid the Land Cruiser in an empty warehouse and linked up with four additional collaborators—three Kuwaitis, the fourth an Iraqi resident of Kuwait. They also put the finishing touches on three plans to kill Bush on April 15. The primary plan was to detonate a bomb by remote control as the former president's motorcade passed by on its way to a public ceremony at Kuwait University. In the event that that plan failed, the principal backup involved positioning the Land Cruiser, packed with explosives and a manual clock-type detonator, on Bush Street near the site of a planned appearance by the former president. If all else failed, Wali al-Gahazali, one of the ringleaders of the group, would as a last resort don a bomb belt and attempt to rush Mr. Bush in a suicide attack.

This daring plot unraveled even before it got fully underway. On April 14, former President Bush arrived in Kuwait. That same day, the conspirators returned to their hiding place after reconnoitering the city to find the warehouse surrounded by Kuwaiti police. A second ringleader, Raad Al-Assadi, managed to flee in a stolen Mercedes but was quickly apprehended. By the end of the day Kuwaiti authorities had taken all of the conspirators into custody. The plot to kill Bush was an abject failure.

The Kuwaiti government made no immediate announcement of the arrests, not wishing to dampen the celebratory atmosphere surrounding the former president's highly publicized visit. Events proceeded according to schedule, although as a further precaution the venue for Bush's principal public appearance was changed from the main university auditorium to a hall in a nearby school for the handicapped. Mr. Bush departed Kuwait without incident on April 16.

Only on April 27 did Defense Minister Sheikh Ali al-Sabah make the arrests publicly known. In revealing that Kuwaiti authorities had successfully broken up the plot, the defense minister announced that two of the Iraqis in custody had confessed that they had been acting not on their own but as agents of the Iraqi government. Some American officials were initially skeptical of the Kuwaiti claims, with press reports indicating that key members of the Clinton administration feared that the confessions might have been extracted under torture. Still, the fact that there had been some sort of plot to kill Bush combined with even the hint of possibility of state sponsorship made it impossible for the United States government to ignore the incident.

In fact, relying on its own sources, the Central Intelligence Agency had already concluded that Baghdad was indeed directly implicated in the plot to kill Bush. The agency's conclusion did not satisfy the White House, however. Senior officials there insisted that any U.S. response should be predicated on evidence that would stand up in American courts—this despite the fact that little serious consideration was given to bringing the alleged perpetrators to the United States for trial.

As a result (and over the objections of CIA Director James Woolsey who argued both that the Justice Department had no appropriate role in the matter and that any delay in U.S. reaction would convey a message of uncertainty), the White House directed the Justice Department, assisted by the Secret Service and the CIA, to undertake a thorough investigation of the incident. Only after the president had reviewed the results of this investigation would he decide whether and how the United States would respond.

Yet even as the Justice Department launched its inquiry, events within the U.S. government moved simultaneously on a second parallel track. Without waiting for the outcome of the investigation, the Pentagon began refining its contingency plans for possible military action against Iraq. Ever since the conclusion of the Persian Gulf War in 1991, United States Central Command (CENTCOM) had maintained a list of seventy to eighty high value targets inside Iraq. On a routine basis, planners on the Joint Staff and in the CIA reviewed and updated this list. Personally persuaded by the CIA conclusion implicating Saddam Hussein's government in the attempt on Bush's life, Secretary of Defense Les Aspin asked General Colin Powell, the chairman of the Joint Chiefs, to identify options for possible retaliation against Iraq. Aspin emphasized that he wanted options that were tailored specifically to the particular circumstances, insuring in essence that any punishment, if administered, would fit the crime.

Powell in turn contacted General Joseph Hoar, the CENTCOM commander in chief, and directed him to nominate a list of targets for a potential strike. As planning guidance, Powell told Hoar that he envisioned neither full-scale war nor even an extended campaign but simply a one-time punitive attack. According to Powell, Secretary Aspin was particularly interested in developing options that would "send a message" to Saddam Hussein. In the JCS chairman's view, the purpose of any military operation mounted by the United States against Iraq was as much symbolic as substantive. With that consideration in mind, Powell wanted to minimize the risk to American personnel. Powell and Hoar agreed that targets nominated should be limited to sites suitable for remote attack by unmanned aerial systems.

To establish a "nexus" between target and the incident providing the basis for a U.S. attack, Hoar decided to give priority attention to agencies of Iraq's large intelligence apparatus, believed by the CIA to have been directly involved in the plot to kill Bush. Acting on the guidance formulated by Powell and Hoar, the CENTCOM staff culled through the existing target list and identified three different intelligence facilities as likely candidates for attack. Of the three, Hoar favored the headquarters of the Iraqi Intelligence Service (IIS). Located in downtown Baghdad in a walled compound known as Mukhabarat, the IIS headquarters had been heavily damaged during the Persian Gulf War. Since the war, however, the compound had been substantially rebuilt.

In Hoar's view, this particular headquarters made for an attractive target on several counts, not least of all because it was a large fixed facility and because CENTCOM had detailed information about the routine within IIS, to include the work schedules of the Iraqis employed there. Hoar knew, for example, that senior intelligence IIS chiefs were in the habit of returning to work in the evening after the majority of the staff is gone for the day. Hoar's concept was to attack Mukhabarat between seven and nine o'clock in the evening Baghdad time in order to take out as much of the intelligence service senior leadership as possible.

Partially offsetting these advantages was Mukhabarat's location in a heavily populated section of the Iraqi capital. Any attack, even one that relied exclusively on precision-guided munitions, would carry the risk of causing noncombatant casualties. For the Pentagon, still smarting from the criticism it received as a result of the destruction of the Al-Firdos bunker during the Persian Gulf War (killing more than two hundred Iraqi civilians in a single incident), this was a serious concern.

Powell concurred with Hoar's recommendation and forwarded it to the secretary of defense with his endorsement. (Powell did not consult the other members of the Joint Chiefs in this process.) Concerned that CENT-COM and the Joint Staff might not fully appreciate the dimensions of the proposed operation, Aspin asked Frank Wisner, Under Secretary of Defense for Policy, to review the option recommended by the military. Wisner met with Powell, emphasizing that the central purpose of any U.S. military action would be to persuade Saddam Hussein that "such behavior is unacceptable." Powell replied that a limited cruise missile attack on a facility such as Mukhabarat would send precisely that signal, a line of reasoning that Wisner found persuasive. Wisner and Powell also discussed the likelihood of any further response by Saddam Hussein against the United States. They both agreed that the prospects of any Iraqi military retaliation were remote at best.

Reassured by Wisner, Aspin signed off on the CENTCOM recommendation and forwarded it to Anthony Lake, the president's national security adviser. With the official investigation of the Bush assassination attempt still underway, top uniformed and civilian leaders in the Pentagon had already reached a firm consensus on how the United States ought to proceed should the president direct military action.

Meanwhile, the very deliberate and comprehensive Justice Department–led effort to establish the guilt of the accused plotters continued. Several teams of investigators from the FBI, the CIA, and the Secret Service visited Kuwait to conduct interviews and examine forensic evidence.

From April through June, prospective U.S. retaliation for the incident in Kuwait City was at best a back burner issue. A leak to the *Washington Post* in early May citing unnamed administration officials claiming that the administration possessed evidence linking the Iraqi government to the attempt on Bush's life did generate a flurry of renewed attention. During a May 9 appearance on *Meet the Press*, for example, Congressman Lee

Hamilton, Democrat of Indiana, referred to the cited alleged Iraqi plot as providing more than adequate rationale for punishing Saddam Hussein. "We cannot tolerate that kind of action against a former President of the United States," declared the highly regarded congressman. "It's outrageous." Appearing on the same program, Senator Richard Lugar, Republican of Indiana, agreed, arguing that force "is the only thing that Iraq would understand." On May 11, *The New York Times* reported that White House officials—again unnamed—were citing "powerful evidence" implicating the government of Saddam Hussein in the attempt to kill his nemesis from the Persian Gulf War. Despite these transparent efforts to prod the administration into action, the attention of political Washington and the mainstream media remained elsewhere.

Throughout the spring of 1993, the young administration of President Bill Clinton found itself mired in controversy due to a combination of missteps and misfortune. The foreign policy issue capturing the most sustained media attention was Bosnia. Escalating violence and instability in the Balkans and reported atrocities perpetrated by the Bosnian Serbs generated intense pressure on a reluctant administration to consider military action. In Somalia, amidst signs of growing local animosity drummed up by faction leaders such as Mohammed Farah Aideed, the United States continued to press the UN to assume responsibility for a well-intentioned humanitarian intervention that had gone well beyond its intended date. At home, in late April, the bizarre fifty-one-day standoff between the Branch Davidians and federal agents in Waco, Texas, ended in fiery tragedy, provoking sharp criticism of Attorney General Janet Reno's Justice Department. The botched effort to flush the Branch Davidians from their compound resulting in eighty-six deaths, including twenty-four children, became a source of major embarrassment. Mr. Clinton's decision in early June to abandon a controversial nomination of Lani Guinier to head the civil rights division of the Justice Department also drew fierce criticism. Even the president's own core constituencies accused him of being fickle and unreliable. Much to the dismay of his key political advisers, the president's approval rating in public opinion polls plummeted.

On June 5, the trial of the alleged conspirators began in Kuwait City. Two of the accused, Wali al-Ghazali and Raad al-Assadi, confessed in open court to having been involved in a conspiracy instigated by Iraq. (Later that same day, one of the two recanted.) The other twelve defendants (nine Iraqis and three Kuwaitis) resolutely proclaimed their innocence.

Not until mid-June did U.S. investigators succeed in wrapping up their report of April's incident. Their interviews and thoroughgoing examination of forensic evidence, especially a detonator identical to a device that had been used in a foiled Iraqi terrorist attack near the Turkish border during the Persian Gulf War, finally persuaded the investigators that Kuwaiti authorities were indeed correct: the plot to kill former President Bush had originated in Baghdad.

On the evening of June 24, with the trial in Kuwait City now approaching its conclusion, Attorney General Reno entered the first family's private quarters to brief the president on the results of the investigation. Others present for this meeting of the administration's "principals committee" included Vice President Al Gore, National Security Advisor Anthony Lake, his deputy Sandy Berger, Secretary of State Warren Christopher, Secretary of Defense Les Aspin, and JCS Chairman General Colin Powell.

The most dovish of the president's advisers, Reno conveyed the impression that she remained less than absolutely certain that the evidence pointed to Baghdad. Yet whatever her doubts, they failed to garner support among the others present. Indeed, the substance of the ensuing discussion focused less on whether or how to punish Iraq than on the likely results of the modest operation conceived by the Pentagon. Once the evidence fingering the Iraqi government had been presented, the imperative of some type of U.S. retaliation was all but taken for granted. Conversation turned instead to considering the specific character of that retaliation and to the problem of anticipating and managing any negative fallout, diplomatic and political, likely to result from any U.S. military action.

To avoid giving needless offense to other Islamic nations, no American military action would occur until after sunset ending the Muslim Sabbath. The option of attacking Saddam's rebuilt headquarters (and implicitly Saddam himself) rather than an intelligence facility was briefly raised and as quickly rejected. The concern of the president's advisers, according to one unnamed senior official, was that "we don't want to get into a cycle of action-reaction where Saddam is trying to target our head of state and we're trying to target him."

For the president, however, the concern looming largest was casualties—Iraqi casualties since the Pentagon's insistence on using unmanned systems had all but precluded the possibility of U.S. losses. The president was adamant that the United States do its utmost to avoid civilian casualties. Lake and Powell assured Mr. Clinton that the planned attack was proportional. To minimize the number of dead and wounded, the attack would occur at an hour when the Iraqi intelligence headquarters was thought to be largely empty—in effect, targeting the facility itself rather than the IIS leadership as Hoar had intended. Still, Mr. Clinton pressed Powell to speculate on the likely number of Iraqi casualties. Uncomfortable at being put on the spot, Powell ventured that a dozen or so might result. Although the JCS chairman hastened to add that "It's a SWAG [wild-ass guess]," the president found this estimate reassuring. He approved CENTCOM's plan for a cruise missile attack on Mukhabarat for late at night (Iraqi time) on June 26. All members of the president's national security team who were present concurred in his decision.

Notwithstanding this presidential decision, a follow-on session occurred the following day to assess the likely domestic political impact of the scheduled attack on Baghdad. Present for this meeting along with the president were three key figures from Clinton's inner circle of political advisers: White House Chief of Staff Mack McLarty; counselor David Gergen; and senior adviser George Stephanopoulos. The members of this troika were uniformly skittish about the potentially negative fallout of the scheduled U.S. military action. With the president leaving the room from time to time to lobby key senators on the budgetary package just then coming to a vote, Lake joined the group and argued vociferously that the issue was "above politics" and that it "demands a response." Expectations that the results of the Justice Department investigation would soon leak and reports that the FBI just hours before had uncovered a terrorist plot to blow up the Lincoln and Holland Tunnels in New York served to reinforce Lake's call for action. Clinton's political advisers acquiesced. In the end, Clinton sided with Lake and reaffirmed his decision of the previous evening. The attack on Mukhabarat would proceed as planned.

CENTCOM was primed to respond. On almost a daily basis during the preceding weeks, Powell and Hoar had discussed the possibility of retaliation against Iraq. The JCS chairman had kept the CENTCOM commander fully apprised of developments in Washington. Hoar, however, had himself played no role in the discussion in the White House, Powell being the sole military participant in the deliberations and the chief conduit of information to Hoar.

Fearing that the French government might well warn Saddam Hussein of the impending American attack, the administration refrained from notifying any of its allies until the very last moment. Likewise, it was only at the last minute that the White House informed congressional leaders and that Powell notified the service chiefs of the president's decision. As a result, there were no leaks prior to actual execution of the operation.

At 4:22 in the afternoon EDT (12:22 Baghdad time), U.S. forces on station in the region commenced their attack on Iraq. As planned by CENT-

COM and approved by the Pentagon, that attack consisted of twenty-three Tomahawk cruise missiles, fourteen launched by the USS *Peterson* (DD969), a Spruance-class destroyer in the Red Sea, and nine by the USS *Chancellorsville* (CG62), a Ticonderoga-class guided missile cruiser in the Persian Gulf. (The attack had originally been intended to include twenty-four missiles but one malfunctioned prior to launch.) Each Tomahawk, a subsonic, precision-guided missile with a 700-mile maximum range, contained a 984-pound conventional warhead. Approximately ninety minutes after launch the missiles reached the target area.

Shortly after 6:00 PM, from his desk in the Oval Office President Clinton appeared on nationwide television to announce the attack. The president described in general terms "compelling evidence" of "an elaborate plan, devised by the Iraqi government" to assassinate former President Bush. Clinton provided the sound bite of the day by reviving a slogan from an earlier era of American history: "don't tread on us." He characterized the attack as "a firm and commensurate response" that would "send a message" to any would-be source of state-sponsored terrorism, deter any future assassination attempts, and "affirm the expectation of civilized behavior among nations." He emphasized that the immediate purpose of the attack had been to "target Iraq's capacity to support violence" and to "deter Saddam Hussein from supporting such outlaw behavior in the future," hence, the targeting of an intelligence facility thought to be directly involved in the plot to kill Bush. The president also offered assurances that the attack had been designed so as to make "every effort to minimize the loss of innocent life."

At a Pentagon briefing that followed the president's televised remarks, Secretary Aspin and General Powell provided amplifying details. The American strike against Iraq, explained Aspin, was "a wake-up call," intended to persuade Saddam's associates that "following this man is not good for your health." Powell revealed that the attack carrier *Theodore Roosevelt* had been ordered to the Persian Gulf to reinforce U.S. forces already in the region, but he indicated that there were no immediate plans for further military action. The next move, if there was to be one, was Saddam Hussein's.

In a strictly military sense, the immediate results of the attack were satisfactory. Inside Makhabarat, one side of the main ten-story building that actually housed the IIS headquarters (and believed also to contain communications and computer centers) was virtually destroyed. The roof was blown off of an adjoining six-story structure. According to press reports, a nearby communications tower escaped unscathed. Still, Rear Admiral

Michael Cramer, the chief intelligence officer on the Joint Staff, briefed reporters that Mukhabarat had sustained "major damage." The IIS as a whole, Cramer said, "has suffered a major setback" although he was careful to acknowledge that the Iraqi intelligence apparatus had "alternate facilities and alternate means" at hand.

On the other hand, seven missiles failed to hit their assigned target. Of those seven, four Tomahawks fell inside the compound but missed the structures within. Three landed outside of the target area altogether and hit residential buildings. The Iraqi news service claimed that the U.S. attack had killed eight Iraqis and injured several others. One of those killed by a stray missile was Layla al-Attar, an internationally renowned Iraqi artist.

Reaction to the U.S. action abroad was generally positive. The governments of Great Britain, Italy, and Germany all promptly issued statements supporting the American attack. Behind the scenes, there was some niggling among several allies that the U.S. had acted unilaterally, not bothering to seek United Nations sanction for the attack. Few were persuaded by the U.S. assertion that unilateral reprisal was justified as an act of self-defense under the terms of Article 51 of the UN Charter. Among friendly nations, the reaction of the French government was notably (but not surprisingly) tepid. By comparison, Moscow gave a ringing endorsement to the American action. Official reaction in the Arab world was less supportive. Among Arab moderates, only the Kuwaitis offered unambiguous support. Others, including Egypt, were officially critical although there were hints that in private several of Saddam's neighbors applauded the American action.

Much to the satisfaction of the president's political advisers, reaction to the strike at home was resoundingly positive. Leaders of both parties in Congress praised Clinton for having demonstrated resolute leadership. According to a CNN/*USA Today* poll, 66 percent of Americans endorsed the president's decision to hit Baghdad. In a CBS News/*New York Times* poll conducted immediately following the attack, the president's overall approval rating shot up from 39 to 50 percent.

The military results of the attack were pretty much as Hoar had expected. He had estimated that about 15 percent of missiles would miss their targets and thus was not surprised that the attack had resulted in some collateral damage and incurred several civilian casualties. In the Pentagon, Aspin and Wisner were privately disappointed that the attack had failed to demolish Mukhabarat completely. When Mr. Clinton two days after the attack remarked offhandedly that "we did, in fact, cripple the

Iraqi intelligence capability, which was the intent of the action," he offered a rationale that undercut the stated position of his own subordinates and also claimed for the reprisal more success than it had achieved; administration representatives were soon obliged to backtrack, explaining that the president had misspoken. Yet for the most part, administration officials viewed the operation with satisfaction: it had been an unmistakable and exceedingly welcome foreign policy success for a team still getting its feet on the ground. Some, like Lake, went so far as to compare its impact to the attack on Libya ordered by President Ronald Reagan. After the raid on Mukhabarat, there would be no further assassination attempts on current or former U.S. officials by Saddam Hussein or anyone else.

Meanwhile the case of the conspirators continued to wend its way through the Kuwaiti legal system. On June 4, 1994, the state security court of Kuwait sentenced six of the accused to death and handed out lengthy prison terms to seven others. One defendant was later acquitted. On March 20, 1995, a Kuwaiti appeals court commuted the death sentence of four of the convicted conspirators. However, the court upheld the death sentences of Ghazali and Assadi, the reputed ringleaders.

In Baghdad, Saddam Hussein remained in power.

Chapter 6

Obligations of Leadership: The Khobar Towers Bombing and Its Aftermath

ELIOT A. COHEN

PART I

A Bomb Explodes

June 25, 1996 was another hot, oppressively humid night in Dhahran, Saudi Arabia. At the Khobar Towers apartment complex located near the sprawling King Abdul Aziz Air Base air conditioners hummed. A block of squat high-rise apartments comprising some fourteen city blocks, bordered on the north by a car park and near a Saudi residential and shopping neighborhood, Khobar housed approximately three thousand military personnel of the 4404th Air Wing (Provisional), together with French, British, and Saudi military counterparts. The Americans occupied thirty-three of one hundred eighty buildings in Khobar Towers, concentrated at the northern end of the sprawling complex. Engaged in the prolonged and fatiguing task of maintaining air patrols over southern Iraq (operation SOUTHERN WATCH), the airmen worked mainly at the King Abdul Aziz Air Base a few miles west of Khobar Towers. Tonight, those off duty were either resting or sleeping in cooled rooms. On top of the Khobar Towers housing complex, however, shortly before 10:00 PM an alert Air Force security police staff sergeant on guard duty, Alfredo Guerrero, noticed a fuel truck drive into the parking lot and stop opposite the concrete barriers on the northern perimeter, which were located eighty feet from Building 131. Its driver jumped out of the truck and into an accompanying passenger car. Instantly, Guerrero called his command center, after which he and two other airmen rushed downstairs, alerting occupants to evacuate the building. Minutes later the truck exploded.[1]

The explosion left a crater between sixty and eighty feet wide and between fifteen and thirty feet deep.[2] It ripped the facade off Building 131, blowing pieces of the low concrete barriers that surrounded the Khobar complex into rooms on the first three floors. On the sides, the floor slabs collapsed when the east and west walls of the building were displaced several feet outward. Nineteen Americans died and some 250 Americans were wounded, 100 of them requiring hospitalization. Hundreds of Saudis, Bengladeshis, and other nationals on the ground and in other buildings also received wounds of varying degrees of severity. Speedy medical care succored most of the wounded, and the 4404th, stunned and grieving, pressed on with its mission of patrolling the skies over southern Iraq. The perpetrators remain mysterious to the present day. Some combination of Iranian intelligence operatives and Saudi dissidents seems a likely possibility, but the Saudi government refused to allow FBI agents to interview suspects that it had apprehended.

No matter who had detonated the bomb, however, its aftershocks would continue for many months to come.

Congress Reacts

The finger pointing began immediately. Members of the 4404th told a *New York Times* reporter, "This building we were in, we constantly joked that we were a fine target, out in this corner, right next to the [car] park."[3] Others told the press that the Saudis had been reluctant to patrol aggressively near the building. Newspapers reported that Major General Kurt Anderson, commander of the Joint Task Force for Southwest Asia, based in Riyadh and Brigadier General Terry Schwalier, commander of the 4404th, had been prepared for a smaller bomb, of the kind that had killed five Americans and wounded scores nine months earlier in Saudi Arabia, in November 1995, but that this had been an altogether more severe, and hence unpredictable attack.

By July 1, 1996, less than a week after the bombing, more critical stories had begun to appear in the press. Extremists had threatened unspecified retaliation for the beheading less than a month before of four men convicted of the November 1995 bombing. A recent "vulnerability assessment" was reported to have shown that Khobar Towers needed a bigger zone of empty space around it—there had been less than a hundred feet between the buildings and the fence that surrounded the complex. Suspicious events in the preceding few months (a car driving up to the fence and dashing off, for example) seemed to indicate rehearsals for an attack.

General Schwalier told reporters that U.S. officials had twice asked the Saudi government to expand the buffer zone around Khobar Towers (400 feet was the figure journalists used), but had been turned down. To be sure, *USA Today* acknowledged, Secretary of Defense William Perry was right to say that American soldiers could not "hunker in their bunkers. But U.S. troops deserve the best protection possible." And, the newspaper added: "They didn't get it at Khobar Towers."[4]

On July 9, 1996, two weeks after the bombing, Senator Strom Thurmond (R-SC) called to order a hearing on the Khobar bombing: before him and the assembled committee members sat Secretary of Defense William Perry, General John Shalikashvili, Chairman of the Joint Chiefs of Staff, and General J. H. Binford Peay, III, Commander in Chief Central Command. For the well-respected and liked Secretary Perry (whom one irate senator had called upon to resign) it was a painful occasion. He began by saying "The responsibility for the safety of our military men and women is mine, and I expect to be held accountable for carrying out that responsibility."

The senators were not content, and in particular, they trained their attention on General Peay. Why, they wanted to know, had the Saudis not acceded to requests to extend the perimeter of the Khobar Towers complex? The general attempted to explain, presenting a common view of Saudi Arabia within the American military:

Over the last several decades, our government has considered Saudi Arabia one of the safest countries in the world. Over 40,000 American civilians live and work in Saudi Arabia this morning. What's more, the U.S. military enjoys a close relationship with Saudi counterparts that is the envy of nations throughout the world. What may appear as Saudi indifference or unwillingness to act on an issue is, in fact, a reflection of their different sense of time. Similarly, what may appear as foot-dragging by various levels of government is often a reflection of the compartmentalized nature of Saudi bureaucracy and decision-making. Decisions at all levels of the Saudi government are slow by U.S. standards and are often reached by consensus. In addition, the King's role as custodian of the two holy mosques produces intense Saudi sensitivity to issues involving their sovereignty. Our sensitivity to these dynamics produces a friendship and internal stability supportive of our national interests. . . . Our relatively small forward presence reflects our recognition that local societies can be easily oversaturated, producing the very instability that we seek to prevent. . . . While some have attempted to compare this bombing with the suicide attack on the U.S. Marine barracks in Beirut in 1983, the differences are simply striking. Saudi Arabia is a viable, prosperous, stable country. Prior to the bombing of OPM SANG last year, there were very few terrorist incidents directed against Americans within the kingdom . . . [5]

After listing the various assessments of security at installations in the Central Command area, General Peay acknowledged that he had "raised the threat from medium to high" following the OPM SANG bombing, "and directed a theater-wide reassessment of security of our facilities in the region."

The Senators did not accept this explanation. Chairman Thurmond asked whether General Peay had visited the complex. He had not. Was the Saudi denial of permission to extend the perimeter passed up the chain of command to him? queried Senator Sam Nunn (D-GA). He was not sure. Senator Carl Levin (D-MI): Should it have been? "I find it difficult today to try to second-guess a forward-deployed commander," Peay explained, saying that the commander of Joint Task Force Southwest Asia, under whose jurisdiction the 4404th came for operational matters, was preoccupied with myriad activities, but above all air operations over Iraq. Senator John McCain (R-AZ) exploded at Secretary Perry: "After the Riyadh bombing in November, it was clear that security at U.S. installations in Saudi Arabia had to be increased, and apparently General Peay did not visit the facilities, did not keep close track of security enhancements, and still doesn't seem to have a good grasp of the situation under his command." Senator Joseph Lieberman (D-CT) seemed to speak for his colleagues when he said: "I think we've got to create a record here that sends an unmistakable message, in spite of all that is going on in a theater like this, that security protection, force protection is so important that once we have designated the security level, the threat level, as high, that any question as fundamental as this one, of extending the perimeter, has to be kicked up almost immediately . . . I want to ask you if you would reconsider . . . your statement about whether in fact that officer should have kicked this upstairs, this decision?" Peay replied that one could not "legislate what should be kicked up" and that one needed to "teach our youngsters to make those value judgments. . . . This is a very competent chain of command that encourages openness. . . . I understand the thrust of your question, but I'm not so sure I'm on your side on this one, sir." Lieberman replied coldly: "I think that's exactly the wrong message to send."

The hearings continued, with all three men coming under close, and sometimes caustic questioning. Senator Charles Robb (D-VA), a Marine Corps Vietnam veteran, wrapped up the public hearing by asking Secretary Perry whether there was an issue of individual responsibility here. Secretary Perry answered that that question was "so portentous, that I want to defer my answer to it until I get General Downing's report. He is looking precisely at that question, and any question that involves culpability." The next step would have to wait nearly two months.

General Downing and Congress Investigate

Three days after the bombing, on June 28, Secretary Perry had appointed retired General Wayne Downing to probe the circumstances of the Khobar Towers bombing. Initially, he did not ask the Downing Task Force to address the issue of personal accountability, but rather the adequacy of security there, the "sufficiency and effectiveness of intelligence" in the Central Command area of responsibility, the adequacy of resources for security against terrorist threats in the area, and, most importantly, recommendations on preventing new attacks or minimizing their damage. Assessing individual responsibility for what had occurred became an additional tasking only later. Downing, an Army general, had served as Commander in Chief of Special Operations Command; he had commanded the elite 75th Ranger regiment, he had had a long and distinguished combat record. He recruited a number of experts, to include retired Air Force Lieutenant General James Clapper, recently retired as Director of the Defense Intelligence Agency, a former Marine, to assist him.

In two intense months Downing's team visited thirty-six sites and conducted four hundred interviews, to include visits with antiterrorism experts in Israel, Jordan, France, and the United Kingdom. Their report, issued on August 30, 1996, was scathing. In twenty-six separate findings it criticized a lack of Department of Defense standards for force protection and urged their creation and dissemination. It criticized the practice of permitting U.S.-based service component headquarters to retain operational control of forward deployed forces, and called for a beefing up of Central Command headquarters which had not set standards for force protection or training in the theater.[6]

The general recommendations, however, attracted less public attention than Finding No. 20: "The Commander, 4404th Wing (Provisional) did not adequately protect his forces from terrorist attack." The report stated that Khobar Towers had been identified to Schwalier as "one of the three highest priority soft targets in the region," and that the November 1995 bombing of an US-Saudi training facility—the OPM-SANG (Office of the Program Manager—Saudi Arabian National Guard) bombing—had served as an ominous warning. In its harsh judgment of General Schwalier's performance, the Downing Task Force put forth the following assertions:[7]

- Schwalier had not raised the issue of expanding the perimeter with his Saudi counterparts or with his superiors, although he had been told by competent technical advisers of its desirability.
- Although he did not have access to an intelligence structure working directly for him, Schwalier still had adequate information pointing to a terrorist threat, to include knowledge of ten suspicious incidents in the last three months.
- Force protection efforts in the 4404th had focused on a "penetrating bomb"—that is, one introduced inside the complex by car or an individual, and had largely ignored the threat of a bomb blast from the outside.
- Schwalier had refrained from introducing important security measures, such as coating windows with shatter resistant Mylar film.
- Ostensibly for reasons of individual comfort and morale, Schwalier and his subordinates did not consider moving personnel out of more vulnerable or exposed rooms to safer areas (which would have entailed putting several individuals in a room).
- Although the 4404th's Air Force Security Police were pulling twelve-hour shifts in trying conditions, and did not conduct special training or terrorist response exercises, Schwalier had made no effort to obtain more security personnel. Furthermore, the Downing Task Force believed that the Wing did not move to a higher threat level in April because of a lack of security personnel—not because the situation did not demand it.
- Schwalier had permitted third country nationals to work in the Khobar complex, despite the risks entailed.
- The 4404th had not rehearsed building evacuations. (The British inhabitants of Khobar, the Task Force noted, conducted monthly drills.)
- The command's arrangements for notifying inhabitants of an attack were cumbersome and bound to fail. A loudspeaker system called "Giant Voice" would, in theory, notify personnel using either voice or a siren. The voice system, however, was barely audible over air con-

ditioning noise, and the siren system was not tested out of deference to Saudi sensibilities. Furthermore, activating Giant Voice required layers of decision making in a situation where every second would count. Only the Commander of the 4404th could authorize Giant Voice after requests had gone to two different command posts.

• General Schwalier's end-of-tour report, written the morning of the bombing (his one-year command tour was just ending) mentioned three areas of focus by the Wing; force protection was not one of them. This Downing took to indicate a lack of commitment to that task.

• The Downing Task Force referred consideration of the actions of General Schwalier and his key subordinates to the chain of command "for action as appropriate." In Downing's view, however, expressed in the report and afterwards in speeches and conversations, Schwalier was not alone to blame. He had not discharged his responsibilities well, in Downing's view, but he had not received the support he should have from his chain of command.

Congress's own staff investigation of Khobar Towers bore fruit two weeks before the Downing Report, on August 14, but attracted far less publicity. The House National Security Committee's (HNSC) staff mentioned some of the shortcomings noted by Downing, but took a different angle. The HNSC staff noted, for example, the failure to activate Giant Voice, but reported the view of Air Force commanders on the spot that an effective evacuation might, ironically, have caused more casualties. As it turned out, personnel in stairwells when the bomb went off survived, when those in the open might not. The HNSC report also credited General Schwalier with having taken numerous actions to improve the security of Khobar, including the placement of concrete barriers on the perimeter of the Khobar complex, internal barriers, sentry posts, and bomb dogs.

But the staff did offer a number of implied criticisms of both the 4404th and its chain of command. It described a pattern of extraordinary scrupulousness in dealing with the Saudis, to the point where new personnel at the 4404th were told that "General Order Number One" is "respecting our hosts."[8] It said that the OPM-SANG bombing, a variety of incidents (including the apprehension of individuals smuggling explosives into the kingdom), and intelligence should have raised the level of alarm. Implicitly, it criticized Schwalier's failure to press the Saudis over the extension of the perimeter into the local area. It did not, however, suggest that Schwalier should be subject to disciplinary or administrative sanctions.

In fact, the HNSC's severest observations of the 4404th had nothing to do with Schwalier or his immediate subordinates. The staff described a unit suffering from destructive personnel turbulence. Schwalier was the first wing commander to serve even for a year: he was, in fact, one of thirteen commanders in four years. Most 4404th personnel served for only ninety days, with the result that 10 percent of the unit turned over every week. The report drew unflattering comparisons with Army units serving considerably longer tours (where Schwalier was one of barely half a dozen individuals in the 4404th to serve for a year in his post, a comparable Army unit at least had 10 percent of its personnel for a year), and more amply supplied with linguists and counterintelligence specialists. Under such conditions security and intelligence personnel at the wing could not hope to develop the relationships with Saudi counterparts essential to protect the facility, the HNSC staff believed.

The Air Force Replies

Even before receiving the Downing Report, Secretary Perry began long-term action to reduce the likelihood of similar calamities. The immediate response to the Khobar disaster included decisions to send dependents home and move U.S. forces into remote areas, away from population centers, a move costing the Pentagon millions of dollars. On September 15, 1996, Perry sent a memorandum to the Chairman of the Joint Chiefs of Staff declaring that "New circumstances require new approaches to the entire scope of how we go about our business."[9] Describing a need for a "more centralized focus and clearer lines of responsibility" in the field of force protection he designated the Chairman his "principal advisor with responsibility for all force protection matters within the Department of Defense." With this move came authority to review service programs, rewrite DOD handbooks, and energize the armed forces to improve measures for protection of U.S. forces in Saudi Arabia.

Several days later, the Senate Armed Services Committee resumed its hearings, this time to consider the Downing Report.[10] In the witness chairs were General Downing, Secretary Perry, and General Shalikashvili. Senator Jesse Helms (R-NC), sitting in for Chairman Thurmond, reported his "grave concerns with what General Downing discovered . . . Mr. Secretary, it appears from the findings included in General Downing's report that we have not learned much from previous investigations or similar incidents." Helms referred thereby to the bombing of Marine barracks in Beirut in 1983, in which a bomb equivalent to some 12,000 pounds of TNT had killed 241 Americans, and which, he believed, should have alerted the Defense Department to these dangers. Senator Nunn also cited Beirut as a case in which an ambiguous chain of command had bred disaster. Once again, the Senators asked why none of General Schwalier's superiors had visited Khobar; General John Shalikashvili, Chairman of the Joint Chiefs of Staff said that both he and General Peay, the CENTCOM commander, regretted this, but that the component commands and staff had had this matter in hand. Senator William Cohen (R-ME) asked if "some sort of institutional opposition" posed an obstacle to aggressive force protection. Like his colleagues, he was baffled that American commanders in the Middle East were not more alive to the threat of terrorism. Again citing the Marine barracks bombing in 1983, he repeated his belief in the existence of institutional opposition in CENTCOM to pressing the Saudis for assistance. He doubted that commanders had taken force protection seriously enough. Once again, Senator Lieberman inquired about command responsibility: Secretary Perry replied that even before reading the Downing Report he had asked the Secretary of the Air Force to review that issue "with a request to determine accountability and consider possible disciplinary actions."

And, in fact, on September 4, the Air Force Chief of Staff, General Ronald Fogleman, and the Secretary of the Air Force, Sheila Widnall, ordered a report to assess the Downing Report. To chair this effort, they selected Lieutenant General James Record, commander of 12th Air Force at Davis-Monthan AFB in Arizona. His charter was to consider and make recommendations on the issues raised in Downing's report and to serve as "disciplinary review and court-martial convening authority for actions or omissions by Air Force personnel associated with the bombing of Khobar Towers."[11] Record assembled a team and conducted over 200 additional interviews, as well as gathered yet more documentation on top of that assembled by Downing. The report came back in two parts, A and B, responding to the two taskings. Part A was delivered at the end of October 1997, and Part B, the accountability review, in mid-December.

Part A dealt primarily with actions the Air Force could take to improve force protection: it included a recommendation to "consider extending tour-lengths for key personnel, including Force Protection personnel," and to improve training. It urged that the Air Force "institutionalize a completely different Force Protection mind-set." Record did, however, make a number of exculpatory observations about the Khobar Towers bombing. The command had taken over 130 measures to improve force protection at Khobar, and these had born fruit. These had, it was true, dealt primarily with the penetrating bomb threat, but the 4404th could not do much beyond the perimeter. "Local Saudi Arabian officials had made it clear to U.S. personnel that security at any installation is primarily a Saudi responsibility; and that U.S. personnel are 'guests' who are not allowed to extend force protection measures beyond the fence line." This relationship, Record noted, remained in place as of October 1996, and General Schwalier could do very little to affect it.[12] This arrangement, moreover, fit the Air Force's traditional doctrine for defense of air bases developed during the Cold War, under which "the Air Force is responsible for Force Protection *inside* the fence."[13] Importantly, Record's task force concluded that "Command relationships had no impact on this terrorist act"—a direct contradiction of the Downing Report, which argued precisely the reverse, and had called for shifting responsibility for force protection to the Central Command chain in the theater, rather than 9th Air Force/Central Command Air Forces in the United States.

Part B of Record's report, the accountability review, had as its purpose determining whether any member of the Air Force chain should be subject to court martial. It was forthright in clearing all of the chain of command of responsibility, leaving only a faint cloud in its appraisal of the performance of senior CENTCOM personnel. Where in the case of the commander of CENTAF, Lieutenant General John P. Jumper, General Schwalier, and his subordinates, the report used the phrase that the individual concerned had "performed his duties in a reasonable and prudent manner. He was not derelict in the performance of his duties," regarding the CENTCOM J-3 (operations officer) Major General Joseph Hurd, Record merely concluded that he "was not derelict in the performance of his duties." Regarding General Peay, Record expressively said even less: "I have not identified any matters of concern regarding General Peay which need to be forwarded to the Secretary of Defense." Again, Record noted that the Air Force Office of Special Investigations had completed two Vulnerability Assessments during Schwalier's tour, one at the very beginning and one in January 1996, six months before the bomb went off. Schwalier had implemented their recommendations with very few exceptions, and had stressed in many ways the importance of base security—for example, initiating weekly security review meetings with his staff, deploying physical barriers, and dispersing key senior personnel (as they rotated through Saudi Arabia) inside the Khobar complex.

Record, whose team had not only had access to the Downing Report but the leisure for a more extensive study of the bombing, believed that some key facts should tend to exculpate Schwalier and his subordinates.

First, they noted that Schwalier had carried out all but three of thirty-nine recommendations of a visiting Air Force Office of Special Investigations security team in January 1996. Second, the Record Report highlighted a Defense Special Weapons Agency (DSWA) study that estimated the yield of the truck bomb at the equivalent of 20,000–30,000 pounds of TNT, as opposed to the 3,000–8,000 figure of the Downing Report, and the 250 pounds of the OPM-SANG bombing.[14] Against a blast of such a magnitude few measures—to include additional walls—would have done much good. DSWA estimated that if the bomb had detonated 400 feet away it would still have shattered glass and inflicted serious structural damage, causing severe injuries and death, albeit on a lesser scale. Third, Record again stressed the importance of Saudi reluctance to expand the perimeter of Khobar Towers into an area used by Saudi subjects and designated for further development in support of a nearby strip mall. He quoted Lieutenant General Richard Neal, USMC, the deputy CENTCOM commander: "the Saudis convinced Brigadier General Schwalier in no short order that they were going to make up for not moving the fence by active patrols, increased patrols and more active vigilance."[15] Record found Downing's other criticisms to be of little consequence. Schwalier had actually programmed the four million dollar acquisition of Mylar lining for windows over a five-year period—this at a time when no other potential U.S. targets in Saudi Arabia had Mylar. The reaction to frequent bomb scares effectively compensated for the lack of evacuation drills. Third country nationals on the compound were placed under additional scrutiny and their living conditions improved to assure their loyalty. Some of the additional measures suggested by Schwalier's critics (e.g., concentrating personnel in a smaller number of interior buildings) would simply have increased the command's vulnerability to an internal bomb. Finally, the "suspicious incidents" leading up to the bombing, in Record's view, soon reduced themselves to only one that could be taken seriously as evidence of hostile intent—the ramming of the external barrier by a truck on the east perimeter. To this incident General Schwalier had reacted by persuading the Saudis to allow his troops to stake the barriers to the ground. In short, General Schwalier had done the best he could with the resources available to him.

Record also reviewed the conduct of Colonel Gary S. Boyle, Support Group Commander, and Lieutenant Colonel James J. Traister, Security Police Squadron Commander. Boyle, he found, had taken an active role in force protection throughout his tenure as commander, and had attempted to move the fence and perimeter out. Regarding Traister, Record noted that many of the deficiencies described by Downing reflected standard Air Force procedures—the twelve-hour shifts for Security Police, and the absence of weapons training in country (personnel were assumed to arrive for their ninety-day tours qualified on their weapons). Traister as well was not, therefore, derelict in his duties.

Record concluded:

It is my firm belief that the tragic bombing of Khobar Towers would have occurred regardless of any chain of command that might have been in effect. Commanders, from General Peay down through the Security Police Squadron Commander at the 4404th Wing (Provisional), knew their Force Protection responsibilities and were actively engaged in carrying them out. This tragedy reflects the harsh reality that a persistent terrorist may be able to wait, watch, and pick the optimum time, place and mode of attack to ensure success.

We have a responsibility to use our very best efforts to minimize the risk from future terrorist acts, but we must also recognize that we will never achieve perfection in Force Protection, or in any endeavor, despite our best efforts. Risks are inherent in military operations. Expecting Force Protection efforts to result in zero casualties could well lead to a situation where military missions are undertaken worldwide only when there are no risks of casualties, or only when such risks are extremely minimal. Evolving to this mindset is neither realistic nor desirable. Our forces must be able to deploy and employ when our national security interests are at stake.[16]

The Record Report, which was leaked but not released, elicited a sharp, and almost universally unfavorable reaction. On December 12, the day after accounts of it appeared in the press, the *New York Times*, like most papers covering the story, noted that when two Air Force F-15s had shot down two Army helicopters over northern Iraq in 1994, killing twenty-six, "only a captain serving as a weapons-control officer in an AWACS control plane went to trial. He was acquitted." The *Times* also noted that although sixteen officers, including two generals, were disciplined in the 1996 crash that killed Secretary of Commerce Ron Brown, no one was court-martialed.[17] Capitol Hill reacted with equal asperity. Floyd D. Spence (R-SC), chairman of the House National Security Committee said that "the Air Force's decision raises the specter of no one within the military chain of command being held accountable." Senator Bob Kerrey (D-NE), and a decorated Vietnam veteran called the Air Force's action "insufficient."[18] A former Deputy Inspector General of the Defense Department, Derek J. van der Schaaf, said, "This kind of thing is almost becoming typical of the Air Force culture. It has the same old odor of the institution protecting its big shots and looking the other way when things screw up."[19] Even before the Secretary of the Air Force officially forwarded Part B of Record's report to the Secretary of Defense on December 20, 1996, word of its findings had already elicited severe criticism, including from some inside the Pentagon. On January 29, 1997, Deputy Secretary of Defense John White, acting in support of a new Secretary of Defense, Senator William Cohen (sworn in on January 24, 1997), tasked the Air Force to evaluate the Record Report. As a result, on February 5, 1997 the Secretary of the Air Force and the Chief of Staff tasked Lieutenant General Richard T. Swope, Inspector General of the Air Force and the Judge Advocate General, Major General Bryan G. Hawley, to conduct yet another study of the Khobar bombing, with a view to exploring several of the recommendations of the Record Report, and, perhaps more importantly, to consider "the propriety of administrative action against the officers involved." The Air Force would convene no court-martial, but a range of administrative sanctions—reprimands and denial of promotion, primarily—remained possibilities.

Another extensive investigation took place, to include a detailed comparison between the actions of Air Force officers and standards as set in Air Force manual and Defense Department directives. It described in great detail everything from the standards for weapons training by personnel on temporary duty to what it described as "the waterfall" method for evacuation of buildings under imminent attack. The conclusions produced by this additional effort echoed those in the Record Report, noting Schwalier's intense efforts to improve force protection at Khobar, and the local geopolitical context. "Historically, within Saudi Arabia there has been no substantial threat from terrorism." A bomb of the size that exploded had been simply "inconceivable."[20] The various deficiencies cited by Downing—an absence of weapon training for security police in Saudi Arabia—simply reflected Air Force norms and procedures, with which Schwalier had complied.

In April 1997, Swope and Hawley reported to Deputy Secretary White. "The issue is not whether, with the benefit of hindsight, responsible officials could have succeeded in preventing or further defending against this terrorist attack. Rather, it is whether those individuals whose duties encompassed force protection met the standards of performance expected of them and acted reasonably and prudently under the circumstances as they existed."[21] In the judgment of Generals Swope and Hawley, they had.

The Office of the Secretary of Defense refused to allow publication of this report, much as it had refused to allow publication of the Record review: some in OSD continued to argue that to publish would only be to compound a terrible public relations problem. Others in the Air Force viewed this embargo as an attempt to suppress a story favorable to Schwalier. Once again, however, the report leaked, and once again, the Air Force came under sharp criticism. The bombing of the Murrah Federal Building in Oklahoma not much more than a year before the Dhahran bombing "showed the power of a large truck bomb placed near but not inside a high-rise building," pointed out one editorialist, noting that that had been warning enough to cause the Secret Service to close off Pennsylvania Avenue near the White House. "Morale is not served by dodging responsibility and circling the wagons around a fellow officer."[22] In the words of the *Washington Post*'s defense correspondent, the Air Force had now presented Secretary Cohen with "a political hot potato. 'The interesting thing now is what Cohen will do with it,' an Air Force official said. 'It's going to be one of his first real challenges as Secretary.' "[23]

Secretary Cohen Decides

The new secretary had, by now, had nearly several months in office. After reading the Downing, Record, and Swope/Hawley reports, he came to a decision, announced in a paper, "Personal Accountability for Force Protection at Khobar Towers," that administrative action was justified.[24] Cohen declared that the Air Force reports did not "reflect a thorough, critical analysis of all the facts and issues," and he contended that in some cases they reached unwarranted conclusions. He acknowledged that the Downing Report had "overstated" some of its conclusions. Still, he found ample grounds to criticize General Schwalier. Khobar Towers had no effective alarm system, even though "Giant Voice"—whose siren had not been tested since 1994—might theoretically have fulfilled that task. There had been no evacuation drills at Khobar Towers, and Cohen did not accept the notion that bomb scares could substitute for them. Schwalier's failure to press the Saudis or his own chain of command on the issue of extending the perimeter around Khobar suggested "a lack of sufficient attention" to the threat of an external truck bomb. What the Swope/Hawley report had implied was a "systematic and organized evacuation method in place at Khobar Towers known as the 'waterfall' method" was no such thing.

"Wing leaders were obliged to have a thorough plan for protecting personnel in the event a perimeter attack materialized."[25] They did not have one, and this Cohen believed to be an unacceptable failure in a senior leader. He therefore recommended to the president that Schwalier, who had already been nominated for promotion to major general, be removed from the list, effectively terminating his career. Noting that Schwalier had never passed some of the problems (above all, extending the perimeter around Khobar) up his chain of command, Cohen decided that he could not blame anyone senior to the commander of the 4404th for the disaster. Only Schwalier would suffer any tangible consequences for what happened at Khobar.

At the news conference announcing his decision, Cohen emphasized his support from senior military leaders. Both the Chairman of the Joint Chiefs of Staff, General John Shalikashvili, and the Vice Chairman, General Joseph Ralston, "recommended to me that it would not be appropriate to promote Brigadier General Schwalier to the rank of major general, and I accepted their recommendation."[26] General Shalikashvili, who was present, confirmed this and endorsed the secretary's decision, saying "We must avoid the temptation to circle the wagons around one of our senior officers." Shalikashvili's support meant a great deal to Cohen. His support, and that of the vice chairman, "made it not quite as high a climb for the President, or for me" Cohen admitted later to a reporter.[27] The secretary had not only Shalikashvili's support: his decision received endorsement from editorialists who wrote approvingly of his unwillingness to "go along with a military culture that indulges failure and places career advancement above honor and duty."[28]

General Fogleman Departs

Many Air Force officers were outraged by the secretary's decision, and by the manner in which it was made—a public decision and announcement that circumvented the Air Force's chain of command, without even the courtesy of a personal interview with the hapless general. They viewed the late release of the Air Force reports as an effort to squelch the pro-Schwalier story, and they viewed Downing as an Army officer prejudiced against a sister service. The most dramatic opposition, however, came from someone who leveled no such accusations, but who simply resigned his office—the uniformed head of the United States Air Force, Chief of Staff General Ronald Fogleman. Fogleman, a decorated veteran of 315 combat missions in Vietnam and former professor of history at the Air Force Academy had, ironically, made his mark as chief by insisting on high

standards of accountability within the Air Force. He had denounced before the Senate a female bomber pilot, Lt. Kelly Flinn, who lied about an
affair with an enlisted man and had resigned rather than face a court-
martial. He had been appalled by the outcome of the shootdown of the
two Army helicopters, and imposed administrative penalties on half a
dozen officers involved. He played an important role in seeing that after
the crash of Secretary Brown's plane senior officers, not just their younger
subordinates, would suffer career-ending administrative actions. But after
his own reading of the record, he simply did not believe that Schwalier
merited deprivation of his promotion.

The tension between Cohen and Fogleman had simmered for some
time, and stemmed from a number of sources, including Fogleman's un-
happiness with the Department's Quadrennial Defense Review and with
other decisions that had gone against Air Force wishes. Some would say
in retrospect that the Khobar decision provided a welcome excuse to a
general who felt himself out of step with the Secretary of Defense in terms
of both policy and personality.

Even before his announcement of the decision to withdraw Schwalier's
promotion, Cohen told a journalist, "There is genuine concern in this
building that Fogleman is pushing this too far. I could say to him now,
'You're fired.' But I don't want to make a martyr of him. If he questions
[my decision] . . . I will relieve him of his duties."[29] Fogleman never gave
him the chance: on Monday, July 28, three days before Cohen's press conference, he resigned his post a year before its term expired, "to defuse the
perceived confrontation between myself and Secretary Cohen."[30] At the
July 31 news conference, when asked if Fogleman had agreed with Cohen's
conclusions, Cohen curtly replied "I would assume the answer is no."

Fogleman's resignation rocked the Air Force. The Khobar disaster came
on top of a series of other embarrassing or tragic episodes—the helicopter shootdown, the Kelly Flinn affair, the Ron Brown crash, the disap-
pearance and apparent suicide of an A-10 fighter bomber pilot, the
courts-martial of two mechanics (and the suicide of one of them) for
maintenance errors that led to a fatal airplane crash, and the forced renunciation by the Vice Chairman of the Joint Chiefs of Staff, General
Joseph Ralston, of promotion to the Chairmanship because of a past act
of adultery. Fogleman had been a popular and well-respected leader. He
was forward thinking, speaking of the Air Force undergoing an eventual
transition to a "space and air force," and he had created the first squadron
of unmanned aerial vehicles. He had, above all, been admired for his can-
dor, integrity, and sense of honor. His decision to resign, newspaper ac-

counts said, came after reading H. R. McMaster's *Dereliction of Duty*, a study of the Joint Chiefs of Staff during the early phases of the Vietnam War, which painted his predecessors as men who lacked the moral courage to stand up to manipulative and dishonest politicians.

He, like Schwalier, had his defenders well after the episode was over. These advocates not only stood up for Fogleman and Schwalier: they took on the Secretary of Defense. In a particularly stinging piece, journalist Matt Labash denounced Cohen as a pseudo tough guy who seemed to have made a difficult decision but had, in fact, taken the easy way out. In this, the lengthiest journalistic piece about the Schwalier affair, Labash quoted a former consul general in Dhahran who had described Schwalier as "the butt of mild kidding" for his obsession with the security of the 4404th. "There's no comparison between the degree of security we had at the American consulate, which by the way, housed the American school with all the children, with what Schwalier had."[31] Labash, who quoted extensively from the Record Report, argued that politics rather than a concern for military principle had actuated the secretary. Given all of the scandals erupting (to include a series of particularly shocking cases of predatory sexual behavior directed at women trainees at the Army's Aberdeen Proving Ground), "military accountability was now, more than ever, on the lips of every soft-paunched editorialist."

Cohen's contention that he could not face the relatives of the dead of Khobar Towers and say that everything had been done for those who had lost their kin was phony, Labash wrote. He never spoke to the grieving kin before making his decision to deny Schwalier's promotion, Labash asserted, and in fact, many of them had praised Schwalier to the reporter. He concluded with the words of one anonymous senior officer:

> This is something that will be on the minds of commanders—how much can they depend on their political leadership to support them when the chips are down. During a fast-moving military situation, you're more worried about covering your six [rear] than taking care of your troops and getting the job done. And I haven't seen the great reassuring statement that says in the future, we'll do better than we did by Schwalier. It didn't come out of the Joint Staff, it didn't come out of the Office of the Secretary of Defense, and it sure as hell didn't come off the Hill.

Secretary Cohen, who had mulled over the Khobar Towers episode for some time, would surely have disagreed, and vehemently. "Personal accountability," he told the press conference on July 31, "is not simply a question of assigning blame. It involves understanding the obligations of leadership, defining command responsibility, and clarifying the high standards of performance that we expect from commanders who are entrusted with the safety of our troops."

PRINCIPAL PLAYERS

Major General Kurt B. Anderson, USAF. At the time of the bombing, Anderson served as the commander of Joint Task Force—Southwest Asia in Riyadh. Among his other duties, he coordinated and oversaw force protection in the Kingdom of Saudi Arabia and the activities of the 4404th Wing (Provisional).

Lieutenant General Carl L. Franklin was replaced by Anderson on April 27, 1996. Before taking up the position, he served in a range of positions. His seven command tours included 48th Fighter Wing, which included command of the Combined Task Force, Operation PROVIDE COMFORT (operations in Northern Iraq), and went on to command 19th Air Force.

Colonel Gary S. Boyle, USAF. In the months leading up to the June 1995 bombing at Khobar Towers, Boyle was Support Group Commander for the 4404th Wing (Provisional). In this position, he had general responsibility for assisting the commander of the 4404th regarding force protection and implementing his directives in this regard.

General Wayne A. Downing, USA (retired). From June through September 1998, Downing headed a commission that investigated the Khobar Towers bombing and overall protection for U.S. forces based in Saudi Arabia. His military career included command of the United States Special Operations Command during the Gulf War and Somalia intervention and, earlier, the 75th Ranger Regiment.

General Ronald R. Fogleman, USAF. Fogleman was Chief of Staff of the Air Force from October 1994 to September 1997. He was a command pilot with more than 6,500 hours of flying time and flew 315 combat missions in Southeast Asia. In the years after his tours in Asia, his commands included 7th Air Force in Korea, and the United States Transportation Command. In July 1997 he became the first Air Force Chief of Staff to resign before the completion of his tour.

Major General Bryan G. Hawley, USAF. Hawley has been the USAF Judge Advocate General since February 1996. Soon after assuming this position, he conducted, along with Air Force Inspector General, Lieutenant General Richard Swope, the second USAF report on personal responsibility in the Khobar Towers bombing. Entering the USAF in 1967, Hawley graduated from the National War College and has spent the preponderance of his career in the judge advocate general corps.

Major General Joseph E. Hurd, USAF. Hurd served as Director of Operations (J-3) for United States Central Command from June 1994 to April 1997, during which he was responsible for managing force protection matters among his other duties. A command pilot with more than 3,500 flight hours, he flew 169 combat mission in South Vietnam. He served as commander of United States air forces in Korea, a position that includes service as deputy commander of United Nations Command, and commander of the 7th Air Force located at Osan Air Base, Republic of Korea.

Lieutenant General John P. Jumper, USAF. From August 1994 to June 1996, Jumper commanded the 9th Air Force and U.S. Central Command Air Forces. In this capacity, he was responsible for operational control over air assets in Saudi Arabia and provided forces to the Commander in Chief of the United States Central Command. A command pilot with more than 4,000 hours of flying time in F-4s, F-15s, and F-16s, he went on to command United States Air Forces in Europe (USAFE).

General J. H. Binford Peay, III. From August 1994 to August 1997, Peay served as the Commander in Chief of the United States Central Command (USCINCCENT), during which he oversaw the reinforcement of U.S. forces in Saudi Arabia in October 1994 (Vigilant Warrior) and the withdrawal of the United Nations Peacekeeping effort in Somalia. During the Gulf War, he commanded the 101st Airborne Division (Air Assault).

Lieutenant General James F. Record. From June 1995 to February 1997, Record commanded 12th Air Force and U.S. Southern Command Air Forces, Davis-Monthan Air Force Base, Arizona. A veteran of 600 combat missions in Southeast Asia, he commanded fighter wings and an air division. In the latter stages of his career, Record served two tours that dealt with the Middle East, including Deputy Commander, Joint Task Force Middle East (afloat) and Director of Operations (J-3), Central Command. Record conducted an inquiry upon request of the Secretary of the Air Force. He retired in February 1997.

Brigadier General Terryl "Terry" J. Schwalier, USAF. As Commander, 4404th Wing (Provisional), Schwalier began his tour in July 1995 and was the first General officer to be assigned there for a full year. He was responsible for implementing force protection guidance received from Central Command and executing measures for security of his command. Before then, he logged more than 3,000 hours of flight time in the RF-4C, T-38, F-16C, F-111 and commanded a squadron and wing, respectively, of the latter two aircraft. He resigned in July 1997 following the revocation of his promotion to Major General.

Lieutenant General Richard T. Swope, USAF. Since April 1996, Swope served as the Inspector General of the Air Force, in which capacity he oversees fraud and abuse programs and counterintelligence operations. Swope conducted along with Major General Bryan Hawley the second USAF inquiry on personal responsibility for the Khobar Towers bombing. Before assuming the Inspector General position, Swope commanded the 13th Air Force at Anderson Air Force Base in Guam and the 316th Air Division and 86th Fighter Wing at Ramstein Air Base, Germany. He has flown F-4s, F-15s, and F-16s and has amassed 3,800 hours of flight time, 320 of which were in combat.

Lieutenant Colonel James J. Traister. Traister commanded the 4044th Security Police Squadron (Provisional) when the Khobar Towers bombing occurred. He was responsible for identifying security weaknesses in his command, providing technical advice to his chain of command, implementing security and law enforcement measures at those facilities.

CHRONOLOGY OF EVENTS

1983

October 23—Shiite suicide bomber, driving a truck bomb with the equivalent of 12,000 pounds of TNT, kills 241 Americans in attack on Marine barracks in Beirut.

1993

February 23—Bomb at the World Trade Center in New York explodes, killing six and wounding hundreds. Explosion is the equivalent of 1,200 pounds of TNT.

1995

April 19—Truck bomb with equivalent of approximately 4,800 pounds of TNT kills 168 at Murrah Federal Office Building in Oklahoma City.

November 13—Bombing of OPM-SANG in Riyadh leaves five Americans and two Indians killed, along with 60 injured.

1996

June 25—Khobar Towers bombing. Truck bomb kills 19 Americans and injures 400 people of several nationalities.

June 28—Secretary Perry appoints a commission, headed by General (ret.) Wayne Downing, former Commander of United States Special Operations Command, to investigate the Dharan incident.

July 9—U.S. Senate Committee on Armed Services holds a hearing on the Khobar Towers bombing. Witnesses include Secretary of Defense Perry and Binford Peay.

August 14—U.S. House National Security Committee releases staff report on the bombing.

August 30—The Department of Defense releases the Downing report.

September 4—Acting upon a request from the Secretary of Defense, Fogleman and Widnall order 12th Air Force commander, Lieutenant General Record to assess the Downing Report.

September 19—U.S. Senate Committee on Armed Services holds hearing on the Downing Commission Report.

October—Lieutenant General Record completes the first half of his report.

December 20—Lieutenant General Record completes report.

1997

January 29—Deputy Secretary of Defense White returns the Record Report to the USAF, calling the probe "not sufficient." White asks for a fuller examination of all applicable standards beyond the Uniform Code of Military Justice.

February 5—Widnall assigns Lieutenant General Richard T. Swope, Inspector General of the Air Force, and Major General Bryan G. Hawley, Judge Advocate General, to report on the recommendations of the Record Report.

April—Swope and Hawley complete report.

June 28—Expecting the Secretary of Defense to deny the promotion of Schwalier, Ronald Fogleman resigns.

July 31—Secretary of Defense Cohen denies the promotion of Schwalier.

PART II

Half a Century Earlier

On December 7, 1941, Japanese forces attacked American forces at Pearl Harbor. Within two hours 2,400 American service personnel had perished, eight battleships had either sunk or been crippled by Japanese bombs and torpedoes, and the enemy had escaped virtually untouched. Within a fortnight the two commanders on the scene, Admiral Husband E. Kimmel, commander of the Pacific fleet, and Lieutenant General Walter C. Short, commander of U.S. Army forces on Hawaii, had been relieved. To the present day, the cashiering of both men, but Kimmel in particular, is a matter of controversy. Their case has some parallels with the far smaller catastrophe of Khobar. They too had received only imprecise intelligence (primarily, a general warning of war ten days before the attack); they too had protected themselves against the wrong, but a reasonable threat (sabotage); they too had done far more than their predecessors to defend their troops against an enemy onslaught quite as unprecedented as General Schwalier's defenders would regard the truck bomb at Khobar; they too were accused of complacency.

There have been many studies written of Pearl Harbor, but none more influential than the massive study by the Joint Congressional Committee investigating that calamity. The following are excerpts from its concluding report in 1946:

the errors made by the Hawaiian commands were errors of judgment and not derelictions of duty . . . [32]

With respect to Hawaii and the fleet, theirs [Kimmel and Short] were the obligations to plan for war, to train for war, and to be alerted for war when it came. The first two of these obligations they discharged in an exemplary manner but in the case of the third, alertness for war, they failed. All of the intelligence, thought, and energies of the field commander are to be devoted to his command. He is to apply all information and intelligence received to his particular situation. He is not privileged to think or contemplate that he will not be attacked. On the contrary, he is to assume and to expect that his particular post will be attacked. He cannot wholly assume that others will inform him when and where the foe will strike. He is "like a sentinel on duty in the face of the enemy. His fundamental duties are clear and precise. It is not the duty of the outpost commander to speculate or rely on the possibilities of the enemy attacking at some other outpost instead of his own. It is his duty to meet him at his post at any time and to make the best possible fight that can be made against him with the weapons with which he has been supplied."[33]

The commanders in Hawaii were clearly and unmistakably warned of war with Japan. They were given orders and possessed information that the entire Pacific area was fraught with danger. They failed to carry out these orders and to discharge their basic and ultimate responsibilities. They failed to defend the fortress they commanded—their citadel was taken by surprise. Aside from any responsibilities that may appear to rest in Washington, the ultimate and direct responsibility for failure to engage the Japanese on the morning of December 7 with every weapon at their disposal rests essentially and properly with the Army and Navy commands in Hawaii whose duty it was to meet the enemy against which they had been warned.

. . . [All] of these deficiencies reduce themselves to principles which are set forth, not for their novelty or profundity but for the reason that, by their very self-evident simplicity, it is difficult to believe they were ignored . . .

1. Operational and intelligence work requires centralization of authority and clear-cut allocation of responsibility . . .
2. Supervisory officials cannot safely take anything for granted in the alerting of subordinates . . .
17. An official who neglects to familiarize himself in detail with his organization should forfeit his responsibility . . .
18. Failure can be avoided in the long run only by preparation for any eventuality . . .
22. No considerations should be permitted as excuse for failure to perform a fundamental task . . .
23. Superiors must at all times keep their subordinates adequately informed and, conversely, subordinates should keep their superiors informed . . .
24. The administrative organization of any establishment must be designed to locate failures and to assess responsibility . . .

25. In a well-balanced organization there is close correlation of responsibility and authority . . .

Notes

1. "Force Protection Assessment of USCENTCOM AOR and Khobar Towers: Report of the Downing Assessment Task Force, 30 August 1996" (henceforth cited as "Downing Report"), p. 54, gives the time as six minutes; Air Force officers say it was less—perhaps three.

2. The various reports differ on this score.

3. Steven Erlanger, "Bombing in Saudi Arabia: The Overview; U.S. Commanders at Saudi Base Defend Efforts to Avoid Attack," *New York Times*, June 28, 1996, p. 1.

4. "Tragic Security Lapses Led to Deaths in Saudi Arabia," *USA Today* Editorial, July 1, 1996, p. 12A.

5. Testimony of General Binford Peay, U.S. Congress, Senate, Committee on Armed Services, "Bombings of U.S. Air Base in Saudi Arabia," July 9, 1996. Henceforth cited as "SASC Hearings."

6. Downing Report, pp. viii–ix.

7. Ibid., pp. 54–60.

8. U.S. Congress, House National Security Committee, "The Khobar Towers Bombing Incident," Staff Report, August 14, 1996, p. 9. Henceforth cited as "HNSC Report."

9. Secretary of Defense, Memorandum for the Chairman Joint Chiefs of Staff, "Subject: Department of Defense Responsibilities for Force Protection," September 15, 1996.

10. "SASC Hearings," September 19, 1996.

11. Lieutenant General James Record, "Independent Review of the Khobar Towers Bombing," October 31, 1996. Henceforth cited as "Record Report."

12. Record Report, Part I, p. 5.

13. Record Report, Part I, p. 9, emphasis in the original.

14. Defense Special Weapons Agency, "Report of Khobar Towers Bomb Damage Survey," n.d. DSWA and the Army Corps of Engineers sent a four-man team to Saudi Arabia July 5–10, 1996 to assess the damage at Khobar.

15. Record Report, Part II, p. 35.

16. Record Report, Part II, p. 51.

17. Eric Schmitt, "Air Force Study Clears All Officers in Saudi Blast That Killed 19," *New York Times*, December 12, 1996, p. 1A.

18. Both quotes from Eric Schmitt, "Lawmakers Assail Clearing of Officers in Saudi Bombing," *New York Times*, December 13, 1996, p. 1A.

19. James Kitfield, "Saudi Blast Rocks the Air Force," *National Journal* 29:1 (January 1997), p. 26.

20. Major General Bryan G. Hawley and Lieutenant General Richard T. Swope, "Report of Investigation Concerning the Khobar Towers Bombing, 25 June 1996," n.d. (April 1997) Part III, pp. 2–3.

21. Swope Hawley report, Part IV, p. 2.

22. "At Fault in Dhahran," *International Herald Tribune* Editorial, April 16, 1997, p. 10.

23. Bradley Graham, "Second Air Force Investigation Clears Officers of Blame in Dhahran Bombing," *Washington Post*, April 13, 1997, p. A7.

24. Dated July 31, 1997. Henceforth cited as "Personal Accountability."

25. Ibid., p. 5.

26. DOD News Briefing, July 31, 1997, Subject: Khobar Towers.

27. Quoted in James Carroll, "War Inside the Pentagon," *The New Yorker*, August 18, 1997, p. 58.

28. "Military Accountability," *New York Times* Editorial Desk, August 1, 1997, p. 30.

29. Carroll, "War Inside the Pentagon," p. 58.

30. Eric Schmitt, "Criticism Over Blast Leads Top Air Force General to Retire," *New York Times*, July 29, 1997, p. A1.

31. Quoted in Matt Labash, "The Scapegoat," *The Weekly Standard*, November 24, 1997, p. 20.

32. "Investigation of the Pearl Harbor Attack," Report of the Joint Committee on the Investigation of the Pearl Harbor Attack, seventy-ninth Congress, 2nd Session (Washington, DC: Government Printing Office, 1946), p. 237ff.

33. This was a quotation from the testimony of Secretary of War Henry Stimson before the committee.

Chapter 7

"To Prevent and Deter" International Terrorism: The U.S. Response to the Kenya and Tanzania Embassy Bombings

WILLIAM C. BANKS

On August 7, 1998 President Clinton received a pre-dawn wake-up call from National Security Adviser Samuel R. "Sandy" Berger, informing him of terrorist attacks on the U.S. embassies in Nairobi and Dar es Salaam. On August 20, retaliatory strikes were launched at targets in Sudan and Afghanistan. The strikes were the product of a tightly controlled decision process, by a handful of officials. Although the United States acted quickly and firmly, questions and criticisms arose early on. What was the decision process? Was the decision to respond with military force effective? Were the strikes lawful? Will the strikes serve the purpose of deterring further acts of international terrorism?

When the United States declined to respond militarily to the 1996 terrorist murder of nineteen American soldiers at Khobar Towers in Dhahran, Saudi Arabia, it was said that our nation's scruples—the need to find convincing proof of who committed an attack before acting against the perpetrators—only served to make us vulnerable to more terrorist attacks. "The message being sent all over the world is that we're vulnerable, and our allies are vulnerable," opined Anthony Cordesman of the Center for Strategic and International Studies. "That won't be solved by more conferences and more gates, but serious thought about how you retaliate and punish."[1] Some suggested that America's threats to retaliate lack credibility because American standards of evidence are too high for this kind of fight.

Still, as former director of counterterrorism William E. Odom opined, "Terrorism at home is a crime; terrorism abroad is war." And if war is thrust upon us, he says, "why not act militarily?"[2] However, what kind of war is it, where cultural or religious fury replaces political and strategic objectives, and sponsorship of the attacks is often hidden? Determining the targets of the response, deciding measures of success, and assessing the deterrent value of a military response are among the hardest issues to wrestle with. This case explores those challenges.

THE ATTACK

When terrorist truck bombs simultaneously struck U.S. embassies in Kenya and Tanzania on August 7, 1998, more than 250 were killed, including twelve Americans, and more than 5,500 were injured. Speculation on suspects and the likely U.S. response quickly focused on law enforcement, the collection of evidence at the bomb sites, and the efforts to build a case to indict, try, and convict the perpetrators in the United States. Some officials and commentators cautioned against any aggressive military response to the attacks, and reminded us that the U.S. public has never been comfortable with unconventional warfare.

Senate Governmental Affairs Committee Chairman Fred Thompson stated: "It certainly seems to me that we're in for something that we're not ready for, as a people."[3] Even in the immediate aftermath of the embassy bombings, Secretary of State Madeleine Albright stated: "We are not a nation that retaliates just in order to get vengeance. . . . [Although] we would all like to go out right this instant and bomb somebody . . . we've got to be careful about what we're doing and why we're doing it . . . so that we can be true to ourselves. . . . We must not forget our own legal system while searching for those who harmed us."[4]

Others pointed to President Reagan's order to bomb Muammar Qaddafi's residence after there was clear evidence of Libyan complicity in attacks on American soldiers at a Berlin discotheque in 1986. Former Assistant Secretary of Defense Richard Perle noted that Quaddafi understood the message and "behaved differently for years."[5] Yet former Director of Central Intelligence Robert M. Gates argued that the Libyan bombing of Pan Am flight 103 in 1988 was in retaliation for the 1986 bombing attack on Libya, and that other acts of terrorism were likely committed with Libyan sponsorship after 1986. According to Gates, retributive violence, "no matter how massive, almost invariably begets more violence against us in response."[6]

According to Paul Goble, a former State Department and CIA official, there is a middle ground: "If you have to make an American legal case, it's hard to do anything. If you say no standards are necessary, then you unleash worse problems. But you have to prove you mean business, and even our courts require no more than excluding reasonable doubt."[7]

But even as the pundits were speculating, a small group—six of President Clinton's most senior national security advisers—convened in the White House situation room beginning on August 10 to plan a counter-attack for the embassy bombings. Investigators had already uncovered evidence that linked the terrorist network of Osama bin Laden, the Saudi exile, to the bombings. Although knowledge about bin Laden and his followers remains sketchy, his core political argument is that American troops should get out of Saudi Arabia. The royal family expelled bin Laden from the kingdom for his political activities at about the same time that U.S. troops were permitted to occupy Saudi soil before the Gulf War. When the Saudi government allowed U.S. forces to remain after the victory, the U.S. "had become to Saudi Arabia what the Soviet Union had been to Afghanistan: an infidel occupation force propping up a corrupt, repressive, and un-Islamic government."[8] The embassy bombings took place eight years to the day after U.S. troops were ordered onto Saudi soil.

The administration was determined to avoid leaks, and hoped to spring responsive raids against bin Laden's cabal that would take the world by surprise. The security precautions worked, or nearly so. On August 20, seventy-nine Tomahawk cruise missiles were fired, timed to explode nearly simultaneously at targets in Afghanistan and the Sudan. One barrage targeted terrorist training camps at Khost, Afghanistan, where intelligence indicated bin Laden and senior lieutenants would be meeting. The second round of missiles targeted a pharmaceutical plant in Khartoum, Sudan, suspected of being a link in the chain of chemical weapons production, also connected to the bin Laden enterprise.

Launched from ships in the Arabian and Red Seas at dusk, with no American casualties, the strikes were the most formidable U.S. military assault ever against a non-state sponsor of terrorism. Damage assessments remain unclear, although the Khartoum plant and some of the terrorist camps were destroyed. Bin Laden and his associates apparently were unharmed.

DECIDING TO TAKE ACTION

After the president's August 7 wake-up call from Sandy Berger, members of the president's national security team began meeting the same day to direct relief efforts, to direct and monitor investigative work, and to consider responsive actions. As early as the 7th, it was reported to the president that the Osama bin Laden group of terrorist organizations was responsible for the bombings. Over the weekend, Berger consulted with Secretary Albright and then asked Secretary of Defense William Cohen, Chairman of the Joint Chiefs of Staff General Hugh Shelton, and Director of Central Intelligence George Tenet to form a small group to begin considering options for responding to the bin Laden network. On August 8, the president's advisers requested the Pentagon Joint Staff and the CIA to create a list of potential bombing targets connected to the bin Laden organization.

President Clinton, Secretaries Albright and Cohen, National Security Adviser Berger, General Shelton, and Under Secretary of State Thomas R. Pickering attended the planning meetings. Attorney General Janet Reno also was informed of the response planning and supplied legal advice to the president. The core of the small group, the National Security Council, is charged by statute to advise the president in the event of a national security crisis.

The Counterterrorism Center at the CIA and other officials prepared an initial list of about twenty targets, and in each instance evidence linking the site to bin Laden was spelled out and the risks of collateral damage were assessed. Because bin Laden was thought to have extensive ties to the industrial sector of the Sudanese government, advisers included in their target list a pharmaceutical facility in Khartoum—Al Shifa.

On Monday, August 10, while traveling in California, President Clinton was briefed by telephone by Berger. On August 12, the president cut his trip short and met in the situation room to consider a winnowed-down list of military options against bin Laden. By the next day, the president was told that other terrorist attacks may be planned against U.S. targets around the world. Clinton was also informed that members of bin Laden's terrorist network would be gathering at three terrorist training camps at Khost, Afghanistan, on August 20. The Afghan camps were already on the winnowed-down list of targets. In addition, advisers presented the president with evidence that the bin Laden network had been actively seeking to acquire weapons of mass destruction—including chemical weapons—for use against U.S. interests.

On August 13, bodies of Americans killed in the bombings were returned to Andrews Air Force Base, where Clinton said, "America's memory is long, our reach is far, our resolve unwavering and our commitment to justice is unshatterable."[9] On Friday the 14th, CIA Director Tenet presented his determination that, while the evidence linking bin Laden to Al

Shifa, the Sudanese factory, was strong, it could be "drawn only indirectly and by inference."[10] According to Tenet, the plant's involvement with chemical weapons was more certain, based on a soil sample taken from near the site that contained a precursor to nerve gas. Attorney General Reno urged that the strikes be delayed, both to give more time for the FBI to gather evidence linking bin Laden to the embassy bombings, and to assure the link between bin Laden and the targets in Afghanistan and Sudan. Secretary Cohen and General Shelton briefed and the president accepted in principle a military plan for responding to the attacks. Clinton ordered the Navy to deploy ships with cruise missiles to the Red Sea and Arabian Sea, and to prepare for the August 20 strikes, but preserved his ability to cancel the raids up to 6 AM (EST) on the 20th.

Alternatives to missile strikes were also considered. Soon after the August 7 embassy bombings, officials in the CIA and the Defense Department considered a raid into Afghanistan to capture bin Laden. Although such a high-risk operation may be so over-the-top that it should not receive serious consideration, former CIA Director Robert M. Gates explained: "Some of the problems you face are really hard, and sometimes people stretch to figure out how to solve them."[11] He noted that whether such plans get a green light depends on a stark calculus of the possible cost in American lives versus the chance of taking out a terrorist who has vowed to kill Americans at every opportunity. In this instance, the plan to abduct bin Laden was shelved by DCI Tenet and other senior officials; it never reached President Clinton.

As planning continued for the August 20 strikes, the White House also responded to the threat of additional terrorist attacks against U.S. targets by ordering the evacuation of the American Embassy in Islamabad, Pakistan. The *New York Times* reported that the American Ambassador to Pakistan, Thomas W. Simmons, Jr., refused to comment when asked at a meeting of Americans about "rumors" that the United States was planning to strike at bin Laden. Ironically, the media attention given to the heightened security in Pakistan, and concerns of U.S. personnel struggling with arrangements at a time when dependent children were beginning a school year, likely alerted the bin Laden group that the United States was planning its own military operation in the region.

Richard A. Clarke, a senior NSC official later explained that it was important to reply to bin Laden in more than one place. Because bin Laden had demonstrated "global reach" through two simultaneous attacks on embassies in two countries, the United States should attack bin Laden beyond his camps in Afghanistan. It was thus decided that bin Laden should be attacked in Afghanistan and at two sites in Sudan: Al Shifa and a tannery in Khartoum that had been linked to bin Laden.[12]

On Monday the 17th, Berger updated the president on the military planning for the strikes, just before Clinton testified to the grand jury in the Monica Lewinsky investigation. Later that evening, the president addressed the nation and admitted to an "inappropriate" relationship with the former White House intern. At the president's family vacation spot on Martha's Vineyard, on Wednesday the 19th, Berger told the president that the Pentagon was awaiting his orders. Meanwhile, on the same day General Shelton told his Joint Chiefs colleagues about the operation for the first time, in part to enlist their help in persuading the White House to drop the tannery as a target. After several calls to the White House objecting to bombing the tannery, Berger relayed the concerns to the president. After consulting other advisers, Clinton ordered the tannery removed from the target list at about 2 AM on the 20th. On the 19th, Berger notified Speaker of the House Newt Gingrich and Senate Majority Leader Trent Lott that the attacks would be made. Senate Minority Leader Tom Daschle and staffers for the unavailable House Minority Leader Richard A. Gephardt were also briefed. After a series of overnight telephone calls, the president gave the go ahead at 6 AM on the 20th. Speaking from Martha's Vineyard an hour after the attacks the president told the nation that "our target was the terrorists' base of operation and infrastructure. Our objective was to damage their capacity to strike at Americans and other innocent people."[13] Interrupting his vacation, Clinton then rushed back to Washington to attend a briefing on the operations and to explain the strikes to the world. The next day, President Clinton formally reported the strikes to Congress.

Late in the afternoon on the 19th, several officials, including a group of counterterrorism experts, were summoned to Clarke's NSC office and told to plan to spend the evening. Although the group had not been involved in selecting targets, and were not then asked to review the targeting decisions, they were asked to prepare talking points for American ambassadors and briefings for Congress and the media after the missile strikes.[14]

THE AFTER ACTION ASSESSMENT

In his August 21 formal letter to the congressional leadership informing them of the mission, the president said that the "strikes were intended to prevent and deter additional attacks by a clearly identified terrorist threat."[15] He reported that the U.S. forces involved in the strikes completed their mission and that no U.S. casualties were incurred. As CNN showed the still-smoldering damage to the Khartoum facility, Berger noted the visible success of the strike in damaging a "so-called pharmaceutical factory in Khartoum, which we know with great certainty produces essentially the penultimate chemical to manufacture VX nerve gas."[16] At the same press conference on August 20, Berger noted that, while it was not then known what damage had been done to the camps in Afghanistan, the target was "perhaps the largest terrorist training camp in the world . . . [T]o the extent we can disrupt it, destroy it and send a very important message at the same time, obviously we think that's advantageous."[17]

A few months later, assessments of the operation had changed. According to Robert B. Oakley, former U.S. Ambassador to Pakistan and former State Department counterterrorism coordinator, "the principal reasons for bin Laden's having popular appeal are growing. . . . People feel they have no voice. They look at a people with great wealth while they live in deep poverty."[18] The seventy-nine missiles deployed, at a cost of about $750,000 each, did not kill bin Laden or his associates in Afghanistan.

Targeting the training camps in Afghanistan affronted several allies in the Islamic world, particularly Pakistan. On August 20, 1998, Pakistani Army Chief of Staff, General Jehangir Karamar, hosted Vice Chairman of the Joint Chiefs General Joseph Ralston. At about ten o'clock, Ralston checked his watch and informed Karamar that about sixty Tomahawk cruise missiles would be entering Pakistani airspace. According to a U.S. intelligence official, Ralston was there to make certain that the missiles would not be mistaken as coming from India and, consequently, be shot down. Karamar's initial anger turned to rage when he learned that, through poor targeting or missing the target, two of the four training camps that were hit and destroyed belonged to Pakistan's own intelligence agency, the Inter-Services Intelligence or ISI. Five ISI officers and about twenty trainees were reportedly killed.[19] Why had Pakistan not been notified earlier? And why was notice given to General Karamar, instead of the Prime Minister?

Despite President Clinton's televised claim that a "gathering of key terrorist leaders" had been expected to take place at the target sites, bin Laden and his associates were more than one hundred miles away when the attack occurred. The "gathering" took place a month earlier, in Jalalabad. One of the six facilities struck was a bin Laden training camp. Thousands of dollars worth of camp facilities were destroyed at a cost of roughly seventy-nine million dollars.[20]

The decision to target Al Shifa was also coming under fire. Questioned a year after the events, NSA Berger did not recall DCI Tenet or anyone else involved in the decision process questioning that Al Shifa was associated with chemical weapons: "No one in the discussion questioned whether Al Shifa was an appropriate target."[21] However, at the State Department Bureau of Intelligence and Research, a report written for Secretary Albright before the strikes questioning the linking of Al Shifa to bin Laden resurfaced after the attack. Although Assistant Secretary of State Phyllis Oakley told her staff to draft a report to reflect their skepticism about the evidence, the report was killed after Oakley met with Under Secretary Pickering. Secretary Albright later stated that she was "not interested in having that debate rehashed."[22]

Suspicions about Al Shifa arose in 1997, when an informant reported to U.S. officials that three sites in Khartoum may be involved in chemical weapons production. Apparently, Al Shifa attracted attention because it had strict security and high fences. Later in 1997, an agent working for the CIA collected a soil sample about sixty feet from Al Shifa, apparently from land that was not owned by Al Shifa. The sample contained about 2.5 times the normal trace amounts of Empta, a chemical used to produce VX nerve gas. Although a 1998 CIA report highlighted apparent links between Al Shifa and bin Laden, the report called for additional information, including additional soil samples and satellite photographs. The report also noted that there was no longer stringent security around Al Shifa.[23]

The evidence linking the pharmaceutical plant to anything other than medicines was found to be inconclusive, at best, according to a report based on thirteen soil samples taken in October 1998 by a team of chemists. Professor Thomas D. Tullius, chairman of the chemistry department at Boston University, stated that "in those samples, to the practical limits of scientific detection, there was no Empta or Empa, its breakdown product."[24] However, Salih Idris, the plant's owner, commissioned the soil study, along with a report by an international security company, Kroll Associates. The Kroll report found no evidence of a direct link between Idris and bin Laden. Nonetheless, Clinton administration officials maintained that they had strong evidence linking Idris to bin Laden, and they dismissed the soil findings, noting that the October samples were taken long after the United States obtained its soil samples, and long after the bombing and rains could have dispersed the incriminating evidence. However, Professor Tullius noted that several locations at the plant were surveyed, including some covered by debris, others protected from rain, and one intact septic tank that provided a historical record of chemicals flushed through the plant drains. Tullius also explained that, while Empta breaks downs within days, Empa remains in the soil and would be detectable for weeks or months after contact with the ground.

The Kroll team found no evidence that the Al Shifa plant had been heavily guarded. Nor was there any sign of secret areas or areas off-limits to outsiders. Their report determined that Al Shifa produced only veterinary medicines and pharmaceuticals for human consumption. Still, the Kroll investigation did confirm Idris's links to Sudan's Military Industrial Corporation, the government entity that makes weapons for the Sudanese Army. The United States charged that the corporation also produced chemical weapons in Sudan, and that bin Laden had supplied financing for the corporation.

NSA Berger later conceded that there were debates at the final targeting meeting concerning the Sudan sites. He maintained, however, that the questions were "geopolitical" and "were not based on any doubts about Al Shifa."[25] Apparently, General Shelton objected to striking the tannery on the grounds that it was not involved in chemical weapons and that civilians might be hit by the missiles. Former CIA Director James Woolsey opined that "this should not be the kind of decision made only with three of four people around you of a Cabinet-level who don't know an EMPTA sample from their left foot."[26]

None of the Joint Chiefs, other than General Shelton, nor FBI Director Louis J. Freeh were privy to the planning of the mission, although the FBI had been actively investigating the embassy bombings in Kenya and Tanzania. Nor was the FBI asked to assess the intelligence that had concluded that the Al Shifa plant in Sudan was involved in making chemical warfare materials. Although CIA analysts say they found evidence connecting the Al Shifa plant to chemical weapons manufacture at some time in the past, others within the Intelligence and Science and Technology Directorates at CIA faulted the rush to reach conclusions about Al Shifa.

Was the small group decision process too insular, too secretive? In assessing the aborted Iran hostage rescue mission in 1980, some speculated that classic groupthink—where "pressures internal to the group result in an overriding concern with maintaining a sense of an amiable in-group, at the cost of individual members ignoring or suppressing their doubts over policy options"—contributed significantly to the rescue mission fiasco.[27] Similarly, following the Cambodian seizure of the *Mayaguez* in 1975, and during the height of the National Security Council debate on the wisdom of air strikes against the Cambodian mainland, the White

House photographer interrupted the conversation to ask, "Has anyone considered that this might be the act of a local Cambodian commander who has just taken it into his own hands to halt any ship that comes by? . . . If that's what happened, you know, you can blow the whole place away and it's not gonna make any difference." President Ford later wrote that, "what [the photographer] had said made a lot of sense," even though it was contrary to the advice of Secretary of State Kissinger, Vice President Rockefeller, National Security Adviser Scowcroft, and the Chairman of the Joint Chiefs of Staff.[28] President Ford then decided against strikes against the mainland in favor of surgical strikes against a Cambodian port.

The responsibility to consult the congressional leadership in these situations is not clear. During this incident, the president made some effort to consult with congressional leaders before the strike was committed. However, the consultative record is mixed. With the 1986 Libyan bombing raid, members of Congress were unhappy that they were notified only once the bombers were in the air. In 1975, Congress was not consulted before President Ford authorized a mission to recapture the *Mayaguez* from Cambodian troops. Nor were members consulted before President Carter's abortive attempt to rescue American hostages from Iran in April 1980.

Given the President's then-ongoing political crisis with the Lewinsky scandal, some surmised that the haste and timing of this decision was at least in part attributable to domestic politics and clouded judgments. The final planning for the raid took place while the president was on a family vacation, trying to heal family wounds inflicted by his recent admission of the Lewinsky affair. A four-star general, reflecting on the decision process, observed: "It's not something to do on a weekend at Martha's Vineyard."[29]

LEGAL AUTHORITY FOR THE OPERATION

In national security crisis situations, the president would normally rely for legal advice on a group informally known as the War Powers Working Group. The group—led by the White House counsel, and made up of the general counsels at the departments of Defense and State, the CIA, and Joint Chiefs, and the NSC, along with the head of the Justice Department's Office of Legal Counsel—meets in national security crisis situations to fashion reports to Congress and to determine the legal strategy for the cabinet secretaries and the president. On this occasion, the group of lawyers with advance knowledge of the strikes apparently was limited to Attorney General Reno and one or two other senior Justice Department lawyers.

On the day the attacks were launched, National Security Adviser Berger sought to offer a legal justification for the cruise missile attacks on targets in Sudan and Afghanistan linked to Osama bin Laden's terrorist network. Berger first cited Article 51 of the United Nations Charter, which recognizes "the inherent right of individual or collective self-defense if an armed attack occurs against a Member of the United Nations."[30] This authority fits the cruise missile strikes if the raid is characterized as "self-defense . . . to pre-empt and deter [bin Laden's] unlawful aggression through terrorist force against the United States and its nationals."[31] If Article 51 includes a right of *anticipatory* self-defense, and not merely the recognized and customary right to respond to an actual attack, this reasoning would likely establish this nation's right under *international law* to use force in these circumstances.

Article 2 of the charter says that no country may violate the territorial integrity of another except in cases of self-defense, raising the question whether the United States violated international law when it shot at the Afghanistan targets through Pakistani airspace without obtaining Pakistan's permission. Moreover, assuming that Article 51 does supply legal authority for the U.S. government to use force abroad, the charter is completely silent about which part of government is authorized to make the decision. In addition, the charter provisions and the customary international law of self-defense have traditionally been construed to apply against state actors. Legal scholars disagree concerning whether the same standards apply where the targets are non-state actor terrorist groups.

Did the president consult adequately with members of Congress before ordering the strikes? Was consultation legally sufficient, or was he required to seek congressional authorization before ordering the mission? The 1973 War Powers Resolution requires that the president consult with Congress in "every possible instance" before committing armed forces "into hostilities or into situations where imminent involvement in hostilities is clearly indicated by the circumstances."[32] While it has never been clear what is meant by the consultation requirement, President Clinton did contact the leadership in advance of authorizing the strikes. While the details of those conversations are not public, Senate Majority Leader Lott and House Speaker Gingrich expressed support for the operation, and Gingrich indicated that he had been included in the briefings in the days following the embassy bombings.

Further evidence of the president's efforts to satisfy the Congress is the letter he sent to them on August 21, the day after the strikes. Reporting "as part of [his] efforts to keep the Congress fully informed, consistent with the War Powers Resolution," Clinton described the operation, and noted the "convincing information from a variety of reliable sources" linking the bin Laden group to the embassy bombings. He stated that the U.S. actions were consistent with the Article 51 self-defense power, and that "these strikes were a necessary and proportionate response to the imminent threat of further terrorist attacks against U.S. personnel and facilities . . . [and] were intended to prevent and deter additional attacks by a clearly identified terrorist threat." The president noted that he ordered the operation "pursuant to [his] constitutional authority to conduct U.S. foreign relations and as Commander in Chief and Chief Executive."[33]

Berger also claimed at a press briefing that a law enacted by Congress in 1996 "instructs" the president to "use all necessary means, including . . . military force, to disrupt, dismantle, and destroy international infrastructure used by international terrorists, including overseas terrorist training facilities and safe havens."[34] However, the actual 1996 language quoted by Berger comes from a congressional finding prohibiting assistance to countries that aid terrorists. The codified law referenced by the administration neither "instructs" or authorizes anything.

As Commander in Chief, the president has the implied constitutional authority to repel sudden attacks. The constitutional text does not say so, but we know from James Madison's notes of the Constitutional Convention that it was to reserve that authority to the President that the framers gave Congress the authority only "to declare war" instead of the first-proposed authority "to make war." Of course, President Clinton was not repelling the kind of sudden attack envisioned by Madison when he ordered the strikes against terrorist installations. But the suddenness and secrecy of terrorist attacks, the unpredictability of their targets, and the difficulty of apprehending terrorists at the scene all suggest that the most effective defense is preemptive.

More expansively, he can argue that he has the authority to fight a war started against us. Bin Laden has actually announced a "holy war" against the United States. Rhetoric alone does not make a de facto war (or else we surely would be in several hundred simultaneously with numerous posturing detractors around the globe), but bin Laden's holy war has already inflicted serious casualties on Americans and hundreds of non-American bystanders besides. When the United States is placed at war by enemy attack, "the President is not only authorized but bound to resist force by force, . . . bound to meet it in the shape it presented itself,"[35] the Supreme Court has said.

Although military reprisals require congressional authorization, Joseph Alpher, head of the Jerusalem office of the American Jewish Committee, opined: "Even if it's revenge, it's meant to send a message that there will be a retaliation, and that is deterrence."[36] To some observers, then, even a reprisal is a defensive measure.

An additional potential source of authority for the strikes is customary national security law. While the dimensions and legitimacy of customary law as domestic law in the United States are by no means settled, commentators have endorsed Justice Jackson's suggestion that "congressional inertia, indifference or quiescence . . . at least as a practical matter, enable, if not invite, measures on independent responsibility"[37] of the president. According to Justice Frankfurter, "a systematic, unbroken, executive practice, long pursued to the knowledge of the Congress and never before questioned . . . may be treated as a gloss on the 'executive Power' vested in the President by § 1 of Art. II."[38] In other words, congressional acquiescence in an executive construction of constitutional powers may, over time, ripen into a kind of constitutional common law.

Whatever the strength of the anticipatory self-defense justification as applied to the Afghanistan camps, the applicability of this approach to the attack on the manufacturing plant in a sovereign capital should be assessed independently. Arguably, the required imminence of a threat should be balanced against the potential damage if the threat is carried out in deciding the president's authority to use force against it preemptively. However, at least one scholar of international law, Professor Francis Boyle, maintains that the attack on the Sudanese facility was unlawful: "The Sudanese government can probably sue the U.S. in the World Court over this."[39]

Some observers also wondered whether the United States legally could and practically should target bin Laden himself in the raids. Since President Gerald Ford first promulgated the rule in an executive order in 1976, U.S. participation or sponsorship of acts of political assassination has been prohibited. Interpretations of the executive order rendered contemporaneously with the contemplated support of a coup against General Manuel Antonio Noriega in Panama reasoned that the death of a foreign leader during an otherwise lawful military operation in which the United States played some part would not render the operation unlawful so long as the leader was not explicitly targeted. Thus, it was probable that the president's advisers predicted that bin Laden would be in the Khost camps on August 20, and that his presence was one reason for selecting the date of the strike.

THE UTILITY OF THE USE OF FORCE IN RESPONDING TO TERRORIST THREATS

According to Senate Judiciary Chairman Orrin Hatch, "There should be nothing that should not be on the table"[40] when it comes to responding to terrorist attacks. Advocating assassination, former Reagan administration ambassador-at-large for counterterrorism L. Paul Bremer wrote: U.S. policy "makes no sense" because "it is permissible to attack a factory in the middle of a city or a terrorist camp inhabited by unnamed operatives, but not to target a man who is proud to kill American civilians."[41]

Among those who disagree is former CIA general counsel Jeffrey Smith, who opined that "the ban on assassination has been widely supported by virtually everyone in the executive branch, from the military through the CIA's clandestine service. First, assassination clearly invites a direct retaliation against not only the President but other senior Government officials and private Americans. Second, we have adequate authority to engage in military actions or covert actions involving the use of lethal force without targeting a particular individual for assassination. Third, it is just not in keeping with American values. . . . To begin to behave like terrorists undermines our role as a leader in respect for the rule of law and respect for human rights."[42] According to Under Secretary of State Thomas R. Pickering, "what we did in clear and careful daylight, in good conscience, on the question of assassination is in my view correct. It distinguishes us from those who adopt assassination and terror as a weapon."[43]

Some plans are so risky that they are not presented to even senior policymakers, much less the president. Still, as former Director Gates noted, "The good thing about the inter-agency process is that it imposes a reality test on these plans. We used to call it the laugh test—can you present this at the NSC without people giggling?" According to Gates, the extravagant planning serves as a "gut check" for the civilians, "that allows the military to ask: 'Are they serious about wanting this? Or are they just playing political games?' "[44]

Some intelligence advisers and senior military officials disagreed with the use of the expensive Tomahawks to send a political message to terrorists. For civilian leaders, the missiles appeal because they are accurate and because there is minimal risk of U.S. casualties. At the same time, some military officials maintained that the coupling between the capabilities of the Tomahawks and their targets in Afghanistan was weak, and that the small payload of high explosives carried by the Tomahawks had little chance of penetrating, much less killing, bin Laden and others in their well-fortified caves and bunkers in Khost. One four-star general went so far as to maintain that there is no evidence that any Tomahawk strike would have a significant impact on terrorists: "When the strong attack the weak, the weak win."[45]

Surgical airstrikes may make sense when the targets are heavy equipment, lethal weaponry, communications centers, and large concentrations of armed forces. Due to the nature of attacks organized by small groups using clandestine methods, terrorist bases generally contain none of these conventional targets. In addition, targeting terrorist bases, which are often in close proximity to populated areas, risks casualties among innocent civilians. Instead, the general argued, if attacking terrorists is the policy choice, then it should be done at some critical point of leverage, "a collapse point."[46] Nonpublic and nonkinetic options should be considered, he said, such as attacking terrorists through the banking system.

Worse yet, six months after the strikes aimed at bin Laden, officials of the State Department, CIA, and NSC say that the strikes may have had no effect, or worse yet, backfired. DCI Tenet told Congress that bin Laden remained capable of striking against the U.S. "at any time."[47] Another senior counterterrorism official said: "I don't think anything we've done has changed the minds of true believers."[48] Clinton administration officials have arrested men believed to be his associates, and officials say that two of bin Laden's plans to attack more American embassies have been thwarted. Nonetheless, according to former Ambassador Oakley, "[I]f we make it into a war, we lose. We'll swell their numbers enormously."[49]

On the positive side, it was maintained that the strikes did at least disrupt the bin Laden network and destroy some training sites and possibly a chemical weapons plant, while killing a few terrorists. If the strikes did indeed reach those who planned the embassy bombings, terrorists are on notice that they are being watched.

Yet it is unclear whether attacks like this one will have any deterrent effect on terrorists. Bin Laden also illustrates the problems inherent in responding to an enemy who is a man and not a state; who has no conventionally structured organization, no headquarters, and no address; and whose adherents live all over the world and are loyal not so much to the man as to an ideology of militant Islam.[50] The U.S. attack may simply constitute part of a cycle of strikes and counterstrikes. While there is no conventional military measure of the success or failure of this form of anticipatory self-defense, some assert that the targets of terror must strike back to demonstrate that they have not been cowed. In the psychological war that is very much part of terrorism, striking back at least boosts the morale of Americans. But is this simply an example of foreign policy by catharsis, where an operation is carried out for short-term political reasons, not to meet carefully crafted national security objectives?

Notes

1. Quoted in Steven Erlanger, "Pursuing Terrorists: Sleuths vs. Rambo," *New York Times*, August 16, 1998, Wk. 5.

2. Ibid.

3. Quoted in Chuck McCutcheon, "Does the U.S. Have the Will and Means for a Sustained War on Terrorism?," *Cong. Qtly. Wkly.*, Sept. 5, 1998, pp. 2352, 2353.

4. Quoted in Erlanger, "Pursuing Terrorists: Sleuths vs. Rambo."

5. Ibid.

6. Robert M. Gates, "What War Looks Like Now," *New York Times*, August 16, 1998, Wk. 15.

7. Quoted in Erlanger, "Pursuing Terrorists: Sleuths vs. Rambo."

8. Mary Anne Weaver, "The Real Bin Laden," *The New Yorker*, January 24, 2000, pp. 32, 36.

9. Quoted in John King, "Events Leading Up to Clinton's Order to Strike Back," http://allpolitics.com/1998/08/21/tictoc.king/.

10. Notes of a participant in the meeting, quoted in James Risen, "To Bomb Sudan Plant, or Not: A Year Later, Debates Rankle," *New York Times*, October 27, 1999, p. A1.

11. Quoted in James Risen, "Pentagon Planners Give New Meaning to 'Over the Top,' " *New York Times*, September 20, 1998, Wk. 4.

12. Risen, "To Bomb Sudan Plant, or Not."

13. Quoted in John King, "Events Leading Up to Clinton's Order to Strike Back."

14. Risen, "To Bomb Sudan Plant, or Not."

15. Text of a letter on Afghanistan and Sudan strikes, 34 Wkly. Comp. Pres. Doc. 1650, August 21, 1998.

16. Press briefing on U.S. strikes in Sudan and Afghanistan, August 20, 1998. http://secretary.state.gov/www/statements/1998/980820.html.

17. Ibid.

18. Quoted in Tim Weiner, "Missile Strikes Against bin Laden Won Him Esteem in Muslim Lands, U.S. Officials Say," *New York Times*, Feb. 8, 1999, p. A13.

19. Weaver, "The Real Bin Laden," p. 37.

20. Ibid.

21. Quoted in Risen, "To Bomb Sudan Plant, or Not."

22. Ibid.

23. Ibid.

24. Quoted in James Risen and David Johnston, "Experts Find No Arms Chemicals at Bombed Sudan Plant," *New York Times*, February 9, 1999, p. A3.

25. Quoted in Risen, "To Bomb Sudan Plant, or Not."

26. Ian Brodie, "American Insists Factory Was Gas Producer," *Times* (London), September 3, 1998, p. 17.

27. Steve Smith, "Groupthink and the Hostage Rescue Mission," *British Journal of Political Science* 15 (1984), p. 117.

28. Gerald R. Ford, *A Time to Heal* (New York: Harper & Row, 1979), pp. 275–84.

29. Quoted in Seymour M. Hersh, "The Missiles of August," *The New Yorker*, October 12, 1998, pp. 34–41.

30. United Nations Charter, art. 51.

31. Statement of Abraham Sofaer, Legal Adviser to the Department of State, "The War Powers Resolution and Antiterrorist Operations," reprinted in War Powers, Libya, and State-Sponsored Terrorism: Hearing Before Subcomm. On Arms Control, Int'l Security and Science of House Comm. On Foreign Aff., 99th Cong., 2d Sess. 26–31 (1986) (commenting on the U.S. bombing of Libya in the wake of a terrorist bomb exploding in a Berlin nightclub).

32. War Powers Resolution of 1973, 50 U.S.C. § 1542.

33. Clinton letter, supra note 10.

34. Press Briefing, supra note 11. The quoted language is from the Antiterrorism and Effective Death Penalty Act of 1996, 22 U.S.C. § 2377.

35. The Prize Cases, 67 U.S. 635 (1863).

36. Quoted in Serge Schmemann, "How Can Terror Best Be Combated?", *New York Times*, August 21, 1998, p. A11.

37. Youngstown Sheet & Tube Co. v. Sawyer, 343 U.S. 579 (Jackson, J., concurring).

38. Ibid., Frankfurter, J., concurring.

39. Quoted in Sam Skolnik, "The Law Behind the Bombs," *Legal Times*, August 24/31, 1998, pp. 8, 10.

40. Quoted in Tim Weiner, "Rethinking the Ban on Political Assassination," *New York Times*, August 30, 1998, Wk. 3.

41. Quoted in Chuck McCutcheon, "Assassination Re-examined," *Cong. Qtly. Wkly.*, September 5, 1998, p. 2353.

42. Quoted in Weiner, "Rethinking the Ban on Political Assassinations."

43. Ibid.

44. Quoted in Risen, "To Bomb Sudan Plant, or Not."

45. Quoted in Hersh, "The Missiles of August," p. 37.
46. Ibid.
47. Quoted in Weiner, "Missile Strikes Won Him Esteem."
48. Ibid.
49. Ibid.
50. Weaver, "The Real Bin Laden," p. 32.

— Chapter 8 ——————————————————————

The Predator

WILLIAM C. BANKS

On the first night of the campaign against Al Qaeda and the Taliban in Afghanistan in October 2001, the United States nearly had a major success. Officials believed that they had pinpointed the location of supreme leader of the Taliban, Mullah Muhammad Omar. While patrolling the roads near Kabul, an unmanned but armed CIA drone trained its crosshairs on Omar in a convoy of cars fleeing the capitol. Under the terms of an agreement, the CIA controllers did not have the authority to order a strike on the target. Likewise, the local Fifth Fleet commander in Bahrain lacked the requisite authority. Instead, following the agreement they sought approval from United States Central Command (CENTCOM) in Tampa to launch the Hellfire missile from the Predator drone positioned above Omar.

The Predator followed the convoy to a building where Omar and about one hundred guards sought cover. Some delay ensued in securing General Tommy R. Franks' approval. One report indicated that a full-scale fighter bomber assault was requested, and that General Franks declined to approve the request on the basis of legal advice he received on the spot.[1] Another report suggested that the magnitude of the target prompted General Franks to run the targeting by the White House.[2] Media reports indicated that President Bush personally approved the strike, although the delay permitted time for Mullah Omar to change his location and thus disrupt the attack.[3] F-18s later targeted and destroyed the building, but Omar escaped.[4] Some speculated that the attack was aborted because of the possibility that others in a crowded house might be killed.

The decision to target specific individuals with lethal force after September 11 was neither unprecedented nor surprising. In appropriate circumstances the United States has engaged in targeted killing for a long time, at least since a border war with Mexican bandits in 1916.[5] In a time of war, subjecting individual combatants to lethal force has been a permitted and lawful instrument of waging war successfully. But new elements of the targeted killing policy emerged in recent years, in response to terrorism and its threats against the United States at home and abroad.

The components of the targeted killing policy quickly took on a sharper focus soon after September 11. For the first time, pilotless drone aircraft were equipped both with sophisticated surveillance and targeting technology and with powerful Hellfire missiles capable of inflicting lethal force effectively from a safe distance. The drones are CIA aircraft, part of the Special Activities division. Thus, the drones were controlled by civilian leaders outside the chain of command. The civilian officials cooperate and share information and decision making with military commanders in a shared campaign against terrorism.

The use of the Predator promised gains in the war against terrorism. If targets as significant as Mullah Omar or even Usama bin Laden could be dispatched with such effectiveness and with little or no risk to U.S. personnel, the objectives of the war on terrorism could be advanced dramatically. At the same time, some questioned the use of the new weapon and its CIA links, as well as several more general short and longer term consequences of an invigorated policy of targeted killing.

This case is designed to raise and explore a few themes that are central to the present and likely future national security posture of the United States. The issues assessed range from host government cooperation, collateral damage, and the locus of decision authority, to tactical questions about the appropriate uses of technology and weaponry. The next section provides a concise narrative backdrop on the conflict triggered by the September 11 attacks. Then the case reviews the emerging policies and procedures that permit targeting terrorists with lethal force, followed by a short section that explores the evolving DOD/CIA relationship in this area. The two final sections assess the legal authorities for and potential limits on targeted killing and the utility of targeted killing in the war on terrorism.

THE "WAR ON TERRORISM"

The worst terrorist attack ever occurred in the United States on September 11, 2001, when nineteen Al Qaeda–linked operatives used knives and boxcutters to kill or wound passengers and pilots and then commandeered four separate but coordinated aircraft in pursuit of preselected targets.[6] Two of the planes struck in New York City at the World Trade Center, causing both towers to collapse, killing approximately 3,000 persons, including hundreds of firefighters and rescue personnel who were helping to evacuate the towers.[7] A third plane was flown directly into the Pentagon in Arlington, Virginia, where 189 persons died, including all who were on board the plane. The fourth plane crashed in Stony Creek Township, Pennsylvania, apparently after passengers overpowered the terrorists, preventing the aircraft from being used as a missile toward its unknown target. All forty-five persons aboard were killed in the crash.

Within hours the hijackers had been linked to Al Qaeda and Usama bin Laden.[8] President Bush visited the World Trade Center site the next day and said, "Freedom and democracy are under attack."[9] On September 17, the president remarked that bin Laden "is wanted dead or alive."[10] In a September 20 address to a joint session of Congress the president also stated, "Our war on terror begins with Al Qaeda, but it does not end there. It will not end until every terrorist group of global reach has been found, stopped, and defeated."[11] The president emphasized that "we will make no distinction between the terrorists who committed these acts and those who harbor them."[12]

The war on terrorism began dramatically and won significant early gains. But as the targeted killing policy evolved from the early days of the war in Afghanistan, not all the signs were positive. After the near miss on Mullah Omar, no verified intelligence reported seeing much less targeting either Omar or Usama bin Laden during the Afghanistan campaign. Senior leaders of Al Qaeda remained at large, and they were likely relocating early and often to elude detection, capture, or death. However, on November 3, 2001, a missile-carrying Predator drone killed Mohammed Atef, Al Qaeda's chief of military operations, in a raid near Kabul.[13] Then, in early May 2002 the CIA tried but failed to kill an Afghan factional leader, Gulbuddin Hekmatyar, an Islamic fundamentalist who had vowed to topple the government of Hamid Karzai and to attack U.S. forces.[14]

The calculus for targeted killing changed dramatically on November 3, 2002, when a CIA drone fired a Hellfire missile and killed a senior Al Qaeda leader and five low-level operatives traveling by car in a remote part of the Yemeni desert.[15] In the first use of an armed Predator outside Afghanistan or, indeed, the first military action in the war against terrorism outside Afghanistan, Qaed Salim Sinan al Harethi was killed. Al Harethi was described as the senior Al Qaeda official in Yemen, one of the top ten to twelve Al Qaeda operatives in the world, and a suspect in the October 2000 suicide bombing of the U.S. destroyer *Cole*, where seventeen American Navy personnel were killed. U.S. intelligence and law enforcement officials had been tracking his movements for months before the attack. Along with al Harethi, killed in the Predator strike were five other Al Qaeda operatives, including an American citizen of Yemeni descent, Kamal Derwish, who grew up in the Buffalo suburb of Tonawanda and who, according to FBI intelligence, recruited American Muslims to attend Al Qaeda training camps.

DECIDING TO TAKE ACTION

The Predator is an ungainly, 40 million dollar, propeller-driven aircraft that flies as slowly as eighty miles per hour and is guided by an operator at a television monitor who may be hundreds of miles away.[16] The drone can hover continuously for twenty-four hours or more at 15,000 feet above any battlefield, and it can send live video to AC-130 gunships or command posts around the world without putting any pilots in harm's way. The drone's radar, infared sensors, and color video camera can track vehicles at night and through clouds, producing sharp enough pictures to make out people on the ground from more than three miles away. The Predator cannot fly in stormy weather, and they have been prone to icing. The drone is also vulnerable to enemy antiaircraft fire. The Predator has been flown by the U.S. military for a number of years. The combat debut of the Predator came in 1995 in the skies over Bosnia, where it provided sharp "real time" images of the battlefield. One year before the September 11 attacks, an unarmed CIA drone captured video in Afghanistan of a man that intelligence officials believe was Usama bin Laden.[17]

The decision to develop the Predator as a combat device was made specifically to attack bin Laden, according to administration officials.[18] The Hellfire missiles are air-to-ground, laser-guided weapons that were used effectively by Apache helicopter gunships against Iraqi tanks in the 1991 Gulf War.[19]

The idea of using the armed Predator drone in counterterrorism combat has been circulating for years. However, lingering disagreements over who should have the ultimate authority for firing the Hellfire missiles—the military or the CIA—slowed the development of the new counterterrorism weapon. It was the possibility that a Predator missed a chance to strike a convoy that apparently included Mullah Omar on the first night of the Afghan war that finally settled the targeting authority dispute, at least for the time being. The missed opportunity, caused by traditional military chain-of-command reviews up to and apparently including the Commander in Chief, gave the CIA its first-ever authority to strike beyond a narrow range of preselected counterterrorism targets.

It has often been said that the September 11 terrorist attacks changed everything. However broad and deep the changes wrought by the cataclysmic attacks, the United States clearly reacted by changing longstanding tenets of its counterterrorism strategy. Where law enforcement and intelligence gathering were the primary instruments of U.S. policy against terrorism outside any designated battlefield, after September 11 the concept of theater of war itself was shelved in the war on terrorism.

In the weeks after September 11, President Bush signed an intelligence finding giving the CIA broad authority to pursue terrorism around the world.[20] A finding contains the factual and policy predicates for the intelligence activities authorized in any significant operation, and the document must be personally approved by the president. By statute, a finding must accompany any covert operation approved by the president, including those that permit targeted killing. However, a finding governs the use of appropriated funds for covert operations by intelligence agencies. (The military use operations orders.) In the classified finding, the president delegated targeting and operational authority to senior civilian and military officials. Precise approval mechanisms remain classified. The authority given in the presidential finding is surely the most sweeping and most lethal since the founding of the CIA. In part, the finding contemplates a high and unprecedented degree of cooperation between the CIA and special forces, as well as other military units. Reacting to the finding, one official implicitly warned the terrorists: "The gloves are off."[21]

Terrorists were first singled out by name in a 1995 Executive Order by President Clinton that introduced a category of "specially designated terrorists" on a list maintained by the Secretary of State and the Treasury Office of Foreign Assets Control.[22] In fact, the CIA has been authorized since 1998 to use covert means to disrupt and preempt terrorist operations planned by Usama bin Laden. The Clinton administration directive was affirmed by President Bush before September 11 and was based on evidence linking Al Qaeda to the August 1998 bombings of U.S. embassies in Africa. The directive stopped short of authorizing targeted killing, but did authorize lethal force for self-defense.

Neither the 1998 directive nor the one issued by President Bush after September 11 exempted the agencies from the 1981 Executive Order provision banning political assassination. The 2001 finding broadens the class of potential targets beyond Usama bin Laden and his close circle, and also extends the boundaries beyond Afghanistan.[23] In permitting explicitly the targeting of an individual with lethal force, the finding also more narrowly focuses the potential to inflict violence. John C. Gannon, retired Deputy Director of Central Intelligence, reacted favorably to the new finding: "The important thing is that the accountability chain is clear. I would want the president's guidance to be as clear as it could be, including the names of individuals. You've got to have the political levels behind you so the intelligence officers are not left hanging."[24]

But was the use of the Predator in Yemen the only way to achieve the administration's objectives? One alternative to the Predator was a "snatch and kill" operation conducted by a squad of commandos, deployed by helicopters from ships in the Red Sea. In discussions with Yemeni officials, it was feared that a ground operation could ignite a guerilla war. U.S. officials commented that armed Predators had been flying over Yemen for some time, awaiting targets of opportunity. Yemeni government officials were aware of the surveillance and of its potential application against Al Qaeda, U.S. officials said.

The Yemeni government increased its cooperation with the U.S. effort in the months before the November 2002 strike, after U.S. officials complained of a lack of cooperation in investigating the *Cole* bombing and other terrorist attacks where suspects hiding in Yemen were potentially involved. Although Yemen sought to conduct its own counterterrorism operations near its remote and largely lawless border with Saudi Arabia, a principal sanctuary for Al Qaeda operatives, a December 2001 operation led to heavy Yemeni casualties.[25]

One key figure in the Yemen Predator strike was outside the traditional circle of those normally involved in planning military operations. U.S. Ambassador to Yemen Edmund Hull, a seasoned counterterrorism expert, personally traveled to remote Yemeni desert territory to seek intelligence on al Harethi.[26] The Arabic-speaking Hull met with local tribesmen and reportedly paid for information on al Harethi's whereabouts. Hull angered local Yemeni officials with his freelancing, and by facilitating a Predator strike that threatened peace in Yemen. But the Yemenis had failed to nab al Harethi in the December 2001 raid, and it appeared that Yemen would not strike again on its own. Aside from insufficient training in counterterror operations, Yemen may have been reluctant to act on its own because of a perceived debt that President Ali Saleh owes to Usama bin Laden's forces, which assisted in putting down a separatist movement in 1994.

Grumbling aside, the Yemen strike was conducted after considerable co-operation between U.S. and Yemeni officials, including the mounting of a joint U.S./Yemen intelligence team.[27] In addition to the intelligence gathered by Hull, the Yemen Predator operation may also have been aided by global positioning coordinates given by one of the several phones held by al Harethi. Once those coordinates were received, targeting officials knew that the Predator had to act quickly, as soon as al Harethi was traveling in a car, away from civilian areas.[28] Apparently, al Harethi had evaded earlier capture attempts and, on that November day, it was suspected that the passengers were going to a target. Deputy Defense Secretary Paul Wolfowitz called the strike "a very successful tactical operation."[29] The wreckage of the car revealed traces of explosives and remnants of communications equipment.[30]

THE DOD/CIA RELATIONSHIP

Part of the buildup toward use of the Predator for the targeted killing operation involved new and still-evolving relations between civilian and military leaders in DOD and the CIA. In July 2002 Secretary Rumsfeld ordered Special Forces commander and Air Force General Charles Holland to develop a plan to capture or kill members of terrorist organizations, on a global scale.[31] When questioned in December about the Predator strike in Yemen and Pentagon policy regarding assassination or killing of Al Qaeda operatives, Secretary Rumsfeld denied that the Special Forces personnel were trained to assassinate: "That is not what they are trained to do. They are trained to serve their country and to contribute to peace and stability in the world."[32]

The evolving Special Forces roles and missions could conceivably find the military carrying out covert operations much the way that CIA has done so traditionally. Some questioned whether such an overlap or redundancy in operation roles and capabilities is desirable, or, if desirable, whether it is workable in practice. According to Defense Science Board (DSB) Chairman William Schneider, Jr., the CIA would execute the operations, using DOD assets. Schneider said that the DSB did not recommend changes in the ban on assassinations, or reductions in congressional oversight. Some members of Congress expressed concern on hearing the DSB report, however, because DOD is not subject to the covert operations reporting requirements.[33]

LEGAL AUTHORITY FOR THE OPERATION; TARGETED KILLING VS. ASSASSINATION

Because the Yemen strike was authorized by the president in an intelligence finding, at first blush, the relevant law is the law of intelligence. Since the Hughes-Ryan Amendment of 1974,[34] Congress has authorized CIA covert operations if findings are prepared and delivered to select members of Congress before the operation described, or in a "timely fashion" thereafter. So long as the intelligence committees are kept "fully and currently informed," the intelligence laws permit the president broad discretion to utilize the nation's intelligence agencies to carry out national security operations, perhaps including targeted killing.[35] Such an operation would follow Hughes-Ryan as an "operation in foreign countries, other than activities intended solely for obtaining necessary intelligence,"[36] and thus presumably would be conducted pursuant to statutory authority.

To some it seemed that the President's "wanted dead or alive" remark about bin Laden ran counter to the longstanding ban on political assassination. Enshrined in an executive order first by President Gerald Ford and unchanged since President Reagan's iteration in 1981, the directive forbids political assassination but does not define the term.[37] Just what does distinguish lawful targeted killing from unlawful political assassination? The answer turns upon which legal framework applies. During war, the law of armed conflict applies, and targeted killing of individuals is lawful, although killing by treacherous—through the use of deceit or trickery—means is not. In peacetime, any extra-judicial killing by a government agent is lawful only if taken in self-defense or in defense of others. But what rules apply when the United States is engaged in a nontraditional war on terrorism?

Although President Reagan's Executive Order 12,333 forbids political assassination, the order does not restrict the lawful use of force against legitimate enemy targets. Without this legal justification, assassination is simply murder and violates domestic and international law. Executive Order 12,333 simply reflects existing law and makes that policy a prominent and explicit part of U.S. law. The defensive use of force—targeted at a known Al Qaeda leader in Yemen, for example—has firm legal roots in U.S. law, the UN Charter, and customary international law. In making operational decisions like the one made to strike with the Predator in Yemen, the law of armed conflict permits targeting Al Qaeda combatants.

Secretary of Defense Donald Rumsfeld opined, "it is certainly within the president's power to direct that, in our self-defense, we take this battle to the terrorists and that means to the leadership and command and control capabilities of terrorist networks."[38]

On the one hand, President Bush asserted forcefully that the September 11 attacks were acts of war directed at the United States, giving our nation the legal right to repel the horrific attacks. Whether waged against us by a state or a non-state terrorist organization, war is defined by what it does, not by the identity of the perpetrator. Still, the law of armed conflict has not yet evolved to account adequately for the twilight zone between conventional war and conventional peace, when nations are subject to the continuing threat of terrorist attack. On the other hand, within this twilight zone of threat from terrorist attacks it is not clear exactly what distinguishes a combatant and, thus, a proper target, from a civilian who may not be targeted. Nor is it known what evidence will suffice that someone who does not wear a uniform and who does not fight for a sovereign state is sufficiently implicated in terrorist activities so as to warrant targeting with lethal force. Clearly someone who is positively identified as an Al Qaeda operative is an enemy combatant, one who may be targeted with lethal force. But, as Yale law professor Harold Hongju Koh asks, "what factual showing will demonstrate that [the target] had warlike intentions against us and who sees that evidence before any action is taken?"[39]

Under the law of war, the selection of individuals for targeted lethal force would not be unlawful if the targets are combatant forces of another nation, a guerilla force, or a terrorist or other organization whose actions pose a threat to the security of the United States. Other international law strictures also come into play, including the United Nations Charter. Article 2 proscribes the violation by one nation of the territorial integrity of another nation, although Article 51 permits measures for "collective self-defense."

In addition to the president's constitutional authorities as commander in chief and his authorities over intelligence activities authorized by statute, the president's finding may also be supported by Congress's September 14, 2001, Joint Resolution giving the president the authority to use "all necessary and appropriate force" against "persons he determines planned, authorized, committed, or aided the terrorist attacks" of September 11. The sweeping authority granted in the resolution is not time-limited; nor does it have a geographic constraint. Nor is his discretion on choice of target narrowed in any way, so long as the target is connected to September 11.[40]

Under what conditions could a U.S. citizen be subject to a Predator attack, ordered by the CIA or the military? Before September 11, the government's authority to kill a citizen outside of the judicial process was generally restricted to situations where the American is threatening directly the lives of other Americans or their allies.[41] Still, the president's intelligence finding does not make any exception for Americans. The authority to target U.S. citizens is thus implicit, not explicit.

Al Qaeda members do not wear uniforms or serve in a nation's army, or fight on a conventional battlefield. But the battlefield against Al Qaeda was declared to be the entire world after September 11. American citizen Kamal Derwish was in the car with al Harethi. Although Derwish was not targeted, National Security Adviser Condoleeza Rice responded to a question about the killing of an American by stating that "no constitutional questions are raised . . . [the president] is well within the balance of accepted practice and the letter of his constitutional authority."[42]

The strike could thus be seen as an airstrike in a combat zone, or it could be characterized as an assassination of a civilian who was innocent until proven guilty. Officials also alleged that Derwish was the leader of an Al Qaeda cell in Western New York. Although several Yemeni-American members of the alleged cell were arrested and criminally charged with providing support to terrorist activities, Derwish was not accused of any crime.

Senator Richard Shelby supported the administration's view that Derwish was an enemy combatant whose constitutional rights as an American were nullified by his actions: "A U.S. citizen terrorist will kill you just like somebody from another country."[43] But Mohammed Albanna, Vice President of the American Muslim Council Buffalo chapter disagreed: Derwish "has not been tried and has not been found guilty . . . he's still an innocent American who was killed."[44] Former Air Force JAG officer and director of the Duke University Center on Law, Ethics and National Security Scott Silliman expressed concern about the implications of the administration's legal and operations theories: "Could you put a Hellfire missile into a car in Washington, D.C., under the same theory? The answer is yes, you could."[45]

WEIGHING THE UTILITY AND IMPLICATIONS OF TARGETED KILLING

There was little doubt among U.S. officials that the Predator strike had material benefits. An important Al Qaeda leader was eliminated, and a strong signal was sent that there is no sanctuary for terrorists. Still, tactically the strike against al Harethi represented an escalation of the war on terrorism.

The Predator depends on reliable intelligence; mistakes happen. In February 2002, a Predator patrolling thousands of feet above Afghanistan fed images to CIA and military officers of a very tall man among a small group. After officials on the ground determined that the man could be Usama bin Laden, a request to launch a Hellfire was made through the chain of command. The request was granted a few minutes later, but by then the group had disbanded. When the man and two others were spotted emerging from a wooded area shortly thereafter, the Hellfire was launched and the three men were killed. Media reports indicated that the three were local men who were scavenging for scrap metal.[46]

Could the Yemen strike be interpreted by other nations and even non-state groups as a justification of their own preemptive attacks on perceived adversaries? Silliman thinks so: "We are basically opening up and crafting a new tool and tactic which is not [only] for the United States to use. . . . We may be putting our leadership at risk." Assassination of a U.S. Secretary of State or another cabinet official cannot be ruled out. Swedish Foreign Minister Anna Lindh expressed similar concerns: "Even terrorists must be treated according to international law. Otherwise, a nation can start executing those whom they consider terrorists."[47] Silliman mused, "if we do this outside the traditional combat area in Afghanistan . . . could we not do it in Germany, Ottawa, or even Cincinnati?"[48]

Should the United States acknowledge that it has conducted an operation like the one in Yemen? Some Yemeni officials reacted angrily to the U.S. strike. General Yahya al Mutawakel, Deputy General of the People's Congress party, maintained that the public acknowledgment of the Yemen strike by the United States violated a secrecy agreement between the two nations.[49] Al Mutawakel argued that the United States did not consider adequately the internal circumstances in Yemen in deciding to go public: "In security matters, you don't want to alert the enemy."[50] He feared domestic unrest in Yemen, and reprisals by Al Qaeda sympathizers still active in Yemen.

How broadly should the targeted killing net be cast? As Vice President Dick Cheney commented, "There's no piece of real estate. It's not like a state or a country. The notion of deterrence doesn't really apply here. There's no treaty to be negotiated, there's no arms control agreement that's going to guarantee our safety and security. The only way you can deal with them is to destroy them. The reach of our efforts must be as broad and deep as the tentacles of the terrorist networks."[51]

As President Bush noted, "We will make no distinction between the terrorists who committed these acts and those who harbor them."[52] Another intelligence official commented, "You have to go after the Gucci guys, the guys who write the checks."[53] Killing them would be especially dramatic, he said, because they do not commonly die for a cause.[54] Although he is opposed generally to targeted killing, retired CIA Inspector General Hitz agreed that going after the funding people "would have a tremendously chilling effect" on Al Qaeda.[55]

Notes

1. See Seymour Hersh, "King's Ransom," *The New Yorker*, October 10, 2001, p. xx.

2. Michael R. Gordon and Tim Weiner, "A Nation Challenged: The Strategy," *New York Times*, October 16, 2001, p. A1.

3. Eric Schmitt, "U.S. Would Use Drones to Attack Iraqi Targets," *New York Times*, November 6, 2002, p. A16.

4. Gordon and Weiner, "A Nation Challenged," p. A1.

5. See William C. Banks and Peter Raven-Hansen, "Targeted Killing and Assassination: The U.S. Legal Framework," U. Richmond L. Rev. 37, 2003, pp. 667, 688.

6. U.S. Dept. of State, *Patterns of Global Terrorism*, May 21, 2002, see http://www.state.gov/s/ct/rls/pgtrpt/2001/html/10235.htm.

7. Ibid.

8. Ibid.

9. Ibid.

10. Barton Gellman, "CIA Weighs 'Targeted Killing' Missions," *Washington Post*, October 28, 2001, p. A1.

11. Ibid.

12. Gordon and Weiner, "A Nation Challenged."

13. James Risen, "A Nation Challenged: The Terror Network," *New York Times*, December 13, 2001, p. A1.

14. Thom Shanker and Carlotta Gall, "U.S. Attack on Warlord Aims to Help Interim Leader," *New York Times*, see http://query.nytimes.com/search/article-page.html?res=9D04E2D91330F93AA35756C0A9649C8B63.

15. John J. Lumpkin, "Al-Qaida Suspects Die in U.S. Missile Strike," *Associated Press*, November 5, 2002, see http://www.timesunion.com/AspStories/story.asp?storyID=68947.

16. See http://www.af.mil/factsheets/fs_122/shtml. See also Schmitt, "U.S. Would Use Drones to Attack Iraqi Targets."

17. Ibid.

18. Bob Woodward, "CIA Told to Do 'Whatever Necessary' to Kill Bin Laden," *Washington Post*, October 21, 2001, p. A1.

19. Schmitt, "U.S. Would Use Drones to Attack Iraqi Targets."

20. James Risen and David Johnston, "Bush Has Widened Authority of C.I.A. to Kill Terrorists," *New York Times*, December 15, 2002, see http://www.nytimes.com/2002/12/15/international.

21. Ibid.

22. Gellman, "CIA Weighs 'Targeted Killing' Missions," p. A1.

23. David Johnston and David E. Sanger, "Fatal Strike in Yemen was Based on Rules Set out by Bush," *New York Times*, November 6, 2002, p. A16.

24. Gellman, "CIA Weighs 'Targeted Killing' Missions," p. A1.

25. Risen and Johnston, "Bush Has Widened Authority of C.I.A. to Kill Terrorists." See also James Risen and Judith Miller, "CIA Kills a Leader of Qaeda in Yemen," *International Herald Tribune*, see http://www.iht.com/cgi-bin/generic.cgi?template=articleprint.tmplh&ArticleId=76077.

26. Philip Stucker, "Yemen Officials Angered by Americans' Methods in Hellfire Strike," *Christian Science Monitor*, November 11, 2002, see http://www.sacbee.com/24hour/special_reports/terrorism/story/616107p-4741358c.html.

27. Seymour Hersh, "Manhunt," *The New Yorker*, December 23 and 30, 2002, p. 66.

28. Stucker, "Yemen Officials Angered by Americans' Methods in Hellfire Strike."

29. Ibid. See also Risen and Miller, "CIA Kills a Leader of Qaeda in Yemen."

30. Ibid.

31. Hersh, "Manhunt."

32. Ibid.

33. Ibid.

34. "No funds appropriated under the authority of this or any other Act may be expended by or on behalf of the Central Intelligence Agency for operations in foreign countries, other than activities intended solely for obtaining necessary intelligence, unless and until the President finds that each such operation is important to the national security of the United States and reports, in a timely fashion, a description and scope of such operation to the appropriate committees of the Congress...." Pub. L. No. 93-559, §32, 88 Stat. 1804 (1974). The amendment was a component of reforms in intelligence operations law designed to make U.S. covert operations decisions directly accountable to the decision makers. See Stephen Dycus, Arthur Berney, William Banks, and Peter Raven-Hansen, *National Security Law*, 3rd ed. (New York: Aspen, 2002), pp. 456–59.

35. Banks and Raven-Hansen, "Targeted Killing and Assassination," p. 713.

36. Pub. L. No. 93-559, §32, 88 Stat. 1804 (1974).

37. Gellman, "CIA Weighs 'Targeted Killing' Missions."

38. Ibid.

39. Ibid.

40. Banks and Raven-Hansen, "Targeted Killing and Assassination," text at n. 482.

41. John J. Lumpkin, "U.S. Can Target American Al-Qaida Agents," *Associated Press*, December 3, 2002, see http://story.news.yahoo.com.

42. Ibid.

43. Ibid.

44. Ibid.

45. Ibid.

46. Hersh, "Manhunt."

47. Ibid.

48. Pamela Hess, "Experts: Yemen Strike Not Assassination," *United Press International*, November 8, 2002, see http://www.upi.com/view.cfm?StoryID= 20021107-042725-6586r.

49. Ibid.

50. Ibid.

51. Bob Woodward, "CIA Told to Do 'Whatever Necessary' to Kill Bin Laden," p. A1.

52. Gordon and Weiner, "A Nation Challenged," p. A1.

53. Gellman, "CIA Weighs 'Targeted Killing' Missions," p. A1.

54. Ibid.

55. Ibid.

Part III
EMERGING SECURITY NEEDS

Separate Powers: The Iraq Liberation Act

LAURENCE POPE

The long-running confrontation between the United States and the Iraq of Saddam Hussein which began with the Iraqi invasion of Kuwait dominated the headlines and the attention of senior American policymakers in the period 1998–99. A cat-and-mouse game between Iraq and the UN Special Commission on Monitoring in Iraq, UNSCOM, led to an initial withdrawal of UNSCOM inspectors in November of 1998, and after much maneuvering and brinksmanship on both sides, to four days of air and cruise missile strikes in December of 1998.[1] With President Clinton caught in a public lie over an affair with a White House intern and facing impeachment, Washington was unusually polarized.

This is the account of legislation adopted during this period, the Iraq Liberation Act (ILA) of 1998. Opposed by the bureaucracy at State, Defense, CIA, and the NSC staff, the ILA was signed into law by President Clinton on October 31, 1998, at one of the weakest moments in his presidency. Without reference to the UN Security Council Resolutions which had been the underpinning of international efforts since the 1990 invasion of Kuwait, the ILA committed the United States to a policy of seeking the overthrow of the Iraqi regime.

ROLLBACK VERSUS CONTAINMENT

In early 1998, the Clinton administration's Iraq policy was under considerable pressure. Its covert support of mainly Kurdish Iraqi opposition groups based in northern Iraq under the banner of the Iraqi National Congress (INC) had collapsed in disarray in 1996 after an attempt by the INC to coordinate an offensive against the Iraqi army ended in a rout, and the imprisonment of hundreds, perhaps thousands, inside Saddam's gulag and torture machine.[2]

Established in 1992 as a vehicle for attracting external support, the INC was the creation of an opposition leader named Ahmed Chalabi. A controversial figure in Washington and in the region, from a wealthy Iraqi shi'a family with deep roots in the old pre-Baath regime, with a Ph.D. in mathematics from MIT, Chalabi had not lived in Iraq since 1958, with the exception of the period 1993–96 when he was the conduit for covert U.S. assistance in the North. Chalabi founded a bank in Jordan in the 1980s, but fled in 1989 to London to avoid prosecution when the bank collapsed with the loss of millions of dollars invested by the Jordanian royal family and other prominent Jordanians. Essentially a lone operator, Chalabi frequently left behind disillusioned supporters. One commented that "a lot of people are fed up with him. He does not listen to anybody. He ran the INC into the ground." Reports of Chalabi's mismanagement of CIA's covert funds were widespread.[3] Because of its close identification with the United States, the INC was shunned by many nationalist Iraqis. As one told the *New York Times*, "How can you side with forces bent on destroying not just the regime but a whole country?"[4]

At the high water mark in 1995, a CIA station in northern Iraq with some fifty case officers and support personnel provided military advice and training to the INC, and the covert funding of the INC is estimated to have exceeded $100 million. But in 1996, the INC was driven out of northern Iraq altogether, after one Kurdish faction appealed for Iraqi help against another. More than 100 INC officials were killed by the Iraqis, and some 7,000 Iraqi oppositionists had to be evacuated to the United States. Promising planning by a second group of CIA-supported Iraqis collapsed when the group was penetrated by the Iraqis and Iraqi intelligence began to transmit mocking messages on the group's CIA-supplied radios.[5]

Chalabi said later that his mistake in 1995–96 was to rely on a covert arm of the U.S. government. In any case, the collapse in northern Iraq led him to turn to the U.S. Congress as a more promising source of funds and support than the CIA, and he found a receptive ear.[6]

On January 26, 1998, a group of Republican former senior foreign policy officials wrote a public letter to President Clinton essentially declaring an end to any bipartisan support for the Clinton administration's Iraq policy. Signatories to the letter included Donald Rumsfeld, Paul Wolfowitz, John Bolton, Robert Zoellick, Zalmay Khalilzad, Elliott Abrams, and Richard Armitage, all of whom were to return to senior positions at State and Defense and on the NSC staff in the Bush administration. Calling for military action against Iraq on the grounds that containment had failed, they argued that "Iraq is ripe for a broad-based insurrection," and urged diplomatic recognition of the INC as a government in exile.[7]

Responding to the pressure on behalf of the administration, Secretary of State Madelaine Albright wrote in the February 23, 1998 issue of *Newsweek* Magazine that encouraging the Iraqi opposition "sounds—but it is not—simple." She argued that the Iraqi opposition was divided, and that "it would be wrong to create false or unsustainable expectations that could end in bloodshed and defeat." Along the same lines, NSC advisor Sandy Berger drew an analogy to the Bay of Pigs: "If you encourage and almost incite people to rise up against their own government, you incur a moral obligation."

Berger and Albright represented the consensus of the foreign affairs bureaucracy at State, Defense, and CIA. At State, there were recriminations about CIA cowboys, and at CIA bitter disagreements about who was at fault for the 1995–96 debacle.[8] At State the focus was on the need to restore a tattered diplomatic consensus in the Security Council as the foundation for the containment policy.

On Capitol Hill, however, proposals for military assistance to the INC continued to gather support on both sides of the aisle as an alternative to the "failed containment policy," and the support of Senator Bob Kerrey (D-NE) added military legitimacy. A planning document for an enclave strategy was drawn up by a retired military officer, General Wayne Downing, formerly commander in chief of the Special Operations Command, who had signed on as an unpaid adviser to Chalabi. General Downing briefed members of Congress, including Senators Lott and Helms and their staffs.[9] Dewey Claridge, a retired senior officer of the operations directorate of the CIA, a veteran of covert action in Central America and elsewhere, was enlisted for the lobbying effort, together with Wayne Marik, who had resigned from the CIA after the northern Iraq debacle.

Invited to appear before a friendly Senate Foreign Relations Committee (SFRC) on March 2, Chalabi offered an attractive proposal for the removal of the Saddam Hussein regime:

The Iraqi National Congress has the operational experience to make such a plan work. Right now, the INC is confronting Saddam on the ground and has the support of thousands of Iraqis. And the INC knows that, given any chance of success, millions of Iraqis are willing to risk their lives to fight Saddam. In March 1991, only seven years ago, 70%

of the Iraqi population, over 15 million people, were in open revolt against Saddam. They will rise again. Give the Iraqi National Congress a base protected from Saddam's tanks, give us the temporary support we need to feed and house and care for the liberated population and we will give you a free Iraq, an Iraq free of weapons of mass destruction and a free-market Iraq. Best of all, the INC will do all this—for free. The US commitment to the security of the Gulf is sufficient. The maintenance of the no-fly zones and the air-interdiction of Saddam's armor by U.S. forces assumed in the INC plan is virtually in place. The funds for humanitarian, logistical, and military assistance requested by the INC for the provisional government can be secured by Iraq's frozen assets which are the property of the Iraqi people. Once established in liberated areas, the wealth of the Iraqi people can be used for their salvation. All the Iraqi National Congress and the Iraqi people ask is the chance to free their country.[10]

No administration witnesses were invited to the SFRC hearings. Among those who appeared in support of assistance to the INC were Wolfowitz, Zalmay Khalilzad, and former Director of Central Intelligence James Woolsey.

On May 29, the same group of Republicans and neo-conservative Democrats that had written to the president on January 26 wrote again to the Republican leadership of the Senate and House denouncing the Administration and calling on the Congress to take matters into its own hands:

Now that the administration has failed to provide sound leadership, we believe it is imperative that Congress take what steps it can to correct U.S. policy toward Iraq. That responsibility is especially pressing when presidential leadership is lacking or when the administration is pursuing a policy fundamentally at odds with vital American security interests.[11]

The letter suggested that Congress should do "whatever is constitutionally appropriate" to change administration policy, and it proposed the creation of a provisional government inside northern and southern Iraq recognized by the United States and protected by U.S. military power— in effect, a unilateral declaration of war by the United States.

During 1998, frustration continued to build within the Beltway as the cat-and-mouse game between Iraq and UNSCOM played out, and the administration repeatedly threatened but failed to carry out airstrikes. UNSCOM inspector Scott Ritter's resignation highlighted the growing ineffectiveness of UNSCOM. The Lewinsky affair moved towards impeachment, undermining the administration's ability to use force without having its motivations called into question—the so-called "wag the dog" effect (after the movie of that name), in which a president starts a war to divert attention from his sexual misconduct.

When Congress returned from the summer recess, the Republican leadership in both House and Senate moved with extraordinary speed to put its stamp on Iraq policy, and to transmute containment into rollback. With no Committee hearings, the Iraq Liberation Act of 1998 cleared both with little or no debate. The Act passed overwhelmingly in the House by a vote of 360-38-36 on September 29.

Introducing the legislation in the House, Representative Gilman (R-NY) noted that ". . . This bill will not tie the President's hands. It does not mandate the actual delivery of military assistance. The only requirement it contains is that the President designate a group or groups as eligible to receive the assistance we are authorizing. I would hope, however, that the President will use the authority we are offering him to begin to help the people of Iraq liberate themselves."[12]

Although there was little debate, and passage of the legislation in the House was a foregone conclusion, but the highly respected Representative Lee Hamilton (D-IN) offered an extensive critique of the ILA—even as he indicated that he would vote for it. Some excerpts:

> . . . What is striking about the bill is the United States, the most powerful nation in the world, would depend on third parties, not even third countries, to carry out its policy objectives. . . . No one should underestimate the difficulties of uniting the Iraqi opposition. It includes some 70 groups and at least three or four major groups. We have tried over many years to unite the Iraqi opposition, and it has not happened. There is, however, modest reason for encouragement. The two main Kurdish groups have a fragile agreement with each other, but they don't want to work with Ahmed Chalabi . . .
>
> . . . there is a wide gap here between means and objectives in this bill. When we declare that our policy is to remove Saddam Hussein from power, we raise the objectives of our policy very high. Yet we provide modest means to achieve what has proven to be a very difficult objective. When you have a gap between goals and means, that often leads to trouble in the conduct of American foreign policy . . .
>
> . . . I wonder whether the bill is at all workable. . . . For example, can we identify any country that is prepared to accept military equipment

in the presence of armed Iraqi opposition groups on its territory? I am not able to do that as of now . . .

. . . the bill could harm the ability of the United States to keep U.N. sanctions in place against Iraq. If it becomes the public policy of the United States to remove Saddam Hussein, as this bill seeks to do, then there will be less unity in confronting Baghdad, more criticism of the United States, and probably more difficulty in getting support for sanctions and for U.N. weapons inspections among Arab States and among Security Council members."[13]

In the Senate, by contrast, the ILA passed unanimously by voice vote, treatment usually reserved for routine business. Senate Majority Leader Lott nevertheless stressed the historic nature of the legislation and its importance:

This is an important step. Observers should not misunderstand the Senate's action. Even though this legislation will pass without controversy on a unanimous voice vote, it is a major step forward in the final conclusion of the Persian Gulf War. In 1991, we and our allies shed blood to liberate Kuwait. Today, we are empowering Iraqis to liberate their own country.[14]

For his part, Senator Helms (R-NC), served notice that he would be watching the administration closely as it moved to implement the legislation:

. . . Opponents of this initiative—I shouldn't call them friends of Saddam—have said that the Iraqi opposition exists in name only, that they are too parochial to come together. They are not entirely wrong—which is why Senator Lott and Chairman Gilman (the lead House sponsor) have carefully crafted the designation requirement in H.R. 4655 to insist that only broad-based, pro-democracy groups be selected by the President to receive drawdown assistance. I would go further, and suggest to the President that he designate just one group, the Iraqi National Congress . . .[15]

Senator Bob Kerrey (D-NE), though he demurred with regard to the INC as an exclusive recipient for assistance, spoke in a similar vein:

This bill, when passed and signed into law, is a clear commitment to a U.S. policy replacing the Saddam Hussein regime and replacing it with a transition to democracy. This bill is a statement that America refuses to coexist with a regime which has used chemical weapons on its own citizens and on neighboring countries, which has invaded its neighbors twice without provocation, which has still not accounted for its atrocities committed in Kuwait, which has fired ballistic missiles into the cities of three of its neighbors, which is attempting to develop nuclear and biological weapons, and which has brutalized and terrorized its own citizens for thirty years. I don't see how any democratic country could accept the existence of such a regime, but this bill says America will not. I will be an even prouder American when the refusal, and commitment to materially help the Iraqi resistance, are U.S. policy.[16]

On October 31, the president signed the ILA. In an effort to square its language with Security Council resolutions promising the removal of sanctions in exchange for good behavior, his statement on the occasion noted that while these were important elements of U.S. policy, they were unlikely to be implemented anyway as long as Saddam Hussein remained in power.

PROVISIONS OF THE ILA

After a catalogue of Iraqi misconduct reaching back to the Iraqi invasion of Iran in 1980, the ILA declares that "It *should* be the policy of the United States to seek to remove the regime headed by Saddam Hussein from power in Iraq and to promote the emergence of a democratic government to replace that regime."[17] As Representative Gilman noted, its only requirement was that within ninety days the president designate groups eligible to receive U.S. assistance. The president was not obliged to provide any assistance to them—nor did the ILA appropriate any funds for this purpose. Even $2 million in funds to be used in grant assistance for broadcasting inside Iraq by the "Iraqi democratic opposition" was not new money, but an authorization to use existing funds.

Section 4 of the Act authorized the president to "direct the drawdown from stocks" of defense articles and services, including training, up to a value of $97 million, for which he was authorized to reimburse the Department of Defense. But the ILA appropriated no funds for this prospective reimbursement. Moreover, the "drawdown from stocks" would have to involve only what are known as excess defense articles, or military surplus—items the military had certified it could do without, and which could be provided to worthy foreign recipients, provided they could pay the shipping costs.

The president was, however, directly enjoined by the Congress in one matter. Section 5 of the ILA reads as follows: "Not later than 90 days after the date of the enactment of this Act, the President *shall* designate one or more Iraqi democratic opposition organizations that satisfy the criteria set forth in subsection (c)" as eligible for assistance. And what were the criteria? That the group or groups in question include a "broad spectrum" of Iraqi individuals and groups, "committed to democratic values, to respect for human rights, to peaceful relations with Iraq's neighbors, to maintain Iraq's territorial integrity, and to fostering cooperation among democratic opponents of the Saddam Hussein regime."

The problem was that no organization or group inside or outside Iraq could meet these criteria. Neither of the two feuding Kurdish groups in the North, Talabani's Popular Union of Kurdistan (PUK), and Barzani's Kurdish Democratic Party (KDP), was remotely democratic in nature, let alone broad-based in an ethnic sense. Nor could the Iranian-backed Supreme Council for the Islamic Republic in Iraq (SCIRI)—the only effective guerrilla group active on the ground inside Iraq—be described as democratic or containing a broad spectrum of Iraqis. As for Chalabi's INC, an April 21, 1999 headline in the *Washington Post* summarized the situation: "Congress's Candidate to Overthrow Saddam Hussein, Ahmed Chalabi, Has Virtually No Other Backing."

The Act was silent as to what would happen if the president should be unable in good faith to locate a group meeting the criteria. But it was clear that if he didn't, there would be hell to pay, and Senator Helms was quite direct about what he was looking for in the way of a designation: "The President need not look far; the Iraqi National Congress once flourished as an umbrella organization for Kurds, Shi'ites and Sunni Muslims. It should flourish again, but it needs our help."[18]

ZINNI SPEAKS OUT

General Anthony C. Zinni, USMC, the regional Commander in Chief or CINC, had not been consulted by anyone in the Pentagon, the State Department, or the White House about the decision to sign the ILA, and he took strong issue with it. At a breakfast meeting with reporters in his Tampa headquarters before the ILA became law, Zinni said he saw no viable opposition to Saddam, and warned against the possible fragmentation of Iraq. Asked about the so-called Downing plan, Zinni said he knew of no ongoing military planning for assistance to the opposition. "I don't think these questions have been thought through or answered," he told the reporters. "If they have, no one's asked me about it." Zinni went on to warn against allowing Iraq to splinter into a collection of states, citing the need for a strategic balance with Iran, and he said that Arab leaders in the region were wary of a U.S. plan that would "arm everybody in sight" and result in the creation of a power vacuum in Iraq.[19] "I think a weakened, fragmented, chaotic Iraq—which could happen if this isn't done carefully—is more dangerous in the long run than a contained Saddam is now," Zinni said.[20]

Zinni's remarks angered backers of the ILA on the Hill, and generated calls in the press and on the Hill for his resignation. The INC charged angrily that "the general claims to have studied the Iraqi opposition yet neither the general nor anyone from his staff has ever been in contact with the Iraqi National Congress."[21] His remarks also embarrassed the administration, and were at odds with its declared policy of "dual containment" against both Iraq and Iran which rejected any notion that one state could be used to balance the other.

The youngest son of Italian immigrants, Zinni was a decorated Vietnam veteran who had commanded troops at every level. No stranger to Iraq, he had spent several months in the north as Chief of Staff for Operation Provide Comfort, the rescue operation for the Kurds. In Somalia in 1993 he commanded the naval task force which extracted UN peacekeepers under fire without a casualty, earning the gratitude of the Clinton administration.

Like many Marines, and more than most, Zinni had a sharp sense of the importance of the congressional role in foreign policy and national security matters. In an effort to gain greater support for the administration's Iraq policy, Secretary Cohen had asked him earlier in the year to brief the Senate leadership and House Speaker Gingrich. As the military leader with responsibility for the 20,000 or so U.S. military personnel in the Persian Gulf region, Zinni resented the absence of any consultation with him over the ILA by the administration internally or by the Congress. He believed it was his duty to speak out, mindful that he had sworn at his confirmation hearing that he would give his personal assessment to the Congress when asked to do so.

DESERT FOX AND THE "ROLLBACK FANTASY"

Tensions with Iraq over UNSCOM finally came to a violent conclusion at year's end. On December 15, Executive Chairman Richard Butler withdrew UNSCOM observers, and on December 17 air and cruise missile strikes were launched in Operation Desert Fox, with Zinni commanding. The Desert Fox attacks failed to bring about the collapse of the regime, which was in any case not their intent, but they did cause significant damage to Iraqi military and regime targets.

On December 16—the day before the Desert Fox strikes—six Republican senators, including Senators Helms and Lott, wrote to the president about a "perceived drift" in U.S. policy toward Iraq. They complained about Zinni's statements, as well as statements by Secretary of Defense Cohen, and urged the President to "move swiftly" to designate "a group such as the Iraqi National Congress" as a recipient under the Act. The letter asked angrily why no cabinet secretary had met with General Downing to discuss his plan for assistance to the opposition, which he had spent "considerable time" drawing up.[22]

At year's end, in the bi-monthly *Foreign Affairs*, organ of the Council on Foreign Relations, three prominent analysts published a devastating critique of what they called "The Rollback Fantasy." They wrote that

> Even if rollback were desirable, any policy to achieve it would have to pass three tests to be considered seriously. It would have to be militarily feasible, amenable to American allies whose cooperation would be required for implementation, and acceptable to the American public. All current rollback plans involving the Iraqi opposition come up short. Those who tout these nostrums as superior to existing U.S. policy are therefore either engaging in wishful thinking or cynically playing politics.[23]

One of the authors of the article, Ken Pollack, a veteran analyst of Iraqi affairs at CIA, was subsequently hired to handle Iraqi affairs on the NSC staff, further angering ILA proponents on the Hill.[24]

NONIMPLEMENTATION

On February 5, 1999, a week after the deadline set by the ILA, with the administration in technical violation of Section 5 of the Act, the president designated seven groups as meeting the criteria, presumably collectively, although this was not spelled out: the Iraq National Accord, composed of former military officers based in London, once seen as a promising coup vehicle, but revealed to have been penetrated by Iraqi intelligence; three

Kurdish groups, including the PUK and the KDP, SCIRI, and the Movement for Constitutional Monarchy, headed by a member of the Hashemite family.

Of the seven groups designated, only three had any presence on the ground, and they all announced that they would not accept U.S. assistance under the ILA. As for the monarchists, the U.S.-funded Radio Free Iraq based in Prague commented, they "have no army, very little organization, and no known support among the people in Iraq." That essentially left the INC.

In an effort to give expression to the new "regime change" policy and to deflect congressional pressure, the administration appointed Frank Ricciardone, a career Foreign Service officer, to serve in a new position with the optimistic title of "Special Representative for the Transition in Iraq." Efforts were made to lobby the Arabs in support of the new "regime change" policy, first by Martin Indyk, the Assistant Secretary, and by the Secretary of State in a January tour of the Gulf with Ricciardone in tow, but they failed to gain a hearing. Chalabi's INC was unable to establish a presence in any of the Persian Gulf states. Even Kuwait, host to some 5,000 U.S. military personnel, refused permission to the INC to set up an office. The *Washington Post* quoted an Arab diplomat as saying of Chalabi's efforts that "we Gulf Arabs live in the desert and we know what a mirage is."[25]

Secretary Albright's January tour coincided with an appearance by General Zinni before the Senate Armed Services Committee in which he was questioned about his views on the ILA. While careful not to take direct issue with the Act, which was after all law, Zinni repeated his criticism of support for the opposition. His testimony produced an embarrassing juxtaposition of headlines in the *New York Times* of January 29: "Albright Introduces a New Phrase to Promote Hussein's Ouster (regime change)," and "U.S. General Warns of Dangers in Trying to Topple Iraqi." The article on Zinni's testimony noted that "General Zinni's criticism of Iraqi opposition groups is in fact widely shared within the administration, although no other senior official has been willing to state that view so publicly since President Clinton, under pressure from Congress, signed the aid to dissidents into law last year."

Unsuccessful efforts continued by Ricciardone and other U.S. officials to unify the Iraqi opposition. An April meeting in London of eleven opposition groups under INC auspices, attended by Senator Bob Kerrey (D-NE), generated a statement papering over rifts between various factions but little else. SCIRI boycotted the meeting. (Senator Kerrey is reported to have hinted to the group that the United States was determined to get rid of Saddam Hussein before the end of the year in light of the presidential elections.)[26]

In May, after Secretary Albright met with INC representatives in Washington and promised "nonlethal" assistance, an anonymous U.S. spokesman, presumably Ricciardone, was quoted as saying that "these are the day-after guys"—in other words, not people who could bring about a change of regime. A November meeting of an INC "assembly" was finally held in New York, financed by the State Department to the tune of $3.1 million paid to the public relations firm. Again, SCIRI boycotted the meeting.[27] (Chalabi had wanted to hold the meeting in Kurdistan, but the administration declined to offer the necessary security guarantees, and no state in the region would host it.) In an internal coup engineered behind the scenes by Ricciardone intended to deflect criticism of his autocratic style, Chalabi was barred from assuming the chairmanship of the INC in the future. Despite this, disarray among the 300 or so Iraqis present was painfully evident.[28]

Meanwhile, the administration wrangled internally over how to implement the ILA. Broadly, State favored cosmetic measures in order to deflect congressional criticism, while DOD, which controlled the equipment and training, opposed any action at all. The resulting bureaucratic compromise bordered on farce. The INC was provided with surplus fax machines, computers, and filing cabinets, and four INC staffers were trained for twelve days at a Florida air base in "nonlethal" skills—principally public affairs. Chalabi's bitter complaints to the Hill led to high-level meetings with Senators Lott, Helms, and others, generating expressions of outrage but no moves towards arming the INC. On June 26, 2000, Vice President Gore met with the INC to "discuss the methods by which the INC could make the most effective use of assistance available under the authorities of the Iraq Liberation Act and related legislation."[29] As the Clinton administration drew to a close in October of 2000, a "cooperative agreement" was signed with the INC for "public information activities," "preparations for humanitarian relief operations," and "training in protective skills."

The ILA was not without cost to the administration's efforts to maintain international support for the containment of Iraq. By establishing it as the declared policy of the United States to seek the removal of the Iraqi regime, the ILA complicated the effort which finally led to the adoption of UNSC Resolution 1284 in December 1999. As one senior participant remembers it, "the French, the Russians and the Chinese, regularly brought up the ILA, and asked whether in light of it we could say that we would adhere to Security Council resolutions and international law. We said of course we could. They chose to view this as a renunciation of the ILA. We meant nothing of the sort, of course. But it amused them to make us say it."[30]

The ILA was also damaging in the region. Some Arabs in the Gulf and elsewhere found it impossible to believe that the United States was serious about the removal of Saddam Hussein if its chosen vehicle was a discredited emigre group based in London. Paradoxically, the ILA worked to reinforce the widespread Arab conviction that keeping Saddam Hussein in power and under sanctions served American interests.

THE BUSH ADMINISTRATION AND THE ILA: WHAT GOES AROUND . . .

In its first year in office, the Bush administration has followed an approach to the ILA which is difficult to distinguish from that of the Clinton administration, even though it is almost entirely staffed by officials who once were strong supporters of the INC (Secretary of State Colin Powell is a notable exception). A June 10, 2001, article in the *Washington Post* commented that:

> Another element of Bush's Iraq policy—backing for Iraqi opposition groups—remains under review despite predictions by some officials that they would move quickly to boost American support. An administration official said U.S. officials realize that a policy of supporting opposition activities inside Iraq faces skepticism from U.S. allies in the region and that the Iraqi National Congress, an umbrella of opposition groups, has yet to prove itself. The official said the administration is looking at "gradually" building support for the INC.[31]

In the aftermath of the terrorist attacks of September 11, 2001, debate within the administration over rollback versus containment has revived, and there have been new calls for support for the INC and an enclave strategy in Iraq. Internal divisions within the administration between proponents of an overthrow strategy at Defense and those who favor a continued containment strategy at State are apparent. In the *New Yorker* of December 24, 2001, Seymore Hersh writes that the plan outlined to Congress by Chalabi in 1998 has been revised by the INC, and that it would now involve the insertion of "several thousand" U.S. special forces personnel. In addition, Chalabi is reported by Hersh to have secured the agreement of Iran to operate across the Iranian border into southern Iraq.[32]

The Bush administration has so far continued to refuse to provide the INC with lethal assistance or assistance for use inside Iraq. In a December 5 letter, leading members of Congress including Senators Lott, Helms, Lieberman, and McCain, complain that:

> Since the passage of the Iraq Liberation Act three years ago, we have fought to provide support for Iraqis inside Iraq. The Iraqi National Congress (INC), an umbrella group of all the significant anti-Saddam forces inside Iraq, has consistently requested Administration assistance for operations on the ground in Iraq ranging from the delivery of humanitarian assistance and information-gathering to military and technical training and lethal military drawdown. Despite the express wishes of the Congress, the INC has been denied U.S. assistance for any operations inside any part of Iraq, including liberated Kurdish areas. Instead, successive Administrations have funded conferences, offices and other intellectual exercises that have done little more than expose the INC to accusations of being "limousine insurgents" and "armchair guerillas."[33]

At year's end, press reports suggested that the success of the military campaign against the Taliban in Afghanistan had led to a reconsideration of the 1998 Downing Plan, on the premise that a strategy of support for an insurgent group combined with air power could also succeed in Iraq. One article suggested that the Downing Plan had become a "lightning rod" for a new debate within the administration between ILA (and INC) supporters and opponents, who reportedly included "much of the State Department, CIA, and the professional military."[34] The INC was described as "a London-based confederation of Iraqi opposition groups that enjoys considerable backing on Capitol Hill but is seen as largely ineffectual by many in the administration."[35] Accounts of the alleged debate within the administration recycled old quotes from General Zinni, now recast as the Bush administration's representative to Palestinian-Israeli security talks, in which he referred to the INC as "silk-suited, Rolex-wearing guys in London."

In fact, there was evidence that even its most ardent supporters within the administration had arrived at a realistic appreciation of the limited capabilities of Chalabi's INC. Senior officials in the State Department were wondering whether the department could legally continue to fund the INC at all, following a report by the State Department Inspector General of INC accounting deficiencies,[36] and rival Kurdish leaders Ahmed Barzani and Jalal Talabani both are reported to have told a State Department emissary in December that they would refuse to have anything to do with any U.S. plans involving the INC.[37]

Notes

1. See David L. Wise, "Scott Ritter v Saddam Hussein: The Crisis over UN Weapons Inspections in Iraq," Maxwell/SAIS National Security Studies Case CS 0600-18, Syracuse University, June 2000.

2. See Jim Hoagland, "How the CIA's Secret War on Saddam Collapsed," *Washington Post*, June 26, 1997, p. A21.

3. Dana Priest and David B. Ottaway, "Congress's Candidate to Overthrow Saddam Hussein Has Virtually No Other Backing," *Washington Post*, April 21, 1999, p. A3.

4. Ethan Bonner and Youssef M. Ibrahim, "The World: Battles Joined—A Country at War, Both Abroad and at Home; A Tough New Goal in Iraq," *New York Times*, December 20, 1998, Section 4, p. 1.

5. Hoagland, "How the CIA's Secret War on Saddam Collapsed."

6. Priest and Ottaway, "Congress's Candidate to Overthrow Saddam Hussein Has Virtually No Other Backing."

7. http://www.newamericancentury.org/iraqclintonletter.htm.

8. Hoagland, "How the CIA's Secret War on Saddam Collapsed."

9. Vernon Loeb, "Congress Stokes Visions of War to Oust Saddam, White House Fears Fiasco in Aid to Rebels," *Washington Post*, October 29, 1998, p. A1.

10. Chalabi's testimony can be found on the INC's website, at http://209.50.252.70/English/news/98/inc980302a.htm. See also Daniel Byman, Kenneth Pollack, and Gideon Rose, "The Rollback Fantasy," *Foreign Affairs*, January/February 1999, pp. 24–41.

11. The text can be found at the INC's website, at http://209.50.252.70/English/news/98/oth980529a.htm.

12. The Congressional Record, E1857, October 1, 1998.

13. The Congressional Record, H9498, October 5, 1998.

14. The Congressional Record, September 9, 1998, S11123–24.

15. The Congressional Record, October 7, 1998, S11812.

16. Ibid.

17. The text of the ILA, which became P.L. 105–338, can be found in the Congressional Record at H9498, October 5, 1998.

18. The Congressional Record, October 8, 1998, S11812.

19. Bradley Graham, "U.S. General Attacks Aid for Groups Seeking to Topple Iraqi Leader," *Washington Post*, October 22, 1998, p. A32.

20. Reuters, "Plan to Aid Opponents of Iraq Criticized," *Washington Times*, October 22, 1998, p. A4.

21. See INC website, http://209.50.252.70/English/news/99/inc990130a.htm.

22. The text is on the INC website at http://209.50.252.70/English/news/98/oth981216a.htm.

23. Byman, Pollack, and Rose, "The Rollback Fantasy."

24. For criticism of Zinni and Pollack, see Jim Hoagland, "Virtual Policy," *Washington Post*, March 7, 1999, p. B7.

25. Priest and Ottaway, "Congress's Candidate to Overthrow Saddam Hussein Has Virtually No Other Backing."

26. See the Iraq Report at the website of Radio Free Iraq, http://www.rferl.org/iraq-report/1999/04/15-160499.html, an excellent source for detailed coverage of exile politics.

27. http://www.rferl.org/iraq-report/1999/10/40-291099.htm.

28. John Lancaster and Colum Lynch, "Iraqi Exiles Meet to Mount an Opposition in New York, Pledges of Unity," *Washington Post*, November 2, 1999, p. A15.

29. The White House statement is at http://www.fas.org/news/iraq/2000/06/000626-iraq-wh1.htm.

30. E-mail from a senior participant to the author.

31. See for example Robin Wright and Doyle McManua, "Bush Camp Split on Anti-Terror Policy," *Los Angeles Times*, September 21, 2001, p. 1.

32. Seymore M. Hersh, "The Iraq Hawks," *The New Yorker*, December 24, 2001.

33. Steve Mufson, "Ten Leading Lawmakers Urge Targeting of Iraq," *Washington Post*, December 6, 2001, p. A28.

34. Michael Dobbs, "Old Strategy on Iraq Sparks New Debate," *Washington Post*, December 27, 2001, p. A1.

35. George Gedda, "Saddam's Rivals Have Plans for Ouster," The Associated Press Wire Service, December 30, 2001.

36. Associated Press, "U.S. Suspends Aid to Leading Iraq Opposition Group," *Washington Post*, January 6, 2002, p. A22.

37. Personal communication with the author.

Chapter 10

Squeezing a Balloon: Plan Colombia and America's War on Drugs

VOLKER C. FRANKE AND JUSTIN REED

February 13, 2003, 9:00 AM. The single-engine Cessna 208 landed hard after the pilot reported engine trouble minutes before the plane was scheduled to reach the provincial capital Florencia. The plane was carrying four Americans on contract with the CIA and a Colombian military intelligence officer. The men were photographing Colombia's southern coca fields for tracking and targeting purposes as part of the Bush administration's intensifying war on drugs in Latin America. Colombian soldiers, who arrived at the rugged crash site within thirty minutes of the accident, found two of the passengers—one American and the Colombian—shot to death. The other three were missing. The plane was riddled with rounds from an M-60 machine gun, but Colombian investigators claim the gunfire did not cause the crash.

The plane had crashed in a traditional stronghold of the Revolutionary Armed Forces of Colombia (known by their Spanish acronym *FARC*), a Marxist-oriented guerilla group classified as a terrorist organization by the State Department. Soon after the crash, the FARC admitted to killing the two observers at the scene and taking the others hostage. The three Americans, the FARC offered, could be exchanged in a broad prisoner swap, however, the Colombian and U.S. governments both refused.[1] The guerrilla attack comes as part of a renewed escalation in the violence that has tormented the entire Andean region for more than five decades.

Colombia, the world's leading producer and distributor of cocaine, provides about 90 percent of the cocaine entering the United States and some two-thirds of the heroin found on the East Coast. In addition to supporting independent traffickers and cartels, the drug trade serves as a major source of funding for the FARC and the National Liberation Army (ELN), the hemisphere's most prominent guerrilla groups, and the right-wing paramilitary United Self Defense Forces of Colombia (AUC). The AUC and the FARC each control areas of massive coca and poppy cultivation and their involvement in the drug trade continues to fuel violence as each group vies to gain or retain profitable territory.

This case chronicles a half-century of violence in Colombia, describes the nature and magnitude of U.S. involvement in its bloody civil war, and explores connections between America's war on drugs and its more recent war on terrorism. The case focuses specifically on the merits of Plan Colombia, the Clinton administration–initiated strategy of source-country drug eradication, and the effects and implications of the Bush administration's decision to intensify previous U.S. counter-drug efforts. Questions raised by this case include: What threats does Colombia's civil conflict pose to U.S. national security? How does Plan Colombia address those threats? Is Plan Colombia effective in achieving Washington's counter-drug objectives? Are drug interdiction and eradication legitimate national security concerns? How does the war on drugs affect the traditional roles and missions of the U.S. military? Finally, what is the connection between America's drug war and its war on terrorism?

COLOMBIA'S CIVIL CONFLICT

Although the guerrilla war has plagued Colombia for some fifty years, cocaine has dramatically raised the stakes and the level of violence over the last two decades. With the world's highest murder rate—some 30,000 homicides in the past ten years are attributed to the war—Colombia suffers the worst political violence in the Western hemisphere.[2] The seeds of Colombia's civil war were planted in the 1940s when the elite Liberal and Conservative parties successfully repressed efforts for democratic reform by the country's peasants. Massive violence erupted in 1948, however, when leftist presidential candidate Jorge Eliecer Gaitan was assassinated by right-wing extremists. By the early 1950s, some 200,000 Colombians had been killed as a result of the civil strife, known as "La Violencia."[3]

Escaping the state military's offensives, leftist peasants declared "semi-autonomous rural communities" in the previously uninhabited eastern regions of Meta and Caqueta (see Map 10.1). Labeling these Marxist-inspired separatist peasants "gangs of communist bandits," the state campaigned aggressively to dismantle the communities. The leftists responded in kind, forming armed self-defense movements that avowed the use of militant tactics against the state for the purpose of radical social change.[4]

Map 10.1
Colombia

Maps provided by www.worldatlas.com.

The most prominent insurgencies are the *Fuerzas Armadas Revolu-cionarias de Colombia* (FARC), which began in the 1960s as an armed self-defense movement interested primarily in land reform, and the *Ejercito Liberacion Nacional* (ELN), formed in 1964 by Cuban Revolution–in-spired students. Over time, however, the political ideologies of both guer-rilla groups have become increasingly contaminated by drug trafficking, kidnappings, extortive "taxes" on peasants, and terrorist activities.[5] For in-stance, the ELN has recently adopted a strategy of attacking industrial sites such as the Caño-Limón oil pipeline, a campaign that is costing the state millions of dollars in revenue each month. The FARC, says former U.S. Ambassador to Colombia (1998–2000) Curtis Kamman, "like to use leftist rhetoric but they are now basically a bunch of thugs that like to grow their power. 'Keep this thing going, it is the best game in town,' given the easy drug money."[6]

Kidnapping remains a major source of income for both the FARC and the ELN. Alfonso Cano, a member of the FARC's ruling secretariat, explains "We know that this is bad, but we have a very large force that needs to eat and to dress, and we need arms and munitions."[7] Kidnappings occur in accordance with the FARC's so-called "Law 002," announced in March 2000, which requires persons with more than the equivalent of $1 million in assets to volunteer payments or risk detention.[8] As one member of the FARC's secretariat explains: "Our struggle is to do away with the state as it now exists in Colombia, preferably by political means, but if they don't let us then we have to carry on shooting."[9]

A testament to its enormous influence, then-President Andres Pastrana (1998–2002) awarded the FARC control over a Switzerland-sized "demilitarized" zone called the *despeje* on November 7, 1998, as a conciliatory effort to engender peace negotiations.[10] Far from bringing peace, however, the territory became an "untouchable training and recruiting ground for FARC guerillas."[11] With some 18,000 members today, the FARC earns annual revenues of nearly $600 million in drug money, and controls some 120,000 hectares of coca.[12]

By the 1970s, powerful cartels had transformed drug production from a cottage industry into a global smuggling juggernaut, employing some 300,000 Colombians. The booming drug business gave rise to a class of elite narco-trafficking aristocrats who settled their operations in the rural provinces occupied by the guerrillas. The leftist groups vehemently opposed the cartels and their pursuit of FARC-controlled drug cultivation plots.

To advance their interests and fight the guerrillas, many of the traffickers aligned themselves with Colombia's landed gentry who had established the nationalist paramilitary *Autodefensas Unidas de Colombia* (AUC). Today, the AUC continues to use violence and torture against the guerrillas and their civilian supporters, targeting even human rights workers, trade union leaders, academics, and journalists as well.[13] The AUC, which has recently been added to the State Department's list of international terrorist organizations, receives about 70 percent of its funding from the drug trade, and is responsible for some 70 percent of Colombia's annual human rights violations.[14]

COLOMBIA: A FAILING STATE?

By the late 1980s, Colombia had become a near shell of a nation, run by a government mired in corruption and dependent on the whim of powerful drug cartels and guerrilla groups. "The corrosive effect of narcotics money on Colombian society," explained Ambassador Kamman, "has distorted the economy, weakened the democratic political process and eroded confidence in the country's stability."[15]

Today, estimates suggest that 60 percent of the Congress have received illicit campaign contributions from the drug cartels.[16] Some 70 percent of crimes remain unsolved. Only around 40 percent of murders are investigated, one in ten result in arrest, and the conviction rate is merely 7 percent. The statistics paint a dismal picture: 1.5 million displaced persons and 3,500 annual deaths resulting from civil war.[17] Each year, the FARC, AUC, and ELN alone are responsible for more than 3,000 killings.

Explains Paul Simon, Acting Assistant Secretary of State for International Narcotics and Law Enforcement Affairs,

> The ongoing internal strife that Colombia has suffered has hampered its economic progress, severely strained both military and civil institutions, and wreaked havoc on the civilian population who must live with the constant threat of terrorist violence. It has also resulted in a flood of illicit drugs into the United States.[18]

Serving as Commander in Chief of the U.S. Southern Command from 1997–2000, General Charles Wilhelm was reminded by the complex situation in Colombia of the United States' ill-fated war in Vietnam. But, he explained, "this ain't no Vietnam. I wish it were; it would be easier."[19] For Kamman, one thing is clear: "We don't want to repeat the experience in Vietnam. But neither do we want to commit the error of neglect that allowed the Taliban to rise in Afghanistan." Colombia, he admits, is a "prime example of the symbiotic relationship between narcotics trafficking and politically motivated violence."[20] One other observer even suggests that "the future of military conflict—and therefore of America's global responsibilities over the coming decades—may best be gauged in Colombia . . . If left unmolested, they [guerilla groups] will likely establish strategic links with al Qaeda."[21]

Is Colombia on the verge of becoming a failed state? "State failure" and "state collapse" are new labels for a type of severe political crisis in which "the institutions of the central state [are] so weakened that they [can] no longer maintain political authority or political order beyond the capital city, and sometimes not even there. Such state failures usually occur in circumstances of widespread and violent civil conflict, often accompanied by severe humanitarian crises."[22]

AMERICA'S WAR ON DRUGS

The history of U.S. military involvement in Central and Latin America dates back some 175 years to the inception of the Monroe Doctrine, which stipulated that Latin American affairs were to be considered of vital interest to the United States.[23] During the Cold War, Colombia was viewed by Washington policymakers as a stable democracy capable of serving as a bulwark against the specter of communism infiltrating Latin America. By the mid-1990s, however, sustained peace and democracy had turned SOUTHCOM into a regional command struggling to stay relevant. As General Wilhelm explained in 2000,

> Every military in the region is rethinking its role . . . There is no external threat to this region right now. Most internal threats are laid to rest. They are refocusing on internal security, on regional peacekeeping and counterdrug operations. I'd like to play a larger role in the actual restructuring of the militaries.[24]

Few in the United States initially approved of this notion. Since the mid-1970s Congress had enacted laws restricting U.S. military and police training operations around the world. For instance, an amendment sponsored by Senator Patrick Leahy (D-VT) and enacted as part of the FY 1997 Foreign Operations Appropriations Act, stipulates that no funds are to be provided "to any unit of the security forces of a foreign country if the Secretary of State has credible evidence that such unit has committed gross violations of human rights."[25] The legislation attempted to ensure that the U.S. military would never again be associated with abusive armies as it was in El Salvador during the 1980s.

By the 1970s, drug abuse and trafficking had become a problem steadily tearing at America's social fabric.[26] President Reagan, in April 1986, signed National Security Decision Directive 221 declaring drug trafficking a threat to national security[27] and vying "to halt the production and flow of illicit narcotics, reduce the ability of insurgent and terrorist groups to use drug trafficking to support their activities, and strengthen the ability of individual governments to confront and defeat this threat."[28]

The military leadership disliked Reagan's securitization of the drug problem as "they wanted no role in what was ultimately a social problem ill-suited to military solutions." The true solution, they told Congress, namely stopping the demand for drugs "was a mission that rightfully belonged to police and local drug-rehabilitation programs."[29] But, faced with mounting drug-related violence, President George H. W. Bush decided in August 1989 to make the Defense Department the single lead agency for detecting, monitoring, and interdicting drugs entering the United States.[30] According to Ambassador Melvyn Levitsky, the Assistant Secretary of State for International Narcotics Matters at the time, "the implementing mission statement signed by then Defense Secretary Richard Cheney made it clear that the U.S. military was to have only a supporting role in the drug war. U.S. armed forces were to assist law enforcement personnel but had no power to arrest individuals or seize aircraft or ships."[31]

General George Joulwan, who was leading the military's anti-drug charge as CINC-SOUTHCOM from 1993 until 1997, described the drug problem as a balloon: "Squeeze it in one place and it pops up somewhere else."[32] Local squeezes simply move the industry to other parts of the country or across the border, thereby further spreading violence and corruption. The only answer, Joulwan believed, lay in a concerted regional strategy which, of course, would be much harder to implement.

To reduce the flow of illegal drugs into the United States, the Pentagon initiated a strategy of source-country interdiction, supporting efforts to destroy drugs and dismantle trafficking organizations at their origin. The "War on Drugs" was based on three major strategies: (1) extradition of traffickers to the U.S., (2) drug crop eradication campaigns, and (3) decertification of Colombia as a recipient of U.S. counter-drug aid.

Extradition

In 1979, the Carter and Lopez administrations signed a treaty allowing drug traffickers charged with smuggling in the United States to be extradited and tried in U.S. courts.[33] The drug cartels were furious. Traffickers waged a massive campaign of violence against the Colombian state, killing hundreds of police investigators, journalists, and public figures that threatened the drug business.[34] Continuous cartel pressure resulted in the incorporation of a clause into the 1991 constitution banning the extradition of Colombian citizens. The extradition ban was finally lifted in December

1997 near the end of the Samper administration through an amendment to the constitution, requiring successive favorable votes in two sessions of Congress in both houses. The first extradition, however, did not take place until the Pastrana administration. Since then, Colombia has extradited more than 100 of its nationals charged with high-level narcotics traveling, drug-related money laundering, hostage taking, and the murder of a retired New York City police officer. Said Paul E. Simons, Acting Assistant Secretary of State for International Narcotics and Law Enforcement Affairs in his June 3, 2003, testimony before the Senate Drug Caucus, "we have no better extradition partner."[35]

Drug Crop Eradication

Crop destruction was intended to eliminate the supply of drugs at their source before they could be processed and smuggled into the United States. Articulating the intent of this strategy, Ambassador Kamman explained that "eradication was designed to drive up the price on the street in order to prevent the average teenager from getting started on drugs, but it didn't significantly increase the price or reduce demand."[36]

The unintended effect in Colombia was that once cultivation plots had been sprayed, rural farmers simply moved to other parts of the countryside and began replanting their crops.[37] Coca, referred to by many Colombians as "the blessed plant," continues to be cultivated because, as one farmer articulated, ". . . it is the only one which gives us enough to live on."[38] Despite the fact that farmers receive only US$140 per month for a small patch of coca, cultivation of this crop remains their most profitable enterprise.[39] As a result, overall coca cultivation steadily increased between 1998 and 2001, as did eradication efforts.

In 2002, Colombia's newly elected President Alvaro Uribe lifted limits on aerial eradication, leading to the spraying of 43,000 hectares of coca in the first four months of his presidency (see Table 10.1).[40] It is too early to tell whether Plan Colombia is working, according to Rand Beers, Assistant Secretary of State for International Narcotics and Law Enforcement Affairs (1998–2002). "The idea was to cap and then reduce the cultivation in Colombia without increasing it in Peru and Bolivia. And 2002 was the first year in which the full resources allocated for Plan Colombia were actually available."[41]

Alternatives to cultivating illicit crops exist, but have made little progress in the guerrilla-controlled areas.[42] On the one hand, explains Beers, illicit drug cultivation typically happens "at the end of the trans-

Table 10.1
Hectares of Coca Estimated under Cultivation and Eradicated in Colombia[43]

Year	Hectares under Cultivation	% Increase	Hectares Eradicated
1998	101,800	28	49,641
1999	122,500	20	39,113
2000	136,200	11	42,283
2001	169,800	25	77,165
2002	144,450	−15	TBD

portation network and not necessarily on the most productive land. On the other hand, the alternative development aspect of Plan Colombia was not just to provide alternative livelihood to the people but also to bring institutions of government to the area. But before you can bring control and livelihood to the area, you need to bring security."[44] A small alternative development farm can earn an income at least three times Colombia's minimum wage. But, says Francisco de Roux, the director of *Desarollo y Paz,* a nongovernmental organization in the Magdalena region that assists some 5,000 farmers in implementing alternative development, "nothing is more profitable than coca, but the farmers know it has a very high social cost. They say: show me an alternative that offers a reasonable living, and I'll leave coca."[45]

Decertification

Deeply frustrated with a Samper government steeped in corruption and humbled by the drug cartels—as evidenced by the fact that Samper's campaign manager was arrested for funneling $6 million from the Cali cartel into the election campaign—the Clinton administration cut aid (but not counter-narcotics assistance) to Colombia in 1996 and 1997. This so-called decertification expanded on the provisions of the 1988 Anti-Drug Abuse Act, restricting certification from countries not in compliance with U.S. anti-drug policies.[46]

U.S. pressure forced the Samper Administration (1994–98) to enforce the extradition treaty and fight the cartels with greater vigor than any previous president, while at the same time mandating Colombian support for future U.S. counter-drug policies.[47] However, Samper's cooperation with the United States and his focus on dismantling the cartels came at a heavy price: the surmounting influence and threat of the guerrilla insurgencies, specifically the FARC, was not fully addressed.[48] As violence continued to rise in Colombia and drug supply soared on American streets, critics of the "War on Drugs" grew more vociferous. In response, the Clinton administration opted to modify previous counter-drug strategies with a new focus.

PLAN COLOMBIA

Recognizing the enormity of illegal drug activities in Colombia, the newly elected Pastrana government tried to improve strained relations with the United States. "What we need, said Pastrana, is a Marshall Plan for Colombia."[49] Drafted over the course of only a month, the government announced in October 1999 a $7.5 billion integrated strategy known as Plan Colombia, "to meet the most pressing challenges confronting Colombia today—promoting the peace process, combating the narcotics industry, reviving the Colombian economy, and strengthening the democratic pillars of Colombian society."[50]

Among other things, Plan Colombia proposed to reduce the cultivation, processing, and distribution of narcotics by 50 percent over six years through interdiction and eradication efforts, restore government authority and control over the drug producing regions of southern Colombia, and offer alternative and economic development programs to assist small farmers make the transition to legal economic activity.[51] To assist these efforts, the United States committed to providing $1.3 billion in a total U.S. interagency assistance package. The remaining funding was to be provided by the Colombian government ($4 billion) and the international community.

Supporting the new focus, Senator Joseph Biden (D-DE) asserted in a May 2000 report to the House Committee on Foreign Relations:

Never before in recent history has there been such an opportunity to strike at all aspects of the drug trade at the source. . . . Helping Colombia is squarely in America's national interest. It is the source of many of the drugs poisoning our people. It is not some far-off land with which the United States shares little in common. It is an established democracy in America's backyard—just a few hours by air from Miami.[52]

Similarly, Brian Sheridan, Assistant Secretary of Defense for Special Operations and Low-Intensity Conflict, testified before the House Committee on International Relations on September 21, 2000:

> The targets are the narco-traffickers, those individuals and organizations that are involved in the cultivation of coca or opium poppy and the subsequent production and transportation of cocaine and heroin to the U.S. Only those armed elements that forcibly inhibit or confront counter-drug operations will be engaged, be they narco-traffickers, insurgent organizations, or illegal self-defense forces.[53]

Despite supporting the enhanced role for the U.S. military, Congress restricted the number of U.S. personnel implementing the program in Colombia: no more than 400 U.S. military personnel and no more than 400 U.S. citizen civilian contractors.[54] However, according to Ambassador Levitsky, "U.S. advisors are prohibited from engaging in operations or active combat."[55]

But while Plan Colombia intensified the traditional strategy of crop defoliation, reducing coca cultivation in 2002 for the first time since the mid-1990s (see Table 10.1), significant challenges remain. Paul Simon, Acting Assistant Secretary for International Narcotics and Law Enforcement Affairs, explained in a July 2003 testimony before the House Committee on Government Reform that:

> In Colombia, the drug security control has a clear advantage since the bulk of coca and opium poppy grows in zones that fall beyond the firm security control of the central government. As eradication squeezes the industry, ground fire from narco-terrorist groups has increased. . . . Accordingly, we expect that these groups will increasingly use their firepower and ingenuity to protect and expand their drug interests in Colombia.[56]

Overall support for Washington's counter-drug initiative has been mixed. Hard-line "drug hawks" such as Rep. Dan Burton (R-IN) initially supported Plan Colombia, as similar programs focused on source-country eradication and counterinsurgency had succeeded in the neighboring Andean nations of Peru and Bolivia. For many hard-liners in the war on drugs, Plan Colombia's problems stemmed from Congressional restrictions limiting aid from funding U.S. military engagement with the guerrillas and paramilitaries. Former CINC-SOUTHCOM and Clinton administration "drug czar" General Barry McCaffrey argued,

> There was always an artificiality to this policy that endorsed helping a democratically elected Colombian government against drug criminals but refused to help them when they are threatened by people who are blowing up oil pipelines, murdering mayors, and kidnapping politicians.[57]

In addition, hard-liners argued that the scope and intensity of crop defoliation campaigns were too limited to effectively deter farmers from moving and replanting crops. At an April 10, 2002, hearing of the House Appropriations Subcommittee on Foreign Operations, Representative Nita Lowey (D-NY) opined that the "area of coca cultivation increased significantly last year, despite our aerial spraying campaign . . . We may be putting a Band-Aid on a hemorrhaging wound."[58]

Other observers question the Colombian government's ability to effectively implement Plan Colombia. In a 2002 study on the effectiveness of efforts to develop alternatives to cultivating illicit crops in Colombia, the Government Accounting Office (GAO) found that

> While Colombia uses aerial spray operations to carry out an active eradication program, the government's lack of control over many coca-growing areas limits its ability to carry out sustained ground-based interdiction operations . . . Colombian military and law enforcement units destroy some cocaine laboratories and seize narcotics and precursor chemicals during individual counternarcotics operations; however, they lack sufficient forces to maintain the permanent presence to sustain such operations on a day-to-day basis. Further complicating the problem is that a large land area ceded to one of the guerilla groups is off limits to U.S. and Colombian agencies, but is reportedly an increasing source of coca and precursor supplies. Throughout these areas, insurgents and paramilitaries operate largely with impunity. The experiences in Bolivia and Peru showed that sustained interdiction operations are necessary to disrupt coca markets and thus produce declines in the prices of coca. Without these declines, alternative development efforts are not as effective.[59]

Heralding successful efforts to reduce coca cultivation in Bolivia and Peru,[60] the report finds that success in the war on drugs demands: (1) host government control and security in project areas; (2) effective interdiction operations; and (3) careful coordination of eradication, interdiction, and alternative development efforts. However, the report concludes, "the Colombian government does not control large parts of the coca-growing areas, limiting its ability to carry out sustained interdiction operations, and the Colombian government's ability to effectively coordinate eradication and alternative development activities remains uncertain."[61]

Other critics assert that Plan Colombia's failure lay not in its enforcement and implementation, but in its conception, citing the destructive results of indiscriminate spraying operations as evidence. For instance, residents of the town of La Hormiga in the province of Putumayo claim that aerial fumigation has killed "hundreds of acres of food crops, scores of cattle, and hundreds of fish that washed up the banks of the Guamez River" because planes sprayed pesticides indiscriminately on legal and illegal crops.[62] Said Leandro Romo, the human rights ombudsman for La Hormiga, "some of these people had started the process of pulling up their coca. They were getting ready with corn, yucca, and then the fumigation started. We're not arguing with the goals, just the methods. This has been indiscriminate. And until now the farmers have received virtually nothing."[63]

While recent reports show some success in the drug war in Colombia, the "balloon" is squeezed elsewhere. A "turning point" was the phrase used by John Walters, Director of the Office of National Drug Control Policy, to describe figures released in March 2003 that indicate a 15 percent drop in Colombia's crop of coca in 2002 (see Table 10.1). Yet, at the same time in Bolivia, which experienced a 23 percent increase in coca cultivation as of June 2002 (see Table 10.2),[64] the candidate of the powerful coca growers' movement received 21 percent of the vote in the 2002 presidential election, and in January of 2003, protests by coca farmers brought much of the country to a standstill for two weeks. In Peru, the drug war's other "success story," the government decided in September 2002 to restart forcible eradication in hardcore coca areas, "a policy Peru eschewed in the late 1980s, after Shining Path terrorists exploited discontent over it."[65]

Ambassador Curtis Kamman reiterated the danger of overemphasizing eradication successes in one geographical area: "Now that spraying has been carried out in a more effective way, it has had an effect on total crop cultivation in Colombia, but also in Peru and Bolivia. And some people

Table 10.2
Net Hectares of Coca under Cultivation[66]

	Bolivia	**Colombia**	**Peru**	**Total**
1996	48,000	67,200	94,400	209,700
1997	45,800	79,500	68,800	194,100
1998	38,000	101,800	51,000	190,800
1999	21,800	122,500	38,700	183,000
2000	14,600	136,200	34,100	185,000
2001	19,900	169,800	34,000	223,700
2002	24,400	144,450	36,000	204,850

fear that it might spread further across the Andes and even to Brazil."[67] The drug industry, *The Economist* concluded in a recent story on the success of Plan Colombia, "has an unerring eye for institutional weaknesses. As long as cocaine is demanded, victories over it involve defeats elsewhere."[68]

DRUGS AND TERRORISM

Entering office in January 2001, President George W. Bush elected to intensify the Clinton administration's counter-drug efforts. The terrorist attacks of September 11, 2001, influenced policymakers in Washington to view the guerrilla insurgencies and paramilitary groups in Colombia through the larger lens of the new global "War on Terrorism." As the rebel forces demonstrably profit from the drug industry while resorting to terrorist acts to further their respective agendas, the Bush administration linked these two policies, amalgamizing drugs and guerrillas into the singular "narco-terrorist" threat.[69]

On March 21, 2002, the Bush administration sent Congress its wartime request that propounded allowing U.S. support of all Colombian counterterror operations. On May 1, Attorney General John Ashcroft asserted the administration's linkage of the guerrilla organizations to such groups as Al Quaeda: "Just as we fight terrorism in the mountains of South Asia, we will fight terrorism in our own hemisphere."[70] As one SOUTHCOM official explained, ". . . the fundamental center of gravity for the terrible problems afflicting Colombia are the guerrilla groups and their paramilitary foes. Until you go after that root cause of instability, you are only treating symptoms like drug trafficking."[71]

Recognizing the complexity of Colombia's security challenges, Ambassador Kamman concluded, "we are thus faced with a witches' brew in Colombia that bodes ill for our counter-narcotics goals and eventually could result in an even more powerful sanctuary for terrorist groups whose political objectives are contrary to our own." Explaining further, Kamman warns, "Unlike the Islamic extremists in other parts of the world, the terrorists who operate in Colombia have not explicitly declared the United States to be their target. But their political and economic objectives are incompatible with our values, and they could ultimately present a force for evil no less troublesome than Al Qaeda or irresponsible forces possessing weapons of mass destruction."[72]

BUSH'S QUIET WAR

In 2003, Congress funded $700 million of a requested $731 million for the Andean Counterdrug Initiative (ACI) budget, allocating $433 million in counter-drug aid to Colombia alone. Approximately 65 percent ($284 million) of the ACI's budget is earmarked for "counter-narcotics military assistance and training for federal military and police units" in the country. The remaining 35 percent ($149 million) of the aid is designated for alternative crop development, support for the rule of law, and institution building.[73] The most controversial component of the ACI plan is the administration's proposal to tack on an additional $98 million to help the Colombian army protect the Caño-Limón oil pipeline from attacks by the FARC and the ELN.[74] The additional allocation request practically removes restrictions for U.S. troops to train Colombian forces to protect the 484-mile-long pipeline. Voicing his support of the ACI, Senator Christopher Dodd (D-CT) conjectured: "If we turn our backs on this corner of the world, I fear that we may see another situation arise like that which we saw when we ignored Afghanistan."[75]

While the director of the Office of Drug Control praises coca crop reductions, violence and anti-American sentiment are on the rise in Colombia. On January 21, 2003, the ELN kidnapped a British reporter and an American photographer at a roadblock between the towns of Saravena and

Tame in Colombia's Arauca province.[76] Although both journalists were released after eleven days, the incident raises questions concerning the future nature of American military involvement in Colombia's civil war. Many Colombians believe the kidnapping occurred as an aggressive reaction to the unwanted arrival of seventy U.S. Special Forces "advisers" and Huey II helicopters sent to aid local forces in Arauca. Said Jose Murillo, President of the Joel Sierra Regional Committee for Human Rights, "it's a deplorable act, but it is the result of anger among the people here over the militarization of Arauca. You don't need some deep analysis to tell you what the U.S. troops are going to bring, a worsening of the government's dirty war . . ."[77]

Worsening indeed, as the killing and kidnapping of the five plane crash victims in February 2003 illustrates. The FARC demanded that the Colombian army immediately suspend military operations and overflights and that Colombian military forces retreat from a cluster of eight towns nearby. In response, the Bush administration ordered 150 additional Special Forces troops to Colombia, raising the total number of military personnel above the 400-troop limit established by Congress in 2001. The administration justified exceeding the limit so as "to carry out emergency evacuation of U.S. citizens or any search-and-rescue operation for U.S. military personnel or U.S. citizens according to the legislation."[78] Anti-American violence in Colombia is escalating, as U.S. involvement in the civil war deepens.

Notes

1. Scott Wilson, "Congressmen, in Colombia, Urge Reply to Kidnapping," *Washington Post*, February 21, 2003, p. A16; Scott Wilson, "Hunt Expands for Missing Americans in Colombia," *Washington Post*, February 16, 2003, p. A17; Scott Wilson, "5 Missing After U.S. Plane Goes Down in Colombia," *Washington Post*, February 14, 2003, p. A18. As of July 2003, the exact whereabouts of the three Americans are still unknown.

2. Julia Sweig, "What Kind of War for Colombia?" *Foreign Affairs*, September/October (2002), pp. 1–11.

3. Russel Crandall, *Driven by Drugs: U.S. Policy toward Colombia* (Boulder, CO: Lynne Rienner, 2002); Sewall H. Menzel, *Cocaine Quagmire* (Lanham, MD: University Press, 1997).

4. Gary M. Leech, "Fifty Years of Violence," *Colombia Report*, 1999, at http://www.colombiareport.org.

5. Menzel, *Cocaine Quagmire*.

6. Interview with the authors, July 16, 2003.

7. Michael Reid, "Colombia: Drugs, War and Democracy," *The Economist*, April 21, 2001, pp. 3–16.

8. In addition, the FARC often purchased victims kidnapped by common criminals and then negotiated ransom payments with their families. See Paul Simon, "U.S. Narcotics Control Initiatives in Colombia," testimony before the Senate Drug Caucus, June 3, 2003, at http://www.state.gov/g/inl/rls/rm/21203.htm.

9. Reid, "Colombia: Drugs, War and Democracy." p. 10.

10. Crandall, *Driven by Drugs*, p. 73.

11. Dana Priest, *The Mission: Waging War and Keeping Peace with America's Military* (New York: Norton, 2003), p. 207.

12. See Raphael Pardo, "Colombia's Two-Front War," *Foreign Affairs*, July/August (2000), pp. 64–73 and "The Gringos Land in Colombia," *The Economist*, 31 August 2000.

13. See Crandall, *Driven By Drugs*, p. 85 and Reid, "Colombia: Drugs, War and Democracy," p. 12.

14. James Kitfield, "Giving War a Chance," *National Journal*, June 1, 2002, p. 1634; Winfred Tate, "Colombia's Role in International Drug Industry." November 1999, at http://www.foreignpolicy-infocus.org, last accessed July 29, 2002.

15. Curtis Kamman, "Narco-Terror: The Worldwide Connection between Drugs and Terrorism," Testimony before the Senate Committee on the Judiciary, March 13, 2002, at http://judiciary.senate.gov/print_testimony.cfm?id=196&wit_id=333, last accessed July 16, 2003.

16. See Michael Stohl and George Lopez, "Westphalia, the End of the Cold War and the New World Order: Old Roots to a 'NEW' Problem," Paper presented to a Symposium on "Failed States and International Security: Causes, Prospects, and Consequences," Purdue University, West Lafayette, IN, February 25–27, 1998. For further information see http://www.ippu.purdue.edu/failed_states/1998/papers/stohlz-lopez.html, last accessed April 2, 2003.

17. See Reid, "Colombia: Drugs, War and Democracy," p. 6 and Ann C. Mason, "Colombian State Failure: The Global Context of Eroding Domestic Authority," Paper presented to a Symposium on "Failed States and International Security: Causes, Prospects, and Consequences," Purdue University, West Lafayette, IN, February 25–27, 1998. For further information see http://www.ippu.purdue.edu/failed_states/1998/papers/mason.html, last accessed April 2, 2003.

18. Simon, "U.S. Narcotics Control Initiatives in Colombia," p. 2.

19. Quoted in Priest, *The Mission*, p. 206.

20. Kamman, "Narco-Terror." See also Rand Beers, "Narco-Terror: The Worldwide Connection between Drugs and Terrorism," Testimony before the

Senate Committee on the Judiciary, March 13, 2002, at http://judiciary.senate. gov/print_testimony.cfm?id=196&wit_id=331, last accessed July 16, 2003.

21. Robert Kaplan, "Supremacy by Stealth." *Atlantic Monthly*, July/August 2003, p. 66.

22. Daniel Esty, Jack Goldstone, Ted Robert Gurr, Barbara Harff, Pamela Surko, Alan Unger, and Robert Chen, "The State Failure Project: Early Warning Research for U.S. Foreign Policy Planning," Paper presented to a Symposium on "Failed States and International Security: Causes, Prospects, and Consequences," Purdue University, West Lafayette, IN, February 25–27, 1998. For further information see http://www.ippu.purdue.edu/failed_states/1998/papers/gurr.##html, last accessed April 2, 2003.

23. American military interventions in Latin America include the Dominican Republic (1905 and 1965); Nicaragua (1912 and during the 1980s); Mexico (1914); Cuba (1961); El Salvador (throughout the 1980s); Grenada (1983); and Panama (1989). For further detail see Priest, *The Mission*, especially Chapter 9.

24. Quoted in Priest, *The Mission*, pp. 199–200.

25. Ibid., p. 185.

26. Ambassador Melvyn Levitsky, Assistant Secretary for International Narcotics Matters (1989–93) notes that "U.S. government drug strategies make it clear that reduction in the use of illegal drugs through prevention, education and treatment is the goal of U.S. drug policy. Supply reduction is designed to ensure that drugs are not cheap and widely available to the public. There is both a push and a pull factor involved; interestingly, push gets much more press and Congressional attention while pull receives much more government funding." E-mail correspondence with the authors, August 14, 2003.

27. Ted Galen Carpenter, "Perilous Panacea: The Military in the Drug War," *Policy Analysis*, February 15, 1990, at http://www.cato.org, last accessed July 29, 2002.

28. See http://www.fas.org/.

29. Priest, *The Mission*, p. 204.

30. National Security Decision Directive 18, Section 124, Title 10, U.S. Code.

31. E-mail correspondence with the authors, August 14, 2003.

32. Quoted in Priest, *The Mission*, p. 204. See also *The Economist*, "The Balloon Goes Up," March 8, 2003, pp. 37–8.

33. Bruce Bagley, "Colombia and the War on Drugs," *Foreign Affairs*, Fall 1988, p. 79.

34. Tate, "Colombia's Role in International Drug Industry." Notably, cartel-funded gangs like the Extraditables assassinated Justice Minister Rodrigo Lara Bonilla in April 1984, and Liberal Party presidential candidate Luis Carlos Galan in August 1989. As well, the group exploded a passenger plane, assassinated a

Supreme Court Justice, detonated car bombs in shopping malls, and destroyed the headquarters of the Colombian investigative agency. See Crandall, *Driven By Drugs* and Pardo, "Colombia's Two-Front War."

35. See http://www.state.gov/g/inl/rls/rm/21203.htm, last accessed June 9, 2003.

36. Interview with Ambassador Curtis Kamman conducted by the authors on July 16, 2003.

37. Bagley, "Colombia and the War on Drugs," p. 80.

38. Council on Hemispheric Affairs, "Drugs Replace Communism as Point of Entry for U.S. Policy on Latin America," August 24, 1999. See http://www. derechos.net, last accessed July 29, 2002.

39. Janet Lloyd, "Report On: Plan Colombia and Indigenous Peoples," *Amazon Watch*, December 2001, at http://www.amazonwatch.org.

40. Marc Grossman, "Press Conference in Bogota, Colombia," March 5, 2003, at http://www.state.gov/p/18438pf.htm, last accessed July 3, 2003.

41. Interview with the authors, conducted July 22, 2003.

42. For instance, in January 2002, Congress passed the Andean Counterdrug Initiative, providing $625 million for counter-narcotics programs, including alternative development, in Andean countries. Title II of the fiscal year 2002 Foreign Operations appropriation bill (P.L. 107–115). For an analysis of the effectiveness of the program see GAO-02-291.

43. See Bureau for International Narcotics and Law Enforcement Affairs, "International Narcotics Control Strategy Report—2002," at http://www.state.gov/g/inl/rls/nrcpt/2002/html/17944pf.htm, last accessed July 7, 2003.

44. Interview with the authors, July 25, 2003.

45. Reid, *Colombia: Drugs, War and Democracy*, p. 9.

46. The 1988 Anti-Drug Abuse Act specified that all certified countries must sign a treaty demonstrating progress in "drug eradication, interdiction, demand reduction, chemical control, and cooperation with U.S. drug enforcement agencies. See http://www.usdoj.gov/dea/pubs/history/deahistory.html.

47. Crandall, *Driven By Drugs*, p. 128.

48. Ibid., p. 131.

49. Interview with Ambassador Curtis Kamman conducted by the authors on July 16, 2003.

50. The content of Plan Colombia can be found at http://www.state.gov/p/wha/rls/fs/2001/1042pf.htm.

51. See GAO-02-291.

52. Ibid., p. 150.

53. Crandall, *Driven By Drugs*, p. 149.

54. Karen DeYoung, "Bush Uses Exemption on Colombia Forces," *Washington Post*, February 27, 2003, p. A21. See also Kaplan, "Supremacy by Stealth."

55. Interview with the authors, August 14, 2003.

56. Paul E. Simon, "Disrupting the Market: Strategy, Implementation, and Results in Narcotics Source Countries." Testimony before the House Committee on Government Reform, July 9, 2003, at http://www.state.gov/g/inl/rls/rm/22310 pf.htm, last accessed July 16, 2003.

57. Kitfield, "Giving War a Chance," p. 1635.

58. Ibid.

59. GAO-02-291, p. 13.

60. Amabssador Levitsky notes that "in the late 1980s and early 1990s Peru and Bolivia were responsible for more than 80 percent of the coca leaf cultivation. As efforts to eradicate coca became more successful, the traffickers moved cultivation increasingly to Colombia." Interview with the authors, August 14, 2003.

61. Ibid., p. 12.

62. Scott Wilson, "Aerial Attack Killing More Than Coca," *Washington Post*, January 7, 2001, p. A1.

63. Scott Wilson, "U.S. Doubts Effects of Coca Plan," *Washington Post*, April 7, 2002, p. A13.

64. Ibid.

65. *The Economist*, "The Balloon Goes Up," March 8, 2003, p. 38.

66. Bureau for International Narcotics and Law Enforcement Affairs, "International Narcotics Control Strategy Report—2002."

67. Interview with Ambassador Curtis Kamman conducted by the authors on July 16, 2003.

68. *The Economist*, "The Balloon Goes Up," p. 38.

69. The 2002 National Security Strategy asserts: "In Colombia, we recognize the link between terrorist and extremist groups that challenge the security of the state and drug trafficking activities that help finance the operations of such groups. We are working to help Colombia defend its democratic institutions and defeat illegal armed groups of both the left and right by extending effective sovereignty over the entire national territory and provide basic security to the Colombian people." See text at http://www.whitehouse.gov.

70. Kitfield, "Giving War a Chance," p. 1635.

71. Kitfield, "Giving War a Chance," p. 1634.

72. Kamman, "Narco Terror."

73. Simon, "U.S. Narcotics Control Initiatives in Colombia."

74. The guerrillas attacked the pipeline some 170 times in 2002 alone, costing Colombia as much as $40 million per month in revenue. See "Colombia's Civil War: The Evolving U.S. Role." *Online News Hour*, March 12, 2003 at http://www.pbs.org.

75. Ibid.

76. Scott Wilson, "Journalists Freed by Colombian Guerrillas," *Washington Post*, February 2, 2003, p. A23.

77. Scott Wilson, "U.S. Moves Closer to Colombia's War," *Washington Post*, February 7, 2003, p. A22.

78. Karen DeYoung, "Bush Uses Exemption On Colombia Forces," *Washington Post*, February 27, 2003, p. A21.

Philanthropy vs. National Security: Should CARE Criticize the Military?

ARTHUR C. BROOKS

Jeff Brooks creates direct-mail fundraising appeals for charitable organizations. He is the Creative Director for the Domain Group, a marketing firm based in Seattle that specializes in nonprofits.[1] Jeff has been in the direct-mail business for more than fifteen years. His specialty is overseas humanitarian organizations—foreign aid nongovernmental organizations (NGOs). His clients include both secular and church-based organizations, from America's Second Harvest to World Vision.

Jeff believes in the missions of his clients. After completing graduate degrees in creative writing and literature, he chose to work for an ad firm that specializes in nonprofits in order to make a difference in the world through his work. For his clients, he travels all over the world, meeting with besieged aid workers, religious dissidents, and some of the world's poorest people. He turns what he sees and hears into appeals for donations that usually yield more than these organizations had ever hoped.

Jeff's fundraising success is attracting some of the most prominent players in the humanitarian aid world. In early 2001, for example, CARE International came to the Domain Group and asked Jeff to redesign its fundraising appeals. CARE International is one of the largest private humanitarian organizations in the world. With relief projects in virtually every part of the globe, CARE has a worldwide staff of more than 12,000, has assets of nearly $400 million, and spends nearly half a billion dollars annually on its activities.[2]

Jeff has been working on the CARE account for about a year now, and is considering some important changes to the way the organization portrays itself in its fundraising. Specifically, he is thinking about whether a change in CARE's policy of impartiality on political issues—such as the role of the U.S. military—might be worth reconsidering. He is wondering about the impact of such a change. For example, he is pondering whether an activist stance by CARE against American military activities might have an impact on public opinion—perhaps lowering support for military activities—and consequently impact this country's national security. These questions involve both practical and ethical issues. This case studies Jeff's dilemma.

BACKGROUND

CARE's stated mission is "to serve individuals and families in the poorest communities in the world. Drawing strength from our global diversity, resources and experience, we promote innovative solutions and are advocates for global responsibility."[3] It is best known for its famous "CARE packages," or boxes of food and supplies flown into drought- and famine-plagued areas of the world. However, its work today goes far beyond food drops; the organization offers a wide range of development services, from education to infrastructure. And CARE has frequently provided aid to people in countries affected by military action, as in Bosnia, Kosovo, Somalia, Haiti, and, most recently, Afghanistan. (See Appendix 11.1 for an organizational profile of CARE.)

CARE is not a political organization, at least not overtly so. According to Andy Pew, CARE's Director of Advocacy and Policy, CARE feels strongly about "impartiality" in international conflicts. He views it as a matter of simple professional ethics: An impartial CARE—unfettered by political ties—has maximum access to communities in which problems exist, and hence is as effective as possible in meeting its mission.[4]

This stance has set CARE apart from many other "competing" international humanitarian organizations, which have often taken distinct positions on political issues. For example, the medical aid group *Medecins Sans Frontieres* (Doctors Without Borders [MSF]) began in 1971 when a group of French doctors became frustrated—for ethical reasons—with the political neutrality of the International Red Cross in humanitarian crisis situations.[5] The organization has not been afraid to express itself in non-neutral terms in conflicts since that time. For instance, in describing civilian casualties in Afghanistan in December of 2001, *MSF*'s language was strongly value-laden: "MSF is increasingly seeing evidence of an unacceptably high toll on civilians due to the military operations . . . [It is] all the more disturbing as the leaders of the war against terrorism affirm that the conflict is being waged in the name of civilization and respect for humanitarian values."[6]

Given this example and others like it, Jeff is considering whether CARE's political neutrality might be an anachronism, a liability. While it is not clear that organizations such as MSF are more effective fundraisers than CARE, many seem to be gaining a higher international profile.

Jeff has been looking at a recent independent study of CARE's "brand" among current and potential donors which made some provocative suggestions regarding CARE's optimal fundraising target group. Based on the data from a series of focus groups, the study built the following "conceptual" portrait of the *ideal* CARE donor:[7]

- Interested in world events and issues, he or she is well-traveled.
- He or she believes that the world can be better and wants to be part of making it so.
- He or she is "politically progressive."
- He or she is skeptical that the fundamental issues of poverty and social injustice can be overcome, especially by first-world governments and agencies that often seem to work only for the betterment of their *own* people.

The study labeled these target donors "skeptical progressives." The firm clearly intended this label for political liberals that are especially skeptical of American foreign policy interests that might involve humanitarian concerns.

This is particularly relevant in the late fall of 2001 and early spring of 2002: The United States is involved in a military campaign to topple the government of Afghanistan in the wake of the September 11 terrorist attacks on New York City and Washington, D.C., and to destroy Afghanistan's terrorist infrastructure, replacing it with a regime less hostile to the West. In addition, it seems clear that the United States will soon be looking to other targets around the world, which the U.S. government believes are implicated in terrorism against the United States and its allies. The hardships of war—and the subsequent nationbuilding efforts—will require the intervention of NGOs like CARE in the affected countries.

Afghanistan (as well as most other potential targets, such as Iraq and Iran) is a poor country, and a natural candidate for CARE's operations.[8] CARE has been operating in Afghanistan since 1961, only suspending its operations during the Soviet occupation and civil war from 1980–89. At present, CARE runs projects in many parts of the country that focus on issues from emergency food relief, to sanitation, to primary education. CARE also operates Flight Operation for Humanitarian Assistance in Afghanistan (FLOFA), which aids other NGOs by air-transporting them in and out of remote regions of the country.

There would appear to be plenty in the Afghanistan conflict—and related future conflicts—to concern a "skeptical progressive" who has traditionally been suspicious of U.S. involvement abroad. Should CARE develop a critical stance to advertise its services to those Americans who are at least cynical about, if not openly opposed to, America's so-called "War on Terror?" Would such a strategy be effective, or counterproductive? Beyond its potential effectiveness, this strategy poses an ethical dilemma for Jeff. Could such a strategy, while garnering more donations for CARE, possibly compromise American national security interests?

If Jeff decided it was a good idea, a new marketing strategy for CARE might be to ratchet up its criticism of the U.S. military in Afghanistan and elsewhere. And indeed, other humanitarian aid organizations seem to be taking this approach. Chief among them is Amnesty International (AI),[9] which frequently criticizes U.S. conduct in its annual *Amnesty International Report* and periodic memoranda.[10] AI has frequently criticized the United States over the years, and itself has absorbed criticism for what some have perceived as leftist, anti-U.S. political bias.

Regarding the war in Afghanistan, AI's 2002 *Report* states (among many other examples of criticism of the U.S.-led military efforts) that

> An unknown number of civilians were killed or had their homes or property destroyed during the U.S.-led bombing campaign which started in October. The U.S. and its allies may have breached the rules of war.

AI's efforts have not gone unnoticed in the NGO community, nor by the U.S. military itself, which frequently seems on the defensive regarding AI's charges and criticisms. For example, on November 30, 2001, Defense Secretary Donald Rumsfeld was asked in a press briefing,

> Could you respond to some of the concerns that have been raised by human rights groups? Amnesty International said . . . that they were concerned that the response of the opposition when the Taliban prisoners took over or overpowered their capturers at [the military prison at] Mazar-e-Sharif may not have been proportionate. What's your view of that?

Secretary Rumsfeld replied,

> Well, I wasn't there. . . . It's a—your question's too tough for me. I don't
> know what "proportionate" would be.

What could be better for attracting a "skeptical progressive" to an NGO
than this kind of publicity about alleged military abuses? And CARE certainly could produce its own stories about the U.S. military for potential
donors. But might this strategy, especially at a time of national security
crises, have secondary consequences for national security and military effectiveness? It is clear that NGOs and citizen activism in the past have pro-
foundly influenced issues such as the Vietnam War, turning public
opinion against the U.S. government, and hastening (if not provoking)
changes in policy. In Vietnam, for instance, the American Friends Service
Committee, a Quaker NGO, paired anti-war lobbying in the United States
with direct aid to Vietnam in a high-profile—and ultimately effective—
way. In the words of Benjamin Ferencz, Chief Prosecutor of the Nurem-
berg War Crimes Tribunal, "In the United States . . . civil society brought
the Vietnam War to an end. . . ."[11]

Some might worry about contributing to these effects—by adding
CARE's voice to a chorus of criticism that currently contains mostly
smaller NGOs such as AI, MSF, and Human Rights Watch—at a time of
such grave security crisis. Criticizing for fundraising purposes might be
opportunistic, or even unethical and dangerous. Indeed, it might play into
the so-called "CNN effect," in which public focus is directed to the most
difficult and unsavory aspects of war fighting, lowering the public's ap-
petite for these unhappy, but arguably necessary, parts of a military operation. Many argue, for example, that this effect led to truncated,
suboptimal operations in the Gulf War and Somalia.[12]

On the other hand, if the convictions of the "skeptical progressive" are
legitimate, might not CARE's critical stance be fundamentally ethical?

Jeff's personal suspicion is that national security concerns about
CARE's fundraising tactics are not well-founded. In his words, "CARE is
too small . . . I doubt that even if we could make it work that we could influence behavior and attitudes beyond giving."[13] Others are not so san-
guine, seeing at least the possibility that CARE and similar organizations
could have a subtle, but real, impact on public support—and thus national
security. Eric V. Larson, a Policy Analyst for the RAND Corporation who
is an expert in national security public opinion issues, details this possible link:

CARE and other NGOs tend to be good policy entrepreneurs; they routinely have access to congressional staffers, and are often asked to testify, and their views can provide support to members who are seeking policy change. They also are good media entrepreneurs, and regularly opine on issues of noncombatant casualties and collateral damage, essentially expressing a "zero tolerance" policy on the matter and thereby possibly influencing that class of viewers who largely will be swayed by emotional arguments of this kind. . . . They also are well-connected to their sponsors, many of whom are activists and happy to engage in fax, letter-writing, or email campaigns; thus, these organizations can mobilize supporters to provide evidence of grass roots support for their positions, and political leaders (and especially members of Congress) who also are entrepreneurs, always are looking for an issue that will gain them media attention.[14]

Bill Smullen, a retired Army Colonel and Chief of Staff to Secretary of State Colin Powell, agrees with Larson. He is in the unique position of having hands-on expertise in both the national security and nonprofit worlds, having served Powell in activities ranging from the Gulf War to America's Promise (a human development organization for underprivileged youth). In his words,

[CARE] can definitely influence public opinion against the U.S. military, which I would argue is committed to the same kind of nation building effort. [However, CARE] should be using its time and talent to convince that same constituency of potential donors in question that what they're doing as an NGO to influence things for the betterment of the people is worth supporting for the difference it is making in the life of the nation.[15]

Jeff has been in the advertising business long enough to know that such questions are best informed by more than opinions. Data are an invaluable tool in understanding markets. And it so happens he has data at his disposal on these issues.

Using the following data, Jeff seeks to probe three main issues:

- What impact might a fundraising stance that is critical of the U.S. military by a major humanitarian organization like CARE have on national security, if any at all?
- Is the fundraising/marketing strategy suggested here likely to be successful?

• What are the ethical issues he should take into account, from all sides?

DATA

Jeff is looking at several sources of data, not all of which necessarily illuminate the question of whether he should change CARE's political framing; some of it is just general data on public perceptions of how and where the government and NGOs are active overseas.

The first main data source is a poll performed by CARE itself. In an effort to understand the feelings and beliefs of potential donors, CARE sponsored a nationwide survey in March of 2002 on the role of America and its NGOs in the alleviation of global poverty.[16]

The poll began by asking the opinions of respondents regarding how much the U.S. government spends, and should spend, on foreign aid (see Table 11.1).

Note that the actual figure for 2002 is 1.1 percent of the Federal budget.[17] That is, while 1 percent of the population underestimates foreign aid, 77 percent overestimates it (while 13 percent has no opinion). With this in mind, consider the accompanying question: "Does the U.S. spend too much money, too little money, or about the right amount of money on foreign assistance?" The responses to this question were:

Too much: 41%

Too little: 16%

Just right: 32%

Don't know: 11%

Regarding the role of private NGOs, the CARE poll went on to ask where respondents felt the principal responsibility lies for foreign humanitarian aid. The answers were

Mainly governmental responsibility: 11%

Mainly responsibilities of NGOs and individuals: 12%

Responsibility that should be shared by both: 72%

Don't know: 5%

Finally, suggestive of the "skepticism" of potential donors, the poll asked for reactions to the statement, "Although poverty does not lead di-

Table 11.1
Percentage of the U.S. Federal Budget That Americans Believe Is
Spent on Foreign Aid

Percent of budget spent on foreign aid	Percent of respondents that believe it is this amount
0	1%
1–2%	9%
3–5%	13%
6–10%	15%
11–15%	8%
16–20%	11%
21–25%	5%
26–30%	7%
31–40%	6%
41–50%	6%
Over 50%	6%
Don't know	13%

rectly to terrorist activities, when governments fail to meet the most basic needs of their people, poor nations can become havens for terrorists." The reactions were:

Strongly agree: 47%
Somewhat agree: 33%
Somewhat disagree: 11%
Strongly disagree: 6%
Don't know: 3%

The CARE poll results can be further contextualized by a July 2002 poll undertaken by the Program on International Policy Attitudes (PIPA) at the University of Maryland.[18] PIPA asked a random sample of 1,352 Americans questions about defense spending priorities. Several results are salient. First, when asked whether the United States spent too much on defense, too little, or about the right amount (compared to the FY2002 level of $331 billion), the responses were:

Too much: 24%

About right: 52%

Too little: 24%

More telling than this, though, was a comparison between the actual ratio of spending on defense versus foreign aid to that favored by respondents. Currently, the ratio is 11.5:1; respondents favored a ratio of just 3:1.

Another data source that Jeff is considering is the General Social Survey (GSS). The GSS has been administered approximately semiannually since 1972 to a random sample of about 3,000 Americans, and asks a wide variety of social, political, and demographic questions. In 1996, the GSS featured a battery of questions on charitable giving, as well as attitudes about different institutions, including the U.S. military.[19]

Two questions from 1996 are of primary interest (Table 11.2).[20]

1. "Would you say you have a great deal of confidence, only some confidence, or hardly any confidence at all in the military?"
2. "Did you or a member of your family make a charitable contribution of time or money to foreign/international cause in the past year?"

In other words, the small percentage of the population that gives to causes like CARE are more than twice as likely to express little or no confidence in the U.S. military. This proportion, however, is still only about 23 percent of givers.

It may be that the perceived pattern—low confidence in the military predicts a lot of giving to international relief charities—conflates the effects of other, related forces, such as age, education, or political views (which are also germane to the question at hand). The GSS data can be employed more intensively with the aid of binary regression analysis.[21] This technique allows one to separate out the individual impacts of different variables.

When the effects on giving of age, gender, marital status, education, race, political views, and confidence in the military are considered simultaneously, most of the variables have no measured impact on charitable giving. However, the following two results appear:

Table 11.2
GSS Data on Charity and Confidence in the U.S. Military

Characteristic	Percentage of population
Little or no confidence in the military	11.4%
Contributed to foreign/international charitable cause	4.1%
Contributors to foreign charitable causes with little or no confidence in the military	23.1%

Note: Sample size=2,904 respondents.

1. One extra year of education (by itself) pushes up the average probability of giving by a little less than a point, to about 5 percent. An extra four years of education pushes up the average probability of giving to about 8 percent.
2. Expressing "no confidence" in the military (by itself) pushes up the probability of giving by over four points, to about 8.5 percent.

In other words, lack of confidence does appear to have a strong, independent relationship with giving. While this analysis does not establish a *causal* relationship between low confidence and giving, it does establish a link between people with these characteristics, independent of other variables. And this suggests that the "low confidence" group may be a natural fundraising constituency. Whether fundraising with a skeptical progressive message could actually compromise people's confidence in the military is not clear.

Finally, Jeff is looking at a nonprofit marketing report based on a survey on charitable giving motives conducted in the Atlanta area in 2000.[22] Approximately 2,000 people were randomly interviewed about their charitable giving in the prior year, particularly focusing on humanitarian relief. The data were compiled and analyzed, and yielded Table 11.3, which matches stated reasons for giving with particular demographic groups that were especially likely to give for each reason.[23]

These data tell us which fundraising strategies are likely to be most effective for different groups. These groups include people in high and low

Table 11.3
Reasons for Giving Charitably: 2000 Atlanta Survey[24]

Demographic	Community[1]	Effectiveness[2]	Duty[3]	Tax[4]	Religious[5]
High Income				X	
Low Income			X		
Younger				X	
Practicing Faith			X		X
Married				X	
Single					
Nonwhite		X	X		
Women		X	X	X	X
Conservative		X			
Volunteer	X	X	X		X

Reasons for giving: 1. Giving is important for a community. 2. Charities are more effective than governments at what they do. 3. Giving is my duty. 4. Giving provides tax benefits. 5. It is my religious obligation to give.

income categories, younger people, those that practice their religious faith, married people, single people, nonwhites, women, self-described political conservatives, and those that volunteer their time to charities.

Note that beyond information on how a CARE fundraising campaign might be targeted, Table 11.3 also provides clues on constituencies that might be influenced politically by fundraising messages. For example, if a message takes a form such as favorably comparing CARE in its nation-building efforts with those of the U.S. military, we might see certain demographic segments—specifically, those that tend to be swayed by "effectiveness" arguments—impacted in their attitudes toward American military forces.

JEFF'S REACTION

Initially, Jeff is discouraged by these data about the prospect of adopting a politically confrontational focus in CARE's fundraising. This is due mostly to what he considers a weak connection between lack of confidence in the military and giving to groups like CARE. In his words,

> The group that shows a correlation between lack of confidence in the military and probability of giving to international causes is small. [Furthermore,] if you're going to be oppositional, you have to be dramatically so . . . to totally demonize the enemy—otherwise, it's boring. I think demonizing the military would seriously turn off all except a minority of progressives. "Lack of confidence" is a long way from seeing them as the enemy.

However, he notes,

> I could easily imagine a situation where I or somebody would take these data and draw the conclusion that an oppositional anti-military message was the right way to go . . . In that case, I'd test the message in direct mail, limited quantities, and see what happens.

In the matter of ethics and the effects on national security, Jeff remains unconvinced that a confrontational fundraising would have any effect whatsoever. However, he is open to differences of opinion, and seeks guidance on these issues.

APPENDIX 11.1: CARE ORGANIZATIONAL PROFILE

CARE Mission Statement[25]

CARE's mission is to serve individuals and families in the poorest communities in the world. Drawing strength from our global diversity, resources and experience, we promote innovative solutions and are advocates for global responsibility. We facilitate lasting change by:

- Strengthening capacity for self-help;
- Providing economic opportunity;
- Delivering relief in emergencies;

- Influencing policy decisions at all levels;
- Addressing discrimination in all its forms.

Guided by the aspirations of local communities, we pursue our mission with both excellence and compassion because the people whom we serve deserve nothing less.

CARE describes its history as follows:

CARE is one of the world's largest private humanitarian organizations. Headquartered in Atlanta, Georgia, we're part of an international confederation of 11 member organizations committed to helping communities in the developing world achieve lasting victories over poverty.

The scope of our mission has changed considerably since our founding in 1945, when 22 American organizations came together to rush life-saving CARE Packages to survivors of World War II. Thousands of Americans, including President Harry S. Truman contributed to the effort. On May 11, 1946, the first 20,000 packages reached the battered port of Le Havre, France. Some 100 million more CARE Packages reached people in need during the next two decades, first in Europe and later in Asia and other parts of the developing world.

Over the years, our work has expanded as we've addressed the world's most threatening problems. In the 1950s, we expanded into emerging nations and used U.S. surplus food to feed the hungry. In the 1960s, we pioneered primary health care programs. In the 1970s, CARE responded to massive famines in Africa with both emergency relief and long-term agroforestry projects, integrating environmentally sound tree- and land-management practices with farming programs.

Today, our staff of more than 12,000—most of whom are citizens of the countries where we work—help strengthen communities through an array of programs that work to create lasting solutions to root causes of poverty.[26]

CARE's 2001 finances arc summarized in Table 11.4.[27]

APPENDIX 11.2: REGRESSION PROCEDURES

The empirical model used with the GSS data is $y_i = X_i \beta + \epsilon_i$, where

Table 11.4
CARE's 2002 Revenues and Expenses

Revenues		Expenses	
Type	Amount	Type	Amount
Contributions	$127,938,000	Program services	$379,596,000
Government grants	$287,146,000	Administration	$20,965,000
Investments	$7,020,000	Fundraising	$18,112,000
Special events	−$128,000	Other	$3,623,000
Other	$1,292,000		
Total	$423,268,000	Total	$422,296,000

$y_i=1$ if the respondent answers affirmatively to the question of whether he or she gave to international relief charities (and 0 otherwise), X_i is the vector of demographics, and ϵ_i is a random disturbance. This equation was estimated using a logit specification. The marginal impact of each regressor on the probability of giving is defined as $\hat{p}_k = [1 + \exp\{- (\theta + \beta_k)\}]^{-1}$, where $\hat{p}_k$ is the expected probability of a "yes" response, β_k is the regression coefficient on variable k, and hence its marginal impact on $\hat{p}_k$, and θ is the log-odds that $y=1$ for the "average" respondent. θ can be estimated as $\theta = \ln(\bar{p}/1 - \bar{p})$, where $\bar{p}$ is the population proportion for which $y=1$. For charitable giving, $\bar{p} = .041$. The effect on the expected probability owing to a marginal increase in variable k (0 to 1 in the case of the dummy variables; a one-unit increase for the continuous variables) is defined as $\hat{p}_k - \bar{p}$.

The Atlanta survey data allowed respondents to answer affirmatively to as many reasons for giving as they wanted. Each response was coded binarily, similar to the GSS model. Individual probit regressions $y_{ij} = X_{ij}\beta + \epsilon_{ij}$ were run on each motive j for giving. Then, each strategy in Table 11.3 was constructed according to the statistically significant variables in each equation.

Notes

Author's Note: For their cooperation and helpful suggestions, the author is grateful to Jeff Brooks, Eric Larson, Bill Smullen, Andy Pew, Frederic Fournier, Volker Franke, and three anonymous referees.

1. See http://www.thedomaingroup.com.

2. This information comes from CARE's IRS Form 990 tax returns, available at http://www.guidestar.org. For a full organizational profile, see Appendix 11.1.

3. See http://www.careusa.org.

4. This information comes from interviews with the author.

5. See http://www.msf.org.

6. This comes from an MSF press release on December 5, 2001 entitled "MSF Calls Upon Warring Parties to Spare Afghan Civilians: Many Civilian Casualties From Bombing of Tora Bora." See http://www.doctorswithoutborders.org.

7. This information has been altered slightly from the original material for proprietary reasons.

8. See http://www.careusa.org.

9. Started in 1961, AI defines itself as "a worldwide campaigning movement that works to promote all the human rights enshrined in the [United Nations] Universal Declaration of Human Rights and other international standards." AI seeks to "free all prisoners of conscience; ensure fair and prompt trials for political prisoners; abolish the death penalty, torture and other cruel treatment of prisoners; end political killings and 'disappearances'; and oppose human rights abuses by opposition groups." AI is active in more than 100 countries, where it meets victims of human rights violations, observes trials, and prepares international "report cards" on the human rights records of various countries.

10. Amnesty International, *Amnesty International Report* (London: Amnesty International Publications, 2002).

11. See http://www.commongroundradio.org/transcpt/98/9840.html.

12. See Richard Sobel, *The Impact of Public Opinion on U.S. Foreign Policy since Vietnam* (New York: Oxford University Press, 2001).

13. This quote comes from interviews with the author.

14. This quote comes from interviews with the author.

15. This quote comes from interviews with the author.

16. This poll was administered by Peter D. Hart Research Associates. See http://www.hartresearch.com/.

17. This figure comes from the Office of Management and Budget, 2002. See http://www.whitehouse.gov/omb/budget.

18. See http://www.pipa.org/OnlineReports/DefenseSpending/contents.htm.

19. See James Allen Davis, Tom W. Smith, and Peter V. Marsden, *General Social Surveys, 1972–1998: Cumulative CodeBook* (Chicago: National Opinion Research Center, 1999).

20. The wording of these questions is slightly paraphrased here. The contri-

butions question combines separate questions about giving and volunteering for these charities.

21. See Appendix 11.2 for technical details.

22. See David M. Van Slyke and Arthur C. Brooks. *Philanthropy Patterns in Metro Atlanta* (Atlanta: Research Atlanta, 2001).

23. See Appendix 11.2 for technical details.

24. This table is adapted from David M. Van Slyke and Arthur C. Brooks, "Why Do People Give? New Evidence and Strategies for Nonprofit Managers" (Syracuse, NY: Maxwell School of Public Affairs, Working Paper, 2002).

25. See http://www.careusa.org.

26. Ibid.

27. These data were taken from CARE's 2001 990 IRS tax form, which is available at http://www.guidestar.org.

Security and Salvation: Bringing Russia Aboard the Space Station

W. HENRY LAMBRIGHT

As the Clinton administration took power in January and February 1993, national security officials became aware that the Russians were about to transfer rocket technology to India. It was a move fraught with missile proliferation peril. It appeared that the United States might well have to impose severe trade sanctions to head off or punish Russia for the action.

However, the new administration was also acutely conscious that the political situation in Russia was highly volatile and uncertain. Only recently, the Soviet Union had fallen and been replaced in part by a very shaky Russian regime. The Russian President, Boris Yeltsin, was seen by the United States as preferable to any likely alternative. President Clinton wanted to strengthen Yeltsin, not weaken him, and not start off their personal relationship with an affront. What could be done, he wanted to know, to change Russian behavior through positive incentives?

The answer that ultimately came involved the decision to bring Russia aboard the Space Station. This decision, made over the course of 1993, marked a turning point of historic significance for space policy. The Space Station was born in Cold War rivalry. Now it would be reoriented to symbolize post–Cold War cooperation. In both cases, the Space Station linked space and foreign policy, "big science," and geopolitics. However, the foreign policy and geopolitical dynamics to which it was linked had changed enormously in but a few years. So had the Space Station. Originally expected to cost $8 billion, exclusive of launching costs, and be completed in a decade, the Space Station program was initiated by President Ronald Reagan in 1984.[1] In 1988, NASA enlisted Europe, Canada, and Japan as partners, and the station received a name, "Freedom." Freedom, however, burgeoned by billions in cost, forcing a redesign to save money. Under

President Clinton, the Freedom design was abandoned in favor of yet another configuration, called "Alpha," which was subsequently integrated with Russian components when Russia became a partner in the program. The Russian decision "securitized" the Space Station, linking it with post–Cold War foreign policy, as well as aiding NASA at a critical moment to gain funding to keep the program alive.

The largest single international science and technology project in history, the football-field-length Space Station embodies national and international interests. It illustrates the tension between U.S. control of a program and deference to other sovereign nations and their claims. Critics regard the decision to partner with Russia as a Faustian bargain. However, had the decision not been made, the program might well have died in 1993. Linking the Space Station with foreign policy was a matter of salvation.

The Russian decision is, therefore, as problematic as it is significant. While observers may regard it as "good" or "bad," it is a decision everyone agrees was pivotal. Perhaps more than any other single decision in the 1990s, the choice to bring Russians aboard the Space Station symbolizes change in U.S./Russian relations and exemplifies globalization politics where domestic and international issues are closely coupled.

To understand the decision, it is necessary to retrace the steps leading to it, which went back years. Also, it is necessary to see the interplay of various actors—NASA, Russia, the White House, Congress, other nations, and many others. Along the way, concepts of space policy changed, as did views of national security and arms control. Where they converged was in a technological project of vast scale, expense, and controversy. The Space Station is as much an assemblage of political interests as a construction of hardware.

BIRTH OF THE SPACE STATION

After the United States landed a man on the moon in 1969, and the great space race between America and the USSR was won, the question arose for both superpowers, "What next?" In neither country were political conditions remotely ripe for an assault on Mars. In both countries, post-lunar planning led to the conviction that the next major space venture would be an Earth-orbiting facility, a space station, that could have multiple uses. In the United States, however, President Richard Nixon decided that first the United States should build a shuttle, a reusable rocket spaceship, that would provide reliable and relatively inexpensive flight to and from near-Earth orbit. The Soviet Union decided to go first with a Space Station, using expendable rockets as means for access.

In 1971, the USSR launched its initial Space Station, a small facility called "Salyut." Two years later, the United States launched its version, Skylab, making use of Apollo hardware. Skylab was a one-time venture, however, and was abandoned in 1975. In that year, in a moment of warming relations between the United States and USSR, there was a conscious effort to use space to demonstrate that cooperation was possible. In the Apollo-Soyuz Test Project, the U.S. and USSR sent into orbit space equipment that achieved rendezvous, docking and interchange of astronauts.

After Apollo-Soyuz, America focused its energies on the Space Shuttle, while the Soviet Union did the same on Space Stations. As one Salyut ran its course, the USSR launched another—not all of the Salyuts succeeded in reaching orbit. Although not continuously occupied, the Soviet Space Station was used by humans for increasingly long periods.

In 1982, the Space Shuttle was declared operational and NASA lobbied the president for the "next logical step." In 1984, President Reagan agreed, and declared in his State of the Union address that the United States would develop a permanently occupied Space Station within a decade and invite allies to participate in the project.[2] NASA predicted the Space Station would cost $8 billion to construct, not counting Shuttle launch costs. The station would be a huge outpost with separate experiment platforms and a hangar to build other spacecraft. The crew would number about six.

Under Reagan, the relations between the U.S. and USSR again became competitive. Reagan spoke of the Soviet Union as "the Evil Empire." The Space Station was hailed as a demonstration of U.S. national prowess, and there was some thought that the Department of Defense could be a potential user.

In 1986, the USSR launched Mir, a Space Station that marked an improvement over the Salyuts. In the same year, NASA found problems with its initial design and made adjustments. A year later, NASA changed the design again, in part because of congressional budget actions. In 1988, the United States reached agreement with Europe, Canada, and Japan that they become partners and contribute various components to a common enterprise. The United States and international partners named the station "Freedom." It was designed to be larger and more technically advanced than the Russian Mir.

THE FALL OF THE SOVIET UNION

In 1985, Mikhail Gorbachev came to power in the Soviet Union. He soon proclaimed that the USSR had to reshape its economy and reduce rigidity in the Soviet system of government and economics. He stressed a greater "openness" internally, and sought better relations with the United States. Concerned about Reagan's Strategic Defense Initiative ("Star Wars") space-based missile defense, Gorbachev proposed that instead of spending on defense-based missiles, the USSR and United States engage in a long-term peaceful effort in space—with the goal being an unmanned and eventually a manned trip to Mars. While Reagan held to his Strategic Defense Initiative, he did agree to have the United States begin exploring with the USSR, at the technical level, cooperative ventures in space.[3]

In January 1989, George Bush succeeded Reagan. Bush, like Reagan, saw space as an instrument of U.S. leadership in the world. He established an interagency National Space Council and placed Vice President Dan Quayle at its helm. In July, on the twentieth anniversary of the Apollo moon landing, Bush sought to give a long-term direction to NASA by proclaiming the goal of a return to the moon and later trip to Mars. However, he did not give any timetable and NASA came up with a reported cost figure of half a trillion dollars for what was called the Space Exploration Initiative. The Bush decision had little commitment or constituency behind it. Not even NASA, still recovering from the *Challenger* disaster of 1986 and burdened with budget realities of the Space Station, seemed behind it.[4]

Meanwhile, Gorbachev had his own problems as he struggled to keep his empire together. In November, the Berlin Wall came down and Germany moved toward the reunification. Bush now saw space as a way to cooperate with the Soviet Union, bolster Gorbachev, and help the Soviet leader steer the USSR in a peaceful direction.

Any thoughts of cooperation on a grand scale were quickly dashed by Bush's domestic economic and political woes. The budget deficit inherited from Reagan was soaring, causing Bush and Congress in 1990 to reach an agreement to place strong controls on virtually all expenditures, space included. Congress was especially alarmed with reports that the Space Station would cost $38 billion. This latter figure, unlike the first, included launches. Launches, thanks to *Challenger*, were now seen as significant cost and risk elements of the program, no longer a virtual "given."

Bush, meanwhile, stressed the positive in his dealings with Gorbachev. In 1990, he agreed to enter into an "exploratory dialogue" with the USSR on joint ventures in space. In late July 1991, after a long period of planning and lower-level contacts, Bush and Gorbachev met at a Moscow summit. Gorbachev wanted to move fast, boldly in space cooperation. Bush took a more cautious approach. On July 31, the two leaders signed an accord that would lead to flights by Americans aboard the Soviet Space Station Mir, and by Soviet cosmonauts on the U.S. Shuttle. A Bush aide said that space was now being handled "more like arms control."[5]

Just a few weeks later, Soviet recalcitrants seized Gorbachev and attempted to overthrow the Soviet leader and reverse his reforms. Within days, the coup failed. However, Gorbachev was left weakened politically. In December, various Russian republics seceded, and the USSR quickly unraveled. Gorbachev resigned, the USSR ceased to exist, and Boris Yeltsin, President of Russia, emerged as the principal leader within a new Commonwealth of Independent States—open to all states of the former Soviet Union. The United States watched from the sidelines as the extraordinary events progressed; it put all agreements with the former Soviet Union on hold, including those relating to space.[6]

REVIVING SPACE COOPERATION

In the wake of the Soviet Union's fall, a debate ensued within the Bush administration. One faction believed the United States should aid Russia and the other republics, lest their technology (and scientists and engineers) move to new nations that were possible threats to the United States. Others saw no reason to prop up the military industrial complex of Russia and other successor states. In March 1992, Bush indicated he stood with those favoring assisting the former enemy. Among other actions, this meant restarting the stalled discussions on space cooperation.[7]

In Russia, Yeltsin established a new, civilian Russian Space Agency (RSA), under Yuri Koptev. In the United States, NASA also underwent change at this time. The NASA Administrator, Richard Truly, was asked to step down by President Bush. In his place, Bush appointed a little-known TRW executive from California, Daniel Goldin. Koptev and Goldin, both middle-aged men, had been cold warriors their entire professional careers. Their work had been largely in military-oriented space. Now they were expected to forge a civilian partnership, the nature and extent of which were highly uncertain.

In June 1992, Yeltsin came to Washington and met with President Bush. They agreed to the same plan Gorbachev and Bush had reached in 1991, namely, Americans and Russians would fly aboard one another's space-craft. In addition, they agreed to study how Russian technology might be incorporated into the Space Station. It was now up to Goldin and Koptev to implement this agreement. "Mr. Koptev and I have spent our lives building weapons of war," said Goldin. "Now we will beat our swords into plowshares in order to explore space together."[8]

U.S. strategy was to build mutual confidence on the part of the two space powers by a series of progressively more intensive collaborative projects. In November, the United States and Russia signed pacts relating to joint space flights. There would be some U.S. funds provided Russia so that the United States could learn more about Mir technology. Goldin wanted to go beyond astronaut exchange to a docking between Shuttle and Mir. Goldin, however, dismissed journalists' suggestions that a next step beyond that would be merging the two nations' space stations.[9] He wanted to move forward, but did not believe it was possible to go that fast.

LINKING SPACE TO NATIONAL SECURITY

When Bill Clinton became president in January 1993, the world was different. For almost fifty years, competition with the USSR had driven the United States, and, to a lesser extent, its allies. The space program was born and nurtured by the competition. The Space Station was part of this pattern. Now, Cold War competition was removed as a justification. Why spend billions on space, especially a manned space program? Opponents of space spending became more vocal and influential, not only in the United States but also in Europe, Russia, and elsewhere.

Bill Clinton had not thought much about space and foreign policy prior to becoming president. His interest as he came into office was the econ-omy and cutting the deficit. However, his vice president, Al Gore, had ex-perience, as a senator, in space policy. While he was a proponent of NASA, he served in a secondary position and at a point in history when space was declining in national prominence.[10] What would be a justification for multi-billion dollar space expenditures now that USSR rivalry was re-moved? Would exploration for science's sake be enough? Could coopera-tion, as a process initiated by Bush, replace conflict as a spur to action?

These questions came to a head in early 1993, as space and post–Cold War national security became linked as issues. The initial trigger for linkage was the necessity for the United States to act to try to prevent the transfer of a technology that the U.S. regarded as being dangerous for America and the world. The Russia-India "rocket deal" was the issue, and it had been festering since 1992, when Bush was president.

Desperate in the wake of economic collapse, Russia was looking to sell its Cold War developed technology to the highest bidder. In 1992, the Bush administration became cognizant of a contract signed between Glavkosmos, a Russian space trading company, and the Indian Space Research Organization (ISRO). The Russians planned to sell two rocket engines using cryogenic (extremely cold) fuel and also, more significantly, the technology needed for India to manufacture subsequent engines. Bush national security officials pointed out that knowledge about the engines could enable India to mount nuclear warheads on intercontinental missiles. If India did that, Pakistan would do the same. Moreover, such a transfer of technology would be in violation of the Missile Technology Control Regime, an international arrangement recently established whose aim was to prevent proliferation of missile technology. The United States objected to the proposed technology transfer. Russia and India denied the rocket engines would be used for weapons purposes. The United States pressured Glavkosmos and ISRO to get them to step back from the exchange.[11]

In the first month of the Clinton administration, White House officials realized that the Russians were continuing with their plans for the rocket technology transfer and the United States might have to go beyond the Bush administration in decisions about sanctions. Clinton was not disposed to start his relation with Russia and especially Yeltsin with a negative policy. The new administration, which included some national security staff held over from the Bush years, was extremely wary of making Yeltsin's job any more difficult than it already was. They saw him as the best hope the United States had for a leader with a reformist bent. He was in conflict with Russian hardliners who opposed cooperation with the U.S. and who were anxious to make deals with nations and groups the United States regarded as dangerous to its interests.

The president was anxious to know what could be done, via positive incentives, to turn Russia around. There was talk of "strategic partnerships" and an "alliance for reform"—finding ways to merge Russian and U.S. interests over the long haul to achieve positive change in Russia. What could be done? Clinton planned to meet Yeltsin at their first summit, in Vancouver, Canada, in April. He needed something to offer the Soviet president to cause him to change course in policy.

In February and March, staff from the National Security Council, Vice

President's Office, Office of Science and Technology Policy, and various agencies and departments began meeting to put together a list of options. The group was called the "skunk works" team, according to one of its key members, Rose Gottemoeller, a Russian specialist on the NSC staff. The leader of the group was Vice President Gore's national security aide, Leon Fuerth. He cited the Indian arrangement as the Clinton administration's "first test" in halting proliferation from Russia. Unsatisfied with the skunk works team's initial list of "positive incentives," he pushed the group to think more expansively. "We need something big," he said. If Clinton was to get what he wanted, he would have to have something Yeltsin would very much like.[12]

While this activity in the national security field was underway, the Space Station policy question was also rising to presidential level with a new sense of urgency through a domestic policy stream. As Clinton took office, NASA announced the Space Station costs were going to grow by another $1 billion beyond the last estimate. The Space Station had already cost $9 to $11 billion since 1984, depending on what was included in the estimate, but no hardware was yet in space. Redesigned many times along the way, by 1992 the Space Station was projected to be $30 billion to develop, launch, and assemble. Now, the cost was going up again—this at a time when Clinton was determined to cut federal spending to cope with the budget deficit.

In February, Goldin, who was retained as NASA administrator by Clinton, was called to the White House where OMB Director Leon Panetta, a long-time Space Station foe in his previous stint as a congressman, warned that the project might have to be killed in the interest of deficit reduction.[13] Goldin argued for a substantial redesign/cutback as an alternative to termination. Shortly thereafter, Clinton ordered Goldin to come up with three options for redesign that could cut the Space Station from the now projected $31 billion to approximately half that amount. He wanted these by June 1, when the administration would defend its space budget before Congress. Clinton also appointed an independent advisory committee, headed by MIT President Charles Vest, to review the NASA proposal. He directed that the international partners be involved in the redesign process.[14]

What was happening in the United States was mirrored in Russia, only much more so. The new Russian government faced an economic nightmare. Virtually everything was being drastically cut, including space. Plans for a Russian space shuttle, along with further development and use of a huge rocket, equivalent to the Saturn V moon rocket, were shelved. The major program on the Russian drawing board, Mir 2, was also in jeopardy. Koptev, the Russian Space Agency head, was faced with how to keep the Russian space program alive. When he heard that Goldin faced a similar dilemma, at least in regard to the Space Station, he had an idea.

In March, Koptev came to Washington. Sitting in Goldin's office, he asked, "Dan, what if we were to join you in an international space station?" Goldin was initially flabbergasted. "I'll never forget when Yuri dropped the bomb that day," Goldin recalled. But Goldin could quickly see how the Russians could help him. "I was worried we had no experience dealing with [a] station whatsoever—none. We had no major experience in logistics. We knew nothing about the hazards. For Apollo, we had Mercury and Gemini [to learn from]. For a space station, which is more complicated, we had nothing." The Russians, on the other hand, had been building space stations for years. Encouraged by Goldin, Koptev soon followed up the meeting with a formal proposal to the NASA administrator for a merged program. In a letter faxed March 16 by Koptev and his associate, Yuri Semenov, the Russians said, "Billions of dollars could be saved if the Russians and Americans could merge their space station efforts."[15]

Goldin was positive and saw the Russian connection as a selling point for the Space Station, but many in the White House were wary. The international partners—Europe,[16] Canada, and Japan—were already testy because of the redesign ordered by Clinton, and were initially quite negative. Having already invested billions, they saw themselves being marginalized in a US-Russia Space Station and went along with consideration of Russian inclusion only under U.S. pressure. "The (Russians) just want money," one partner official said. Partners also cited, "thorny technical and managerial questions that politicians may not appreciate, especially the reliability and quality of Russian equipment."[17] However, strong backing to explore the Russian option now came from Clinton's National Security Advisor, Anthony Lake.

Lake had cognizance over the nettlesome issue of rocket-technology transfer to India. He was a recipient of the various ideas coming out of the skunk works group concerning positive incentives and the Indian rocket transfer. Fuerth recalled the administration wishing to create a partnership among equals, one of whom was in trouble, with the partnership resulting in an "exchange of equal value" to both countries. These ideas for partnership included the Space Station and, by happenstance, the Russians had now made an overture via NASA for a space station merger. Here,

Lake thought, was an opening to advance administration policy and leverage change in Russia.[18]

DECIDING TO MOVE FORWARD: THE
VANCOUVER SUMMIT

In April, Clinton and Yeltsin met in Vancouver. Prior to leaving for the
meeting, Clinton said he wanted to develop "a strategic alliance with Russian reform." At their private meeting, they discussed canceling the India
rocket transfer in exchange for Space Station participation, and also giving Russia an opportunity at the American satellite market. It was reported
that Yeltsin had broached the possibility the United States would com-
pensate Russia for funds it would forego by canceling the rocket technology transfer to India. The U.S. position was that the Space Station
cooperation and potential access to U.S. and global commercial launch
market should be sufficient incentives.[19] In his remarks at the close of the
summit, Yeltsin declared, in regard to space, "we decided to cooperate . . .
and decided to join forces, the U.S. and Russian administrations," and that
President Clinton had stressed that this was "in support of Russian reforms, a part of the strategic form of cooperation between us."[20]

The comment by Yeltsin, highlighted by the media, provided considerable momentum behind a decision to bring Russia aboard the Space Station. However, it was far from a finished decision. There were many
hurdles along the way, cosmetically and internationally. Clinton had made
a suggestion, not a formal proposal, and it was linked to the rocket technology issue. What Clinton's national security staff wanted was to keep
the process moving forward.[21] Strobe Talbott, Special Advisor to the Secretary of State for Russian Affairs, was anxious the Russian bureaucracy
be engaged in the process. An outcome of the summit was the decision to
establish a "United States-Russian Commission on Technological Cooperation in the areas of Energy and Space." It was to be headed by Gore
and Russian Prime Minister Viktor Chernomyrdin. Various skunk works
staff now became staff to the Gore-Chernomyrdin Commission.

IMPLEMENTING REDESIGN

Just how would the possible Russian connection influence the redesign of the Space Station? A great deal, if Goldin had his way. Goldin

saw the Russian connection as a plus, technically and politically, in saving the Space Station. For Goldin, the Space Station was key to NASA's future. Without the Space Station as destination, why have a shuttle? If manned space went down, why have a NASA? With stakes so high, the NASA administrator worked feverishly, day in and day out, with the single-minded objective of meeting the president's demand for a design that was less expensive. He also thought about how to involve the Russians.

The President's Science Advisor, Jack Gibbons, gave legitimacy to the Russian involvement, telling Goldin after the Summit that he should give "full consideration" to the possible use of Russian technology and expertise as NASA considered alternative ways of redesigning the Space Station. In early April, Goldin provided funds to pay for fifteen leading Russian space experts to join his NASA team as "consultants."

A critical decision in the redesign process involved the seemingly esoteric issue of the station's angle of inclination to the equator. The existing orbital inclination planned was 28.5 degrees. The Russians used an orbit of 51.6 degrees for technical reasons related to planetary geometry and their location. For the Russians to change to the U.S. orbit was extremely difficult—almost impossible, Koptev told Goldin. He warned his NASA counterpart that the two nations "would be doomed to fly separately" if NASA would not go along with Russian requirements. Goldin told his redesign team (50 technical experts) to "shoot for 51.6. If you can't get it, tell us the best you can do."[22]

Goldin seemed to be proceeding as if the Russian connection was a fait accompli. It was certainly getting favorable media attention. The *New York Times* editorialized, "A Russian Bear Hug in Space."[23] Not so fast, said the critics, who observed with alarm the euphoria. Resistance surfaced within NASA (particularly among those human space flight officials close to the existing design), among several lawmakers skeptical of Russian intentions, and among the international partners. Changing to the 51.6 orbit might be good for the Russians, but, it was pointed out, it had negative features. The Shuttle, for example, could lose one-third its payload capacity. Either the Shuttle would have to fly more trips (which added cost and risk) or the payloads (including those of the international partners) would require redesign. In the White House and State Department, even among supporters, there was concern about moving too fast, lest the United States lose bargaining leverage on the rocket technology dispute.

Goldin sought to bring internal NASA resistors aboard—or remove them. He also contacted the partners, who felt neglected, trying to win their support. Meanwhile, Gibbons felt he had to recapture control of the process for the White House. He wrote Goldin that the White House had made no policy decision to focus the Space Station redesign effort around present or future Russian capabilities. "Especially," he declared, "NASA should not limit its redesign options to those compatible with the orbit of the Russian Space Station."[24] Goldin defended himself as an "honest broker." There was "no hidden agenda," he declared.[25]

CLINTON DECIDES

Whatever the United States might want to do with the Russians depended on domestic political decisions, starting—but not ending—with the president.

On June 7, the NASA redesign team reported its findings to the Vest Committee. Clinton had originally set guidelines for three options from which he would choose at $5 billion, $7 billion, and $9 billion over a 5-year period, but NASA estimates ran $11.9 billion for the least expensive option and $13.3 billion for the other two.

On June 10, the Vest Committee declared the three options proposed by NASA were all viable, although none could meet the cost guidelines. Nevertheless, they all would be less expensive than the existing design. It said two options were preferable to the third, which the international partners opposed as making too little use of their equipment.

The NASA options did not explicitly mention Russian participation. The Vest panel, however, declared that "several considerations of safety, flexibility, and redundancy of launch and assured crew return vehicles argue strongly for launching the station at an orbital inclination that allows access by as many spacefaring nations as possible." The panel noted that "an inclination of 51.6 degrees would achieve this and would enable Russian participation thereby potentially reducing costs and enhancing international cooperation."[26]

The president accepted the report and on June 17 announced he would go with a slight variation of one of the Vest-recommended options ("A") that maximized international partner participation and also used substantial hardware planned for Freedom, the existing design. This was the first time Clinton had publicly committed to going ahead with the Space Station, a fact that made all the international discussions with Russia up to this point extremely tentative and contingent. The cost of "Alpha," as the station was now called, was estimated at $10.5 billion over the next five years. The president said nothing about the Russians or the orbital inclination matters in his decision.[27]

"THE HINGE POINT OF NASA'S FUTURE"

Meanwhile, subsequent to the Vancouver Summit, U.S. and Russian negotiators had been discussing the Indian rocket deal—to no avail. On June 10, in an effort to get Yeltsin to change his stance, Clinton and Gore wrote the Russian president, threatening to institute sanctions against Russia that would cost his country potential access to U.S. space markets unless Yeltsin stopped the India rocket arrangement, that was about to proceed. They set a deadline of July 15 for Russian action.[28] Chernomyrdin was scheduled to visit Washington in June for the first meeting of the Gore-Chernomyrdin Commission. The ultimatum caused him to abruptly cancel his visit.

The Clinton administration was using the Space Station as a bargaining chip with the Russians, but there was some question whether the chip would be removed by domestic politics. Clinton was being criticized vehemently by Congress for his handling of the Space Station. A number of long-term Space Station supporters in Congress said they had been "betrayed" by the Clinton administration. They were extremely skeptical that the redesign process would produce a viable Space Station. Many were against involving the Russians. One of the skeptical lawmakers was George Brown, a democratic representative from California, head of the House Science Committee, and the man who had to lead the fight for the Space Station in the House.

Moreover, the makeup of Congress, especially the House, was quite different from what it had been under Bush, with many newcomers unfamiliar with the Space Station. There was a fierce competition for funds at this time and most political pressures were to cut the budget and narrow the deficit. Congress was looking to make a budget-cutting statement and the Space Station was a huge target. Because Clinton had delayed making a commitment to the Space Station so long, NASA and the White House had not mounted an effective campaign on its behalf. Brown gave the Space Station only a slightly better than even chance of surviving. His own support, he made clear, had depended on Clinton's holding relatively closely to the original design.

As the decision process moved to Congress, long-time space analyst

John Logsdon declared, "This is really the hinge point of NASA's future. The overall future of the United States in space is at stake."[29] On June 23, the vote came in the House to continue or terminate the Space Station. The debate was exceptionally intense, with the Space Station cited by opponents as a glaring example of profligate spending. Liberal Democrats and conservative Republicans aligned against the station. Defenders pointed to the Space Station's critical importance for jobs and shoring up America's beleaguered aerospace industry. The Russian issue played little role in the debate as it was still speculative at this point. The program survived, 216–215.[30]

On June 24, Gibbons told Goldin to prepare a plan to implement the president's decision to be delivered to the White House by September.[31] The president's decision had not assumed a Russian connection, but had not precluded it either.

BREAKING THE IMPASSE WITH RUSSIA

While Goldin and others had fought to save the Space Station with Congress, the president's national security aides had worked the diplomatic front with Russia. At the end of June, Lynn Davis, Undersecretary of State; Fuerth, and Talbott, all went to Moscow and met with Yeltsin and his top aides. They were following up on the letter Clinton and Gore had sent earlier in the month, which had caused Chernomyrdin to cancel his visit to the United States. They offered Yeltsin a choice. He could refuse to budge on the Indian rocket deal, in which case the United States would institute sanctions that would cost Russia access to U.S. business; or, he could negotiate on this matter in a way satisfactory to the United States. If Russia took the latter path, the United States would work to make Russia a full partner in the Space Station program and also provide financial incentives so that Russia would not lose money by aborting the Indian arrangement. The message was delivered, but it was not certain Yeltsin would go along.[32]

In early July, Yeltsin traveled to Tokyo to attend an economic summit. There, he and Clinton again discussed the technology transfer issue. Yeltsin gave the impression he was amenable to compromise. A week later, with the July 15 deadline imminent, a delegation from Moscow arrived in Washington and signaled that Russia was ready to negotiate. On July 16, the United States and Russia announced that Russia would abide by the Missile Technology Control Regime (MTCR). It would provide India with the rocket engines (product), but not the know-how (process) as to their making. In return, the United States would not impose sanctions and would give Russia the go-ahead to enter into business relations for the launch of U.S.-made commercial satellites. The other component of the compromise was highlighted the next day, when Koptev and Goldin signed an agreement to "define and determine the feasibility of a cooperative space flight program."[33]

THE GORE-CHERNOMYRDIN AGREEMENT

On September 2, Gore and Chernomyrdin met in Washington, this being the initial Gore-Chernomyrdin Commission meeting. Goldin and Koptev presented their plan of action for a joint Space Station program. Up to this point, recalled Rose Gottemoeller, a lead staffer of the commission, formerly with the skunk works group, Chernomyrdin had been skeptical, and there was a sense he might yet torpedo the talks. But the presentation by the two space agency heads seemed to turn him around. It was a "remarkable moment," Gottemoeller recollected. The saturnine Chernomyrdin suddenly lit up and was an advocate.[34] The two leaders signed an agreement to work together in space that provided a new plan of action. In doing so, Gore declared, "It is time to leave behind the vestiges of Cold War and begin a new relationship between the U.S. and Russia." "We're not asking for handouts—we want to work together," said Chernomyrdin. "We want to make money together."[35]

Under the accords signed that day, there would be three phases in the building of the Space Station. First, American astronauts would fly to Russia's Mir to perform experiments and enhance their understanding of how to work in a Space Station environment. Second, both the United States and Russia would launch new modules into orbit, linking them and assembling an entirely novel outpost. The United States would supply a laboratory module similar to the one envisioned for Freedom. The Russians would supply a habitat for astronauts similar to the one they had foreseen for Mir 2—a program that now would not go forward. Assembly would take place in the higher orbit the Russians wanted. The third phase of the plan would entail expanding the US-Russian Space Station into a truly international station, as Europe, Japan, and Canada added their equipment, modules, and astronauts to the mix.

Finally, the United States agreed to provide the Russians $100 million a year for four years ($400 million). These funds would cover U.S. use of Mir and "mutually agreed upon" activities in the second phase. In exchange, Russia agreed not to sell missile technology to third world countries for military uses.[36]

CONSUMMATING THE MERGER

Talk on how to integrate the U.S. and Russian space programs—Phases 1 and 2 of the Gore-Chernomyrdin agreement—took place in the United States and Russia. The domestic debate about the Space Station in the United States did not stop these planning sessions. Nor did an attempted coup in Russia.

In early October, Goldin and various NASA specialists arrived in Moscow while the capital was in turmoil. Not long before, Yeltsin had dissolved the Russian parliament and ordered a new vote to establish a government. Yeltsin's enemies in the legislature named one of their own as president. Political chaos greeted the visitors.

Yeltsin's opponents sought to take over Moscow's television station; they burned the presidential palace; they opened fire on defenders of the Yeltsin regime. Goldin, from his hotel, called Washington. "What shall we do?" he asked. The message came back that unless personal safety was threatened, it was important to stay the course, not only working out details on the Space Station but also showing support for Yeltsin.

The next day, Goldin and Koptev met, along with their respective teams of experts. As armed fire cracked in the background, Goldin declared, "We feel for the Russian people. But we're here to talk about the future." The meeting went well. The U.S. and Russian negotiators worked out Phase 1 (the Shuttle-Mir Phase) of the program, which would run from 1994 to 1997. As Goldin's group left Russia October 6, Yeltsin's close associates expressed gratitude for the support the U.S. team had shown.[37]

The uprising was put down and Space Station proponents in the United States said Yeltsin's survival showed that working with the Russians was possible. Critics argued the uprising was proof of the fragility of the Russian government. They thought the United States was wading into uncharted and treacherous waters. For many in the United States, the issue was how to partner with the Russians without becoming too dependent on them. Gibbons worried about an exit strategy if the United States had to withdraw from the relationship.

When Goldin returned from Moscow, he divided his time between working on the Phase II plan, to be announced November 1, and lobbying Congress and international partners for the Russian-American space alliance. The assurances of the NASA administrator and others in the administration were not enough for either the partners or Congress. They wanted Clinton.

On October 15, Clinton sent the international partners a letter requesting their support for the Russian arrangement. This letter helped assuage them to some extent. They were miffed about being relegated to a new "Phase III." On October 16, they voted to invite Russia to join the group. As one European official said, "We didn't feel like we had an enormous amount of choice."[38] On November 1, Koptev joined Goldin and Gibbons at NASA to announce the plan for Phase II, the US-Russian design. It would integrate the Space Station announced by the United States in September (Alpha) with elements of what the Russians intended for Mir 2. The exact configuration remained to be finalized, but the general plan indicated that it would take nineteen American Shuttle launches and twelve Russian boosters to assemble the Station, which would still be called Alpha. The project would represent "the largest international venture ever undertaken by countries in history, other than fighting wars," said Gibbons.[39]

Goldin pointed out the United States would remain in command. Asked by media about the junior partner role, Koptev declared, "We spent about 70 years trying to decide who is junior, who is the senior partner. It doesn't seem helpful." Goldin said the time had come for the United States to stop its costly indecision on the issue and make a commitment. "We don't have the resources to keep two separate programs going. . . . The Russians are giving up their independent space station. I believe we in America have an obligation to assure the Russians we're not going to walk away from the space station." Congressman Brown praised the plan, but said, "the devil will be in the details."[40]

NASA said that Russian participation would get the Space Station up in 2001, two years sooner than previously projected without them. It would cost $3 to $4 billion less than the September Alpha station, which had been projected at $19.4 billion. Asked about the stability of the Russian commitment, Goldin pointed to NASA's recent brush with station termination, and said it was the Russians who had to worry about the American commitment.[41]

The reaction to the planned merger was positive in the media. The *New York Times*, which had consistently opposed the Space Station, now switched to support. Hailing "Partners in Space, Not Rivals," it said the amount projected as Alpha's cost meant that the United States would get a better, bigger Space Station more cheaply than it would have gotten without the Russians. It said the greatest benefit was to lessen the Russian inclination to sell dangerous technology to other countries.[42] The *New York Times* endorsement was symptomatic of a turn of the political tide. Launched by Reagan, the Space Station had been most consistently supported by Republican conservatives in Congress over the years who saw it in Cold War terms. Now, with Clinton's belated backing, Democratic liberals were adding their voices to the base of support. For them, the Space Station was an instrument of post–Cold War international cooperation and arms control. Some conservatives were wary, but most went along with the new majority.

A PUSH FOR POLITICAL CLOSURE

Now came a final push for decision, led by the president. There were still key lawmakers who were not satisfied or convinced of Clinton's own personal commitment. Various senior members of the House threatened to reject the Space Station in a letter signed by Representatives Louis Stokes, Jerry Lewis, Robert Walker, and George Brown, unless their reservations were eased. Clinton now took the initiative. He called a meeting the evening of November 29 at the White House. He invited all the congressional leaders and executive branch officials most concerned with the Space Station issue.[43]

The meeting took the form of a consensus-building session. Clinton agreed that the administration would work closely on outstanding technology and budget issues to ensure a sustained U.S. commitment to the Space Station program. Clinton said he would personally back the program over the long haul, and that technical milestones would be developed for Congress to measure progress. In return for Clinton's assurance, the congressional leaders agreed to support the administration's proposal on Russian partnership and seek to consolidate support in Congress.

Some critical details of the White House-Congress bargain included: (1) the Russians would become full partners and the United States would provide $100 million a year for four years for use of Mir and other help; (2) Russia would abide by MTCR; (3) Clinton and Goldin would hold station expenditures to $2.1 billion a year for the next five years; (4) the lawmakers would appropriate that sum every year from Congress; and (5) Congress would release to NASA the $1 billion which had been appropriated but "fenced off" from NASA's use, pending Congressional-Clinton concurrence on the preceding matter.[44]

This meeting broke the deadlock with Congress. Congressman Brown and other critical congressional leaders and executive branch officials not at the meeting subsequently signaled agreement to the plan. Gibbons and Lake now forwarded a "Decision Memo" for the president to sign that formally invited the Russians to join the program, a program that had three phases and which integrated first Russia and then international partners into the U.S. Alpha design.[45]

On December 6, the international partners joined the United States in extending a formal invitation to Russia. "The governments of the international partners are all now agreed to bring in Russia," said a Clinton administration official. "There was a time when we weren't so sure" they would do so.[46] In mid-December, Vice President Gore led a U.S. delegation to Moscow for the second Gore-Chernomyrdin Commission meeting. Chernomyrdin officially accepted the invitation to join the Space Station program. On December 17, Gore signed a formal accord with Russia.[47] Both sides extolled the new relationship. For better or worse, America's long-time rival was now to be its principal partner in building an international Space Station. This was the end of the beginning of an unprecedented, bold, historic, and potentially fragile alliance in space.

Notes

1. Howard McCurdy, *The Space Station Decision: Incremental Politics and Technological Change* (Baltimore, MD: Johns Hopkins University Press, 1990).

2. Ibid.

3. Kathy Sawyer, "Taking Détente to Mars and Beyond," *Washington Post*, May 15, 1988, p. B03.

4. Dan Quayle, *Standing Firm* (New York: HarperCollins, 1994, Chapter 20); Robert Zubrin, *The Case for Mars* (New York: Touchtone, 1997). The Space Shuttle *Challenger* exploded in 1986, taking the lives of all aboard, including the first teacher in space.

5. Kathy Sawyer, "US, Soviets Take Two Small Steps Toward Cooperative Ventures in Space," *Washington Post*, August 15, 1991, p. A19.

6. James Asker, "Soviets Launch New Space Mission as U.S. Puts Joint Projects on Hold," *Aviation Week and Space Technology*, August 26, 1991, pp. 21–2.

7. "White House Blocks Purchase of Soviet Technology," *Baltimore Sun*, March 1, 1992; Frank Murray, "Former Soviets Deserve More Aid, Bush Says," *Washington Post*, June 12, 1992.

8. Kathy Sawyer, "NASA, Russian Official Sign Space Contract," *Washington Post*, June 19, 1992, p. A3.

9. "US-Russia to Team Up in Space," *Washington Times*, October 6, 1992, p. A7; "US and Russia Plan First Joint Space Crews," *New York Times*, October 6, 1992, p. C2.

10. William Broad, "After the Cold War, World's Space Plans Seek a More Down-to-Earth Basis," *New York Times*, January 26, 1993, p. C7.

11. Barbara Crossette, "Russia's Rocket Deal with India Leads U.S. to Impose Trade Bans," *New York Times*, May 12, 1992, p. A8; Bryon Burrough, *Dragonfly: NASA and the Crisis Aboard MIR* (New York: HarperCollins, 1998), pp. 264–5.

12. Interview with Rose Gottemoeller, November 11, 2001. Interview with Dan Poneman, November 30, 2001.

13. W. Henry Lambright, *Dan Goldin and the Remaking of NASA* (Washington, DC: Pricewaterhouse Coopers, 2001).

14. John Gibbons, Memo to Daniel Goldin, "Terms of Reference for Space Station Redesign," March 9, 1993, NASA History Office Files; Kathy Sawyer, "Space Station Redesign Due by June 1," *Washington Post*, March 11, 1993, p. A11.

15. Burrough, *Dragonfly*, pp. 265–266; Y. Koptev and Y. Semenov letter-fax to Dan Goldin, March 16, 1993, NASA History Office Files.

16. The various nations of Western Europe have linked their space programs under a European Space Agency.

17. Andrew Lawler, "Russians on Way to Help NASA Station," *Space News*, April 12–18, 1993, pp. 1, 20.

18. Burrough, *Dragonfly*, pp. 264–5. Fuerth's remarks are cited in John Logsdon and Judith Millar, Eds., *U.S.-Russian Cooperation in Human Space Flight* (Washington, DC: Space Policy Institute and Institute for European, Russian, and Eurasian Studies, George Washington University, 2001), p. 5.

19. Vancouver Declaration and Press Conference, April 4, 1993, cited by John Logsdon, "The Evolution of U.S.-Russian Cooperation in Human Space Flight," Logsdon and Millar, *U.S.-Russian Cooperation in Human Space Flight*, p. 35; Burrough, *Dragonfly,* p. 266.

20. Logsdon and Millar, *U.S.-Russian Cooperation in Human Space Flight*, p. 35.

21. Interview with Rose Gottemoeller, November 11, 2001.

22. William Broad, "Large Role for Russia Expected on Space Station," *New York Times*, April 13, 1993, pp. C1, C10.

23. Memo, Dan Goldin to Director, OSTP, April 13, 1993, NASA History Office files. "A Russian Bear Hug in Space," *New York Times*, April 16, 1993, p. A12.

24. John Gibbons, Letter to Dan Goldin, April 13, 1993, NASA History Office files.

25. Kathy Sawyer, "U.S. Plays Down Russian Space Role," *Washington Post*, April 15, 1993, p. A12. Dan Goldin letter to J. Gibbons with enclosure, May 12, 1993, NASA History Office files.

26. Logsdon and Millar, *U.S.-Russian Cooperation in Human Space Flight*, p. 36.

27. Kathy Sawyer, "Clinton Backs Cheaper, Simpler Plan for Space Station Freedom," *Washington Post*, June 18, 1993, p. A18.

28. Andrew Lawler, "U.S. May Slap New Sanctions on Russia," *Space News*, July 12–18, 1993; Burrough, *Dragonfly*, p. 207.

29. Kathy Sawyer, "Space Station Tethered By Earthly Concerns," *Washington Post*, May 17, 1993, p. A1.

30. Lambright, *Dan Goldin and the Remaking of NASA*.

31. John Gibbons, letter to Dan Goldin, June 24, 1993, NASA History Office Files.

32. Lawler, "U.S. May Slap New Sanctions on Russia"; Burrough, *Dragonfly*, p. 267.

33. Andrew Lawler, "US, Russia Ink Trio of Cooperation Pacts," *Space News*, July 26–August 1, 1993, p. 6.

34. Interview with Rose Gottemoeller, November 11, 2001.

35. Kenneth Bazinet, "US-Russia Sign Space and Energy Agreements," September 2, 1992, UPI press report, NASA History Office files.

36. Steven Holmes, "US and Russians Join in New Plan for Space Station," *New York Times*, September 3, 1993, p. A1.

37. Carla Ann Robbins and Barbara Rosewicz, "U.S. Hopes to Move Moscow into the West through Deeper Ties," *Wall Street Journal*, December 13, 1993. Goldin meeting with Strobe Talbot, "Points to Make." Undated memo in NASA History Office files.

38. Peter deSelding, "Station Partners Accept Russia," *Space News*, October 25–31, 1993, pp. 1, 20.

39. Kathy Sawyer, "U.S. Proposes Space Merger with Russia," *Washington Post*, November 5, 1993, pp. A1, A24.

40. Ibid.

41. Warren Leary, "With Russian Aid, Better Space Lab," *New York Times*, November 5, 1993, p. A20.

42. Editorial, "Partners in Space, Not Rivals," *New York Times*, November 13, 1993, p. A22.

43. Lawmakers who were able to attend were Senators Barbara Mikulski, Phil Gramm, Conrad Burns, Representatives Dick Gephardt, Stokes, Lewis and Walker. Brown was invited but was unable to attend. The president, Gore, Goldin, Robert Clark (NASA Associate Administrator for International Affairs) and Gregg Simon (Gore's domestic advisor) were among the executive branch attendees.

44. William Broad, "Impasse Is Broken on Space Station," *New York Times*, December 1, 1993, p. A20; Kathy Sawyer, "Clinton Wins Support for Space Station," *Washington Post*, December 1, 1993, pp. A1, A8.

45. John Gibbons and Anthony Lake, "Decision Memorandum on Russian Partnership in the Space Station Program," November 29, 1993, NASA History Office files.

46. William Broad, "3 Space Station Partners Agree to Invite Russia," *New York Times*, December 7, 1993, p. C12.

47. Richard Berke, "Gore Signs Pacts in Moscow on Joint Shuttle Crews and Oil and Gas," *New York Times*, December 17, 1993, p. A12.

Dan Goldin's Catch-22: Building a U.S.-Russian Space Station

W. HENRY LAMBRIGHT

In the spring of 1998, the administrator of NASA, Dan Goldin, asked Jay Chabrow, a financial expert, to meet with him in his office. He had charged Chabrow to head a panel to investigate the potential cost-overruns on the Space Station. This was NASA's most important project and was widely criticized in Congress. It was important, however, to President Bill Clinton, who had made it a centerpiece of his post–Cold War Russian strategy. Goldin was under enormous pressure. The agency's own inspector general, the General Accounting Office, and others had said that the budget Goldin had stated for the station was going to be busted in a big way. Goldin had worked intensely to maintain that budget. His NASA lieutenants were telling him they could deal with the costs.

However, a number of segments of the station were backing up at Kennedy Space Center due to delays in launching its first element, a Russian unit called *Zarya*. The third element, *Zvesda*, even more under Russian control, was further behind schedule. There were legislators threatening to kill the project if the overrun grew too great. Goldin wanted to know if Chabrow believed the Space Station was doable for what the NASA administrator had been telling Congress. Chabrow faced a man whom he saw under severe strain, his credibility under attack, his eyes "dark" and "burning." Chabrow told him: "Dan, it's not going to happen."[1]

INTRODUCTION

In 1993, President Bill Clinton directed NASA to bring Russia into the project to build the International Space Station (ISS). Russia thus joined the United States, Europe, Japan, and Canada in the largest civilian, international R&D project in history. The decision was controversial and complicated, as the former foe became America's principal partner. Moreover, the decision meant that the initial assembly in space would unite U.S. and Russian components. The complete International Space Station would be built around a U.S.-Russian centerpiece. In most quarters, the decision to unite the United States and Russia in space was applauded and even seen as historic. A vocal minority warned against putting Russia in a position where it could influence the pace and direction of the project, making the United States and other nations dependent on its actions.

Nevertheless, the president's decision initially helped the project to survive at a time when Congress was more interested in cutting budgets than funding large-scale technological ventures. The Russian decision connected space visibly, dramatically, to larger foreign policy and national security concerns. Clinton's foreign policy aim was to forge Russian technical capability to the United States and its allies, rather than see it transfer to U.S. adversaries. Space policy was connected to missile proliferation policy and the president provided more personal support to the Space Station than he would have otherwise. That White House backing had limits, however. The President also linked the station to his economic policy objectives: cutting the budget deficit, reducing federal expenditures, and downsizing government. It appeared in 1993 that multiple policy goals—space, security, and economic—were compatible where the Space Station was concerned. That is, building a U.S.-Russian Space Station would save NASA money, reduce the time it took to complete the overall project, make the Russians good allies, constrain weapons proliferation, and produce a bigger and better Space Station. The vision of 1993 did not work out as foreseen. Policy and implementation diverged.

In the end, the U.S.-Russian centerpiece did go up—in 2000, two years later than planned. NASA Administrator Dan Goldin thus took a huge step to fulfill President Ronald Reagan's 1984 goal: "a permanently manned space station." Getting the Space Station up, or at least its U.S.-Russian nucleus, was a great technical achievement. It was also a political tour de force. Doing so made it almost impossible to cancel the program.

For Goldin, the U.S.-Russian Space Station proved a colossal leadership challenge. Advocating a U.S.-Russian Space Station helped save the program in 1993. So did agreeing to a budget the administration pressed that was smaller than Goldin's technical cadre in NASA said was needed. The Russians were supposed to help make up the difference in funding. When they did not do so, the decisions that rescued the program came back to haunt the administrator responsible for its implementation. How Goldin coped illuminates the realities of navigating big programs through political, administrative, and technical barriers. For Goldin, integrating a foreign/security policy with a domestic budget policy became a Catch-22. He did get a space station up—but at enormous cost.

DAN GOLDIN

Appointed NASA Administrator in April 1992 by President George H. W. Bush, Goldin served throughout the Clinton years and the first year of George W. Bush's tenure.[2] He left NASA in November 2001, having set a record for longevity among NASA administrators. Universally seen as a leader who made a substantial difference in his agency, Goldin was widely praised and condemned for his performance.

Goldin was fifty-one when he joined NASA in April 1992. Born in New York City, he received a BS in mechanical engineering from City College of New York in 1962. His first job after college was with NASA's Lewis Research Laboratory in Cleveland. In 1967 he left NASA to join the aerospace corporation, TRW. Moving to California, Goldin advanced over the next twenty-five years to become vice president and general manager of TRW's Space and Technology Group.

Most of Goldin's work was in classified military and intelligence space activities. Because of his concentration on the "Deep Black" world of space, he was not well known in civil space circles. However, he was increasingly seen as one of the top technical executives in the classified space community and was extremely active in the 1980s in DOD's Strategic Defense Initiative ("Star Wars"). His advocacy of "faster, better, cheaper" approaches to robotic spacecraft attracted the attention of the first Bush White House, which contrasted the seemingly innovative and nimble work under the Strategic Defense Initiative with the ponderous, bloated space programs of NASA. When President Bush fired NASA's administrator, Richard Truly, in 1992, he looked to the SDI community for a replacement and found Goldin. Goldin was celebrated as smart, decisive, and able. He was also reputed to be abrasive and somewhat unpredictable. His detractors at TRW called him "Captain Crazy." But Bush and his advisers wanted someone to shake up NASA and Goldin was perceived as a change agent.

Goldin quickly asserted himself and made an early impact on the unmanned space science and earth observation programs. When it came to the Space Station, he met a different fate. He sought to initiate a redesign effort, but ran into political opposition from the station's supporters. This was NASA's flagship project, set in motion in 1984 by President Reagan. It was supposed to finish a decade after the Reagan decision for a U.S. expenditure of $8 billion. By 1992, however, NASA had spent more than $10 billion and had little hardware to show—none launched into space. Complicating any change effort was the fact that a number of other nations—Europe, Japan, Canada—were partners in the program.

THE CLINTON-GORE REGIME

In January 1993, Bill Clinton became president and Al Gore his vice president.[3] Goldin stayed on, pending Clinton's appointing his own NASA administrator. Goldin wanted to stay, but did not know Clinton. He did know Gore, who had presided over his Senate confirmation hearings. Gore was favorably disposed to Goldin, whom he saw as carrying out a "reinvention" at NASA that Gore wanted to lead across government as a whole. While both Clinton and Gore had said they would support the Space Station during the election campaign, that meant little now that they were in office. Bringing down the budget deficit and strengthening the economy were the immediate priorities for the new regime. Space was an afterthought for Clinton. Congress also was largely indifferent when it came to space. It was comprised of a substantial number of new lawmakers, and the democratic majority wished to cut back in areas of low priority to deal with the deficit and find money for social and environmental programs.

Leon Panetta, who had opposed the Space Station as a congressman, was now Budget Director. In February, he called Goldin over to the White House and made it clear that he would like to kill the Space Station. The existing design, called "Freedom," had reported yet another overrun, and the time had come to end the misery. Goldin resisted, saying he could redesign the project and save a huge amount of money. Goldin saw the station as NASA's flagship and without a Space Station, the shuttle had little justification. If Station and Shuttle went, manned space would go—and NASA could quickly follow—on Goldin's watch.

Goldin quickly gathered some trusted associates and they worked on redesign concepts. He came back and told Panetta that NASA could bring costs down to a figure Panetta had said was acceptable to the administration. The president followed with a letter directing Goldin to mount a redesign effort, and also appointing a Blue-Ribbon panel to be headed by MIT president Charles Vest to review the NASA report, which was due by June. White House guidelines asked Goldin to come up with design options for $9 billion, $7 billion, and $5 billion, cumulatively over the FY1994–98 period. The existing Freedom design was scheduled to cost $14.4 billion over the same span.

THE RUSSIAN CONNECTION

As the NASA redesign got underway in March, Yuri Koptev, head of the Russian Space Agency, paid Goldin a visit. He proposed that Russia and NASA merge their space station programs. Koptev was working on a MIR-2 design that could be linked with the U.S. Space Station redesign activity. Goldin immediately saw the advantage of learning from Russia's vast experience in space stations. Also, Russian hardware could substitute for U.S. hardware, thereby saving NASA money. As he discussed the idea with administration leaders, he discovered that there was a considerable interest in bringing the Russians aboard the Space Station for foreign policy-security reasons.

The Clinton administration's national security team was worried about proliferation of Russian weapons-relevant technology to American enemies. The Russians were talking about transferring rocket (missile) technology to India, and there was concern that this technology could not only go to India, but beyond to other nations. There were many former Soviet weapons scientists and engineers desperate for work. The national security staff proposed the Space Station as a positive incentive for cooperation on proliferation that Clinton could offer his counterpart, Boris Yeltsin, when they met at an upcoming summit.

Al Gore was the point in the White House where space policy and national security policy converged. He became an advocate of the Russian merger idea, and Goldin saw Gore as an essential ally if NASA, the Space Station, and he himself were to survive. Negotiations on the Russian connection moved at a pace independent of the NASA redesign effort. When Goldin's team produced new design options for a Freedom-successor, called "Alpha," in early June, they were for a U.S. station, not a U.S.-Russian facility. Nevertheless, the design options were such that a linkage with Russia was possible if the negotiations, then underway, were successful.

BUDGETS AND TECHNOLOGY

The Goldin team could not meet the budget specifications the White House had set. There were three options NASA proposed in early June which the Vest panel said were viable. The president's decision at a White House meeting, which Goldin attended, was to go with a scaled-down version of Freedom, which NASA said would cost approximately $12.8 billion for the ensuing five years. The next question was: how much would the administration give NASA? Panetta came out of the meeting believing the president had stuck with a $9 billion limit, the figure Panetta was pushing. Gore and presidential science adviser Jack Gibbons thought Clinton had agreed with a "compromise" figure of $10.5 billion. Panetta said he would not fight the $10.5 billion number, as long as the money came out of NASA's budget—which was going to be held relatively level over the next five years.[4]

That was that! Goldin was told to move ahead with further planning under the $10.5 billion mark. Goldin did not have much bargaining power. He was desperate for White House support.

DEVELOPING A U.S.-RUSSIAN PLAN

The White House told Goldin to engage in technical planning with Koptev, while diplomatic discussions tried to work at the security issues. During the late summer progress on both fronts occurred and in September Vice President Gore and his counterpart, Victor Chernomyrdin, met to agree on a joint program.

By this time, Goldin and Koptev, both worried about the survival of their respective Space Station ventures, had developed an approach to merger. There would be three phases, they told Gore and Chernomyrdin. First, the Shuttle-Mir phase, would be a time when the United States and Russia would learn about one another's hardware and different "cultural" approaches. Astronauts and cosmonauts would train together. Second, the United States and Russia would place modules in space and build a U.S.-Russian Space Station core. Finally, in Phase 3, the international partners would add their modules.

Gore and Chernomyrdin approved this basic plan of action. They also agreed to a U.S. payment of $400 million to Russia for technical assistance. Russia in turn agreed not to transfer rocket know-how to

India (although it would sell the rockets themselves) and to abide by the Missile Technology Control Regime (MTCR). Goldin had little to do with the security aspects of the decision, but knew he and Koptev could not move forward at their level unless these security issues were resolved.

STREAMLINING MANAGEMENT

While planning for a U.S.-Russian Space Station, Goldin was also implementing cost-saving structural changes in the NASA-contractor organization. Goldin argued that he could save a great deal of money on the station by streamlining management. The Vest panel had agreed with him. The general view in Washington was that the NASA-contractor system for the station was overly large and unwieldy. Various centers had achieved a piece of the station pie and engaged their own contractors. An entirely new organizational level had been established at Reston, Virginia, to manage the various center/contractor teams. Then, there was Washington headquarters which, in Goldin's view, had fought his reform of Freedom.

Goldin said he would simplify the management scheme and reduce the number of civil service/industrial jobs associated with the station by thousands. He proceeded to act swiftly, decisively, and, at times, ruthlessly. In August, he announced that the four work packages divided among four NASA centers that had marked Freedom were going, along with the entire Reston office. There would be one "host" center, Johnson Space Center in Houston, which would be the primary locus of operations on the station.[5]

Similarly, Goldin met with the CEOs of the various Freedom prime contractors. As he had with the center directors, he warned that if they did not pull together behind the new Space Station program, and go along with a single prime concept, they risked losing the whole program to congressional opposition. Under the new single prime, they might be able to continue as subcontractors. He got their reluctant concurrence, and subsequently chose Boeing as the single prime.

In October he continued his reforms. He combined the Space Station office in Washington with that of the Space Shuttle under a single Associate Administrator for Space Flight, Jeremiah Pearson. He subsequently appointed Wilbur Trafton director of the Station program. The Freedom executives at NASA were reassigned or forced out. They had fought the redesign and complained about the prospective budget (especially the yearly $2.1 billion cap) as unrealistic. Goldin quelled the dissent.

POLITICAL CONSENSUS-BUILDING

There was by no means full agreement in Congress, even among station supporters, with the Russian decision. Nor were international partners happy. They felt they had little choice but to go along. Congress was another matter.

Once the Gore-Chernomyrdin meeting had reached agreement, the president and Gore more actively helped Goldin in his legislative lobbying. They argued that the station was critical to Clinton Russian policy. It was called the perfect post–Cold War project to bind the two space powers and prevent proliferation of Russian missile capability. Goldin himself made visit after visit to lawmakers.

The administration said that Russian participation would help get the station up in 2001, two years sooner than projected without them. The cost would be $2 billion less than projected with the aborted Alpha program, meaning $17.4 billion. This new figure was the *total* U.S. cost—the first five years ($10.5 billion) plus additional expenses to reach full assembly by 2001. The Russian-American station would not only cost the United States less, but be bigger, thus better, allowing at least six astronauts to work on board.

Gore was also launching his "reinventing government" initiative at this time. He, the president, and Goldin all declared that as the station was being reinvented, so also was NASA. Goldin's bold administrative actions gave credibility to this argument. Nevertheless, Congress, in voting an appropriation for NASA in the fall of 1993, held back most of the allocation for the station pending full understanding of the Russian arrangement and its budget implications.

On November 29, Clinton called a meeting at the White House for key legislative leaders concerned with the station. Gore, Goldin, and other executive branch officials attended. Clinton and Gore emphasized that the Space Station was a critical element in a "strategic partnership" they planned to build with Russia. All agreed that the station needed what it had not had—budget stability. Stability translated into a five-year $10.5 billion budget, allocated in yearly $2.1 billion installments. Clinton pledged to propose such a sum each year, and the lawmakers said they would support Clinton and the station. The lawmakers agreed to remove the restriction they had placed on station spending.

Goldin thus had the go-ahead he needed from Congress. He also got a reluctant green light from international partners who had required Clinton's personal adjuration. On December 17, Gore and Goldin went to Moscow, where the vice president signed a formal agreement with Chernomyrdin inviting the Russians into the station program. Chernomyrdin, on behalf of his country, accepted.

Goldin now had to make the deal a reality—while maintaining the $2.1 billion cap. He told critics that NASA could do the job for the funds provided, and that the Russians would ultimately save the United States money.

HIGH HOPES

Clinton's budget proposal for NASA provided the promised $2.1 billion for the Space Station, but the agency overall was cut from the previous year. Goldin had leeway in apportioning the pain, but the Space Station was off-limits. In a way, this circumstance underlined the fact that there was a presidential commitment to the station, if not NASA.

As the tumultuous year of 1993 gave way to 1994, hopes nevertheless were high at NASA that the agency had turned a corner on the station, with a new political consensus of support. Giving an added boost was the successful repair of the Hubble Telescope. There was no question in Goldin's mind that if NASA could not bring off the Hubble repair, it would have trouble convincing anyone it could build the much more complicated Space Station. The repair went exceptionally well, and television viewers saw unprecedented maneuvers in space by astronauts. "The trouble with Hubble is over," beamed Senator Barbara Mikulski, chair of NASA's appropriation subcommittee, on January 13, 1994. The photos that came back from the repaired telescope were spectacular, and NASA basked in the favorable media attention.[6]

A few weeks later, the U.S.-Russian Space Station program went from planning to reality as Phase 1, Shuttle-Mir, got underway.

On February 3, 1994, the Russian cosmonaut Sergei Krikalev soared into space as a member of the six-person crew of the Space Shuttle *Discovery*. Goldin and Koptev were on hand at the launch to celebrate the occasion. Goldin also announced the name of the two American astronauts who would travel to Russia later that month to begin training for the next mission in Phase 1. Back in Washington, Goldin lobbied Congress relentlessly, arguing that the time when money was spent and nothing happened in space was over. He pointed to the Shuttle-Mir activity as a visible demonstration of progress. Goldin also went with astronauts to the districts of key legislators, speaking at local schools and universities, and providing photo opportunities benefiting the various lawmakers.

As the time for voting on the Space Station approached in the summer of 1994, Goldin stepped up his already frenetic pace. He was joined at times by Koptev, who was Goldin's age and, like Goldin, had once built high-tech weapons during the Cold War. He and the burly Russian hurried from office to office, visiting lawmakers regarded as uncommitted on ISS, pleading their joint cause. Gore and Clinton were also active lobbyists. The vote to kill the Space Station in the House failed by 123 votes. Just one year before, the Space Station had survived by one vote. To go from a 1-vote margin of victory to one of 123 was considered by most observers remarkable. A great deal of political credit went to Goldin, whose star was in the ascendant.[7] It was also clear that the decision to enlist Russia, which came between the two votes, was politically efficacious.

Phase 1 now had the financial resources to advance successfully, one Shuttle-Mir mission after another. Congressional support grew as lawmakers saw progress in space.

THE ENVIRONMENT CHANGES

In January 1995, the Republicans took command of Congress for the first time in decades. Led by Newt Gingrich, House Speaker, they promised a new agenda in which government would be downsized and many tasks privatized. President Clinton, seeing the handwriting on the electoral wall, moved to preempt his opposition. He proclaimed the "end of Big Government" in his State of the Union address, and called for cutbacks in government employment, middle class tax relief, and eventual balancing of the budget.

What these larger events meant for NASA was a $5 billion cut in funding for the ensuing five years beyond those cuts already absorbed. Goldin initiated a major budget/management review aimed at preserving key programs while cutting infrastructure. As this review continued in 1995, the Shuttle-Mir program was active. The International Space Station (ISS) was protected. It received its $2.1 billion appropriation.

However, ISS was affected by the budgetary/management turmoil in its agency setting. Plans were laid to cut back headquarters roles and personnel. Functions were decentralized to the centers, and a privatization process for the space shuttle ensued.

At the beginning of 1996, NASA announced that day-to-day control of the Space Station would shift from Washington to Johnson Space Center. The director of JSC, George Abbey, was formerly Goldin's Special Assistant, and the man seen by NASA insiders as closest to him. There was still an Associate Administrator of Space Flight in Washington, now Will Trafton. However, the real power shifted to Houston, as backed by Goldin.

RUSSIA'S PROBLEMS IMPACT NASA

While there were signs earlier that all was not well with the Russian side of the Space Station program, it was in 1996 that they reached a point of real seriousness for NASA. The issues did not then have anything to do with the Shuttle-Mir program, which continued to give the station a very favorable public image, but rather the less visible technology development effort. Hardware construction in Russia was slowing down, a slippage that impacted on NASA's schedule.

Opponents of the Russian connection had warned about assigning Russia "critical in-line tasks." They said such an assignment showed minimal concern for political and technical difficulties as well as the cost and schedule risks of developing and assembling ISS. This was the first time in the history of manned space flight, said Gene Kranz, former flight director at JSC, that NASA assigned critical path, in-line tasks to another provider with little or no back up.[8] In an effort to make maximum use of Russian capability, save U.S. expense, and contribute to the foreign policy goal of wooing Russia to western nonproliferation values, Goldin had negotiated with Koptev a sequence of development and assembly milestones that made the United States dependent on Russia.

The "critical path" role of Russia was pointed up by the initial sequence of assembly—the first three components. The beginning element was called *Zarya* (for "sunrise"). This was a 20-ton module that would provide start-up propulsion and power. The United States paid for development of *Zarya* with funds going to Boeing, which in turn contracted with a Russian firm, Khrunichev, which was to do most of the work. *Zarya* would be launched by a Russian rocket.

The second element would be *Unity*, a U.S.-funded and -produced hub. It would attach to *Zarya* and serve as a main connector for future pieces of the station. The third element, the service module, called *Zvesda*, would be made by the Russians and funded by the Russian Space Agency. *Zvesda* would provide habitation quarters for three astronauts and a propulsion capability that could endure for the remainder of the scheduled assembly and into the operational lifetime of the station. The essential nature of *Zvesda* lay in the fact that the first two elements would become unstable in orbit after six months. *Zvesda* would have the power to reboost them and maintain the first three elements as a small, but viable space station. The United States would then attach other components, including a laboratory for scientific research, all leading to completing the Space Station core. Once this centerpiece was ready in 1998, the international partners could add their components. It was now projected that full assembly would be finished in 2002.

The significance of Russia's contributions was undeniable. *Zarya* and *Zvesda* were on the "critical path," enabling, not just enhancing, the station. The initial assembly sequence was a huge technical decision, driven by foreign policy and budgetary considerations, and perceived Russian capability. This decision now was getting the United States in trouble because of the interdependency.

In 1996, Koptev told Goldin Russia was suffering from an economic meltdown, the severity of which had been unanticipated in 1993. The central government was funding agencies on a priority basis and RSA was not a priority, or at least not high enough a priority, given Russia's fiscal emergency. Without money RSA could not pay for equipment or even salaries for work.

Goldin informed Congress and Gore. Gore raised the issue at a meeting with Chernomyrdin. The Russian senior official assured Gore that Russia was a reliable partner, and he would look into the matter.[9] The United States agreed to help Russia keep its commitments to the station by adding three space shuttle missions, one to deliver a key Russian component to the Space Station and two to ferry supplies to the existing Mir outpost in space. These would save Russia the expense of several rocket flights—and add to the U.S. expense.[10]

CONTINGENCY PLANS

Goldin had little choice but to develop also a contingency plan.[11] The issue was how much of a contingency plan: how many backup capabilities, at what price? The Clinton administration was still holding the line on federal spending, wherever it could, in the interest of meeting the Republican challenge in Congress and that expected in the forthcoming election. NASA was one place Clinton could cut funds with minimal political cost. Moreover, the White House, Congress, and NASA had locked themselves into the yearly $2.1 billion station appropriations cap. They all lived with that constraint. What NASA could not afford in one year was pushed into the next—or even further out, but now Russia was costing more money than anyone had anticipated.

Goldin directed NASA to explore an Interim Control Module (ICM) as substitute for some of *Zvesda*'s capabilities (guidance, navigation, and propulsion). It would not provide all *Zvesda*'s assets, particularly living quarters for a crew. The Naval Research Laboratory (NRL) had developed a system with some of the propulsion features under the former Strategic Defense Initiative (Star Wars). NASA's contingency plan was to adapt the NRL system. The word "interim" conveyed the fact that this system was limited and temporary, to be replaced by either the Russian *Zvesda*, when ready, or a wholly new substitute which NASA would initiate. Called a U.S. Propulsion Module, the substitute would provide the long-term power that ICM could not supply to keep the nascent Space Station in orbit throughout assembly and into operations.

The issue for Goldin was how to pay for contingencies? He faced painful budget constraints in every facet of NASA's work. Also, Goldin was adamant about staying within the $2.1 billion cap. Forced by reality to act, Goldin created a new line item outside the regular ISS account called "Russian Cooperation and Program Assurance." With administration and congressional approval, NASA reprogrammed funds from other areas of the agency up to $200 million into this account. In addition, Goldin gave the ISS program manager control of money for Space Station research. Money intended for future science could thus be shifted into present hardware.

THE CAP BREAKS

In 1997, however, for the first time Goldin admitted to Congress the cap would not hold.[12] He and his senior management had been trying to keep to the cap through sheer will. "NASA is a can-do agency," he would tell critics.[13] But the limits lay in factors Goldin could not control. The Russian economy was still deteriorating. Moreover, Boeing was facing a $600 million overrun on its Space Station contract. Goldin had to ask for an additional $430 million above the $2.1 billion to keep ISS on target. An unhappy Congress granted $230 million and directed NASA to reprogram funds for the remainder.

Within Congress, James Sensenbrenner, Republican chair of the House Space Committee, demanded to know more about projected Space Station costs. Realizing he faced a test in confidence, Goldin appointed an independent task force under former TRW executive Jay Chabrow to study the financial problem and determine its extent.[14] As this was underway, the Phase 1 program suffered a crisis in space. This crisis, along with the funding issue, brought to the fore the question whether the U.S.-Russian alliance should be maintained.

CRISIS ON MIR

In 1997, a series of accidents on Mir rocked the program.[15] Beginning in February, crews experienced a flash fire and breakdowns in an oxygen generator, carbon dioxide remover, cooling system, and main computer. However, the most frightening event occurred to a mission in June, when a Russian cargo-supply ship crashed into Mir. The resulting loss of air pressure created a potential life-and-death crisis. Thanks to the quick response and ingenuity of the binational crew, disaster was averted, but the events left a legacy of much worry, particularly in the United States. Concern mounted that the United States and Russia had different views about risk and safety. What was acceptable risk in Russia was not acceptable in America.

The policy issue took concrete form in the decision on whether to continue Phase 1 as scheduled. There was another mission intended in 1997 that would send astronaut David Wolf to Mir. Roberta Gross, NASA's Inspector General, expressed grave misgivings about sending Wolf. Representative Sensenbrenner felt so strongly about the issue that he went to Goldin's office to plead his case. He held hearings, went on television, wrote op-eds, and argued vociferously against sending Wolf.

At stake was not only this particular mission, but possibly the entire U.S.-Russian cooperative program on the Space Station. To terminate Phase 1 prematurely would be seen by the Russians as a slap in the face, certainly a lack of confidence in their technical competence. For his part, Goldin had learned from Phase 1 that the Russians really did know a great deal about Space Station technology from which the United States could gain. But he also knew there were legitimate questions about the Russian approach to safety.

Goldin appointed two panels independent of NASA to give him advice as to future action. Goldin was advised by both groups that the problems on Mir—and especially the collision—were aberrations rather than evidence of systemic failure in the Russian program. The Wolf mission, they said, should go forward. Goldin gave the matter personal deliberation and talked to Wolf. Then he called President Clinton and said he had decided to give the go-ahead. Clinton said the decision was Goldin's to make. On September 27 Wolf was launched into space. He returned safely from Mir four months later. The U.S.-Russian space alliance, and thus the Space Station, was preserved, at least for the moment.

PHASE 1 ENDS; PHASE 2 DELAYED

In January 1998, Andy Thomas went up in the final Phase 1 mission. There was another incident—smoke seeped from an overheated atmospheric-cleansing system—but the problem was quickly alleviated. Thomas returned in June, and Phase 1 ended. Goldin proclaimed the Shuttle-Mir program a success. NASA had learned about Russian technology and how better to live and work in space, across cultures. Even the glitches aboard Mir, including the collision crisis, Goldin said, were important learning experiences. NASA was now ready for Phase 2—but Russia was not.

The funding situation in Russia had degenerated further. Delays there and additional problems at home with Boeing were causing mounting cost overruns. NASA now estimated that the overall cost through completion of assembly would not be the $17.4 billion figure projected in 1993, but instead $21.3 billion. Also, rather than achieving "assembly complete" in 2002, closure would come in 2003. Significantly, NASA's budget request in 1998 included a new item, start-up funds to develop a Crew Return Vehicle (CRV). The need for such a vehicle was acknowledged early in U.S.-Russian planning and the question postponed as to who was to build it and when. The CRV was seen as needed for astronaut safety and high-quality science.

Scientists believed it would take 6 or 7 individuals to conduct scientific research that would be truly useful, given the large amount of time astronauts had to spend simply maintaining the facility. But the existing system for escape, a Russian vehicle that could be "parked" at the Space Station, could only accommodate three persons. If the Space Station was to fully realize its scientific goals, there would have to be a CRV that could take all the astronauts to safety, and it was now clear the United States would have to build it.

While Congress was digesting the new request, the Chabrow panel issued its report. It questioned NASA's latest estimate and said the budget for the Space Station would more likely total $24.7 billion for full assembly and not be completed until 2005. The Chabrow figure was thus $7.3 billion more than that foreseen in 1993. While Boeing overruns mattered, Chabrow attributed most of the additional costs to Russian delays, which were continuing, and consequent contingency spending by NASA. He also stated that the $2.1 billion cap had been a mistake from a cost-control standpoint.[16]

Goldin initially rejected the Chabrow findings as too grim. Sensenbrenner, however, hammered Goldin in congressional hearings. The relationship between the two strong-willed men, never warm, became increasingly acerbic in tone.[17]

NASA delayed launch of *Zarya* and *Unity*, which were on schedule, pending credible information about when *Zvesda* would be ready. The Russians kept reassuring Goldin and Gore they would come through. If Russia delivered as promised, it did not make sense to spend money on developing expensive hardware that would not be used. This was especially the case in view of the White House's reluctance to provide additional money to rescue NASA.

GOLDIN ADMITS ERROR

In early May, Goldin conceded to Congress he had erred in assigning Russia the role to provide the long-term propulsion capability to keep the Space Station positioned properly. This was a role the United States should have retained. "We did not, and I accept responsibility and accountability for not doing that," he said. Shortly thereafter, he lashed out publicly at the Russians: "I'm very frustrated and angry at the leadership in Russia who does not do what they say they are going to do." Yes, he admitted, NASA had been "too rosy" in its outlook toward Russia and the Space Station costs, but he still was not ready to say Chabrow's numbers were right.[18] Goldin decided to meet with Chabrow. As Chabrow recalled, Goldin was struggling to decide whether to accept Chabrow's views as to how bad the station funding situation really was. According to Chabrow: "He was under tremendous pressure. He didn't want to let his people down. All his people were telling him they could get the job done. I told him: Dan, it's not going to happen."[19]

Goldin said he would go along with the Chabrow findings, even though there was a risk the International Space Station could be killed as a result. "He had dark eyes and they were burning when he said that," said Chabrow. "He knew he had to take that up to (Capitol) Hill. Obviously, there was a chance they would cancel."[20]

Congress continued to support the Space Station—the vote in the House was 323–109 for the station when a termination bill came up—but both Sensenbrenner and George Brown, the ranking Democrat, warned Goldin that congressional patience was wearing thin. They demanded Clinton get personally involved in pushing the Russians.

PRESSURES MOUNT

Goldin in July proposed a plan to the White House that was a go-it-alone program. He requested new money for a U.S. Propulsion Module, along with funds for other previously designated contingency items. The Clinton administration rejected this plan.[21] It held to its strong foreign policy position that the United States had to nurture the Russian relationship. This was in spite of reports that Russia was not living up to its agreement on missile control and heightened political chaos in Moscow. In August, Yeltsin fired Chernomyrdin, Gore's principal link with Russia's space policy.

In September, Goldin got a call from Koptev. The Russian space official was direct and said, in effect, "I'm out of money." Goldin quickly asked Congress and the White House for immediate authority to transfer $60 million to Koptev with another $600 million over the ensuing four years, as part of a plan to help the bankrupt Russian Space Agency. His concern was that work on *Zvesda*, dreadfully slowed, would come to a complete halt without the immediate infusion of funds. Goldin saw the U.S.-Russian space partnership at stake. Goldin (and Koptev) did not get the "yes" they wanted, at least not from Congress.[22]

By November, Goldin was fed up. It was not clear who or what frustrated him most—the White House, Congress, or the Russians. All seemed unresponsive to the need to move the Space Station forward. Admitting for the first time that he had considered resigning, he demanded that either the White House and Congress provide funds necessary to keep the Space Station effort alive or cancel the program.[23]

Congress this time got the message and quickly authorized the $60 million for Russia that was requested in September. However, it required Goldin to provide a contingency program that would get Russia out of the critical path. Such a plan had already been submitted to Clinton and been rejected. It entailed another $1.2 billion on top of existing planned expenditures, chiefly for additional help to Russia and to fund the new U.S. Propulsion Module.

On November 29, the United States celebrated past glory through the John Glenn shuttle flight. Clinton used the occasion of a television interview by Walter Cronkite to make it known he was aware of Goldin's plight. He declared: "The Space Station is the right thing to do, and we must stay with it." He went on to praise NASA (and indirectly Goldin) as the administration's poster child for government reinvention.[24]

AT LAST: ISS HARDWARE IN SPACE

The Glenn spectacular attracted a huge audience. It showed once again how space had the potential of raising the spirit of a nation. Nevertheless, it was sandwiched between two launches that were much more important to Goldin, Russia, the future of NASA, and the International Space Station. On November 20, Goldin celebrated with Koptev on the plains of Kazakhstan as *Zarya* was launched. *Zarya* was late, but at last in orbit. Then, from Cape Kennedy on December 3, the two men witnessed *Unity*'s launch. Soon after, these first two components of the Space Station were flawlessly integrated. It was a great milestone for the Space Station. At last, components of ISS were in orbit—assembly had begun. But what Goldin really needed was *Zvesda*.

CLINTON HELPS—SOMEWHAT

In January 1999, Clinton announced that for the first time since 1994 he was asking for an increase in NASA's budget. The next year's raise was modest: $13.6 to $13.7 billion. The Space Station got a substantial long-term boost in authorization, however. The previous year, the $2.1 billion cap that Chabrow had derided as having added to the project's costs, was cracked and the budget went up to $2.3 billion. Beginning with this year, Clinton approved an additional five-year increase of $2 billion for the Space Station beyond that allowed earlier. However, only $800 million was approved to come from the White House for the Space Station account. NASA would have to find $1.2 billion from reprogrammed monies within the overall NASA budget. Other programs would bleed to rescue the Space Station.

Clinton expected Goldin to find most of the money to get Russia off the critical path. Goldin was given the go-ahead to spend money for the most important contingency items, especially the U.S. Propulsion Module. The Interim Control Module was already being funded and adapted as a short-term solution. Clinton and Gore also pressured Yeltsin to fund *Zvesda*, making it clear that partnership in space was their preference to going it alone. Goldin, meanwhile, pressed Koptev as best he could.

GOLDIN DEFENDS RUSSIA

Koptev, Goldin insisted, was a "straight shooter." Maybe so, but there were indications that Koptev articulated one policy to Goldin and another to his political masters at home. Russia had informally agreed to deorbit Mir in April, but now this decision seemed to be softening. At a ceremony honoring Russian space achievements, Yeltsin was overheard asking Koptev whether Russia would maintain Mir, and Koptev reportedly said: "Yes, we shall."[25]

Goldin could do only so much. Clinton's national security aides and State Department were heavily involved in negotiations with Russia. Reports surfaced that money the United States supplied Russia for the Space Station was being diverted to Mir.[26] In May, Yeltsin announced that Russia would pay for Mir through August with government money. After that, Mir could stay aloft only with private support.[27] Koptev promised *Zvesda* would go up in late 1999.

Dutiful to Clinton, Goldin defended the U.S.-Russian policy in speeches. In one talk, he told critics to "grow up" and demonstrate "a little bit of knowledge." "The Cold War is over," he declared. It was foolhardy to talk about "critical paths." As he saw it, "without the Russians, I don't know if we would be able to build an International Space Station." There was no doubt in Sensenbrenner's mind as to whom Goldin was directing his barbs. The lawmaker responded with a published article in which he said it was Goldin who was mistaken. The U.S.-Russian relationship in space was based on "outright lies" and he specifically indicted Clinton and Goldin in the mendacity. He admonished Goldin to grow up, "admitting mistakes and taking responsibility."[28]

In late July, Koptev conceded that Russian spending to keep Mir going had contributed to its failure to meet Space Station commitments. He said it was time to deorbit Mir. He did not believe his country could afford two space stations.[29] Koptev's admission bolstered Sensenbrenner's charge about

Russian double-dealing. Also, there were increasing fears among U.S. national security officials that Russia was violating MTCR by transferring sensitive technology to Iran. Clinton issued sanctions on suspected companies involved, but avoided those associated with the Space Station. Rumors surfaced that Koptev himself was a party to the violations—rumors he denied. The Iran issue was potentially devastating to the U.S.-Russia partnership since the avoidance of weapons proliferation was the primary security motivation for bringing Russia aboard the Space Station in the first place.

Zvesda did not go up in late 1999, as Koptev had pledged to Goldin. The reason, said Koptev, was a malfunction in the proton rocket that would launch the component. Because the *Zarya-Unity* facility was losing orbit, and the Interim Control Module was not yet ready, NASA was forced to use the shuttle to provide a needed reboost. Such an unplanned use of the shuttle did not help NASA with its budget problems.

GOLDIN'S WARNING

In early 2000, Koptev informed Goldin that the Russian government was going to keep Mir going with private money and avowed he would launch *Zvesda* by August 2000. He asked Goldin to understand his situation and give him support.[30]

Mir, instead of coming down, was staying up. It had not been occupied since August 1999; now it would be occupied again. A private venture, Mir Corp, was being set up in the Netherlands and largely funded by an American venture capitalist, Walter Anderson. Russia was going to launch a mission to Mir to refurbish the facility and make it suitable for space tourists.

Goldin was utterly furious. In February he publicly warned Russia that it could be headed for expulsion from the Space Station program if it did not launch *Zvesda* by the end of the year. The Interim Control Module, he declared, would go up in December as a substitute.[31] In March, Congress passed the Iran Nonproliferation Act that restricted money sent to the Russian Space Agency unless the president certified Russia was not helping Iran develop a missile capability. Significantly, Congress made an exception of funds related to the completion of *Zvesda*. Russia called the act an affront to its national sovereignty.[32]

In April, two cosmonauts reached Mir to get it ready for the first space tourist, Dennis Tito, an American who paid $20 million for his space excursion. Goldin exclaimed: "I'm highly frustrated by the fact the Russians signed up to a program that put such an incredible emphasis on Mir." He noted sadly: "They always seem to have a little extra money around for Mir, but not the International Space Station." "It's inexcusable," continued Goldin, "for Russia to divert [launch] spacecraft earmarked for ISS to support Mir, particularly since NASA was not consulted. It was not something a true partner would do." He complained that the Russians had lost sight of their "commitment." It was a "breach of relations."[33] But the new Russian president who had succeeded Yeltsin, Vladimir Putin, stated that Russia's priority was to have a "national" space capability, although it would still be a good partner in ISS.[34]

Goldin was in a catch-22. Even if he launched the Interim Control Module in December, that would be just a temporary fix. The U.S. Propulsion Module now being developed by Boeing was not going well and falling behind schedule. Boeing was approaching $1 billion in overruns on its prime contract for ISS (worth close to $10 billion). Highly disappointed with Boeing, Goldin approached TRW to see if it might be an alternative on the Propulsion Module.[35]

But even if it were, the reality was that neither ICM nor the Propulsion Module would yield all the capabilities *Zvesda* would give. *Zvesda* would provide stable, sustained propulsion, and also a habitat for three crew members. The costs of replacing fully what the Russians could deliver with *Zvesda* were much beyond what NASA had and was likely to get from the White House and Congress.

Goldin desperately needed Koptev to deliver on his promises. To help his Russian counterpart, he waived a number of safety rules for *Zvesda* normally applied to U.S. systems: cabin noise, shielding from space debris, risks from pressure drops. If he could get this absolutely critical component up, he could add safety precautions later. Goldin's threat to Koptev was one he did not wish to execute.

ZVESDA GOES UP

Finally, Koptev came through. On July 12, Goldin stood at the Baikonur Cosmodrome complex in central Asia with Koptev, and he watched as a Russian proton rocket blasted off the launch pad. Soon after, it placed *Zvesda* in orbit. The two men gave one another a hug as they witnessed the successful launch.[36] It was two years late and the delays had cost NASA dearly, but these facts did not seem to matter much at this point.

There was a sense of relief among space policy observers in both countries. John Pike, space policy director of the Federation of American Scientists, declared that this event was probably the "single most crucial launch in the Space Station" effort. Russian cosmonaut Yuri Malenchenko remarked: "It provides the complete range of necessary operations to keep the Space Station alive." The size of a Greyhound bus, *Zvesda* was both a command post and living quarters. Its propulsion system would keep the outpost aloft during the anticipated years of further assembly and into operations. U.S. astronaut Ellen Baker summed up a common view when she called *Zvesda* the "heart and soul and the brains of the Space Station."

Amidst the celebrations that accompanied *Zvesda*'s docking with *Zarya* and *Unity*, there was one notable moment of negativism. One of the speakers at the Russian launch site was Yuri Semenov, head of Energia, a rocket builder and contractor to RSA. With Goldin and Koptev sitting behind him, Semenov chastised Goldin and the United States generally for not making the job easier for Russia by supplying more money. He complained that Goldin had provided "moral support," but Russia needed "tangible material support." He lectured the NASA administrator: "This being a joint project, it needs to be financed jointly, Mr. Goldin!"[37]

REACHING FOR REAGAN'S GOAL

Zvesda's launch enabled the United States and Russia to move to the next critical step in Phase 2. All steps were critical but this ensuing one was potentially of even greater historic significance. On October 31, 2000, an American commander and two Russian cosmonauts were placed into orbit by a Soyuz rocket launched from Baikonur. Their mission was called "Expedition 1." Two days later they floated into the U.S.-Russian Space Station. When they arrived, they achieved a milestone for the Space Station and possibly human history.

In 1984 Reagan had set as the goal of the Space Station program a permanent human presence in space. If the Space Station program succeeded in realizing its promise as an outpost and laboratory, ISS likely would be sustained, one way or another, indefinitely. John Curry, who served as NASA flight director, commented at the time of the launch: "I'll say there's a decent chance that [today] may in fact be the last day that we don't have humans in space."[38]

The media and American public gave only fleeting attention to Expedition 1. Those editorialists that did see its possible significance also noted how controversial the program remained. The full realization of ISS was by no means assured. Nevertheless, with all the problems and uncertainties, Goldin felt proud that the centerpiece of the Space Station was up. He had promised the first George Bush, Clinton, and Congress that he would get the Space Station in orbit. What had been accomplished was late, much more expensive than projected, and just the beginning of a Space Station that could be occupied and used. It was "a" space station he had gotten up, not "the" International Space Station. It was a specifically U.S.-Russian Space Station. But it would be almost impossible for a president and Congress to step back now and kill the program. The Space Station program, possibly one congressional vote from death in 1993, was alive and poised for the twenty-first century. Perhaps that was legacy enough for the embattled NASA leader.

GOLDIN DEPARTS IN CONTROVERSY

In late 2000, Mir Corp failed financially and Russia at long last deorbited Mir. It had no choice now but to cast its space future with ISS. At the same time, the United States needed Russia still. The United States depended on Russia for non-shuttle launches and an interim crew rescue capability. However, Russia was no longer in the critical path in terms of supplying modules to be assembled. Plans called for the United States to complete Phase 2 with a range of additional components it would largely supply, setting the stage for Phase 3, at which point the Space Station would go from a U.S.-Russian outpost to a truly multilateral facility.

Unfortunately, the transition to Phase 3 was further delayed. In late November, NASA revealed that the five-year projected costs for assembly pushed ISS way over a $25 billion cap Congress imposed in 2000 as a cost-control discipline. When George W. Bush became president in January 2001, he learned that the five-year overrun could be $4.8 billion or even more. All the requirements for the Space Station that could not be met year-to-year under the $2.1 billion cap, and had been pushed into the future, would have to be addressed by the new administration. Although the Bush White House asked Goldin to remain while it looked for a replacement, it was aghast at the overrun and highly critical (and nontrusting) of Goldin and NASA generally. It immediately cut or postponed various add-ons Goldin had in development, most notably the Crew Return Vehicle.

The Bush administration pressured NASA into sponsoring an independent analysis, led by Tom Young, former aerospace executive, to find out what was financially wrong with ISS and what to do as remedy. Meanwhile, assembly in Phase 2 continued, most notably with the launch in early 2001 of *Destiny*, the major U.S. laboratory. *Destiny* enabled research to be performed with the amount limited by the number of astronauts who could be safely aboard. Nevertheless, the transition to utilization, even as assembly continued, was now underway.

In November 2001, the independent analysis by the Young panel was announced. In a blistering document castigating NASA financial management, the Young report called for slowing down the assembly process. Before starting international partner assembly (Phase 3), NASA was told to pause and gain fiscal control.[39] Goldin received the Young report and downplayed the overrun as just the latest crisis, not as serious a crisis as others the Space Station had encountered on his watch. Moreover, Goldin announced he was already acting to mitigate the financial crisis, beginning with the removal of George Abbey, the powerful director of Johnson Space Center (JSC) he had put in charge of the program in 1996. Once his closest associate at the agency, Abbey was deemed expendable.

The Bush administration was not satisfied with change below Goldin. It wanted new leadership to put NASA's financial house in order. Defiant, Goldin called ISS a great success, and offered "no apologies" for the job he had done.[40] Goldin departed on a date he set in late November after an extraordinary $9\frac{1}{2}$ year record-setting tenure.

Notes

Author's Note: The author wishes to acknowledge support from NSF grant SES-0114689, which relates to space policy, and which yielded material helpful in this case. NSF is not responsible for any views expressed in this case. Thanks also to Anne Hardenbergh for research assistance.

1. Frank Oliveri, "Overruns Slash Heart of Station," *Florida Today*, June 20, 2001, A14.

2. See W. Henry Lambright, *Transforming Government: Dan Goldin and the Remaking of NASA* (Washington, DC: Pricewaterhouse Coopers, 2001).

3. An in-depth study of President Clinton's Space Station decision is found in Chapter 12.

4. Andrew Lawler, "Gore-Panetta Dispute Shaped Space Station Fate," *Space News*, July 26–August 1, 1993, p. 8.; "Clinton Picked Station Matching His Vision, Priorities," *Space News*, August 2–8, 1993, p. 10.

5. Kent Gibbons, "Space Station Jobs Moved to Houston," *Washington Times*, August 18, 1993, pp. A1, A10, A16.

6. Joseph Tatarewicz, "The Hubble Space Telescope Servicing Mission," in

Pamela Mack, Ed., *From Engineering Science to Big Science* (Washington, DC: NASA, 1998), p. 394.

7. Interview with Jeff Lawrence, February 18, 1999, Washington, D.C.

8. James Oberg, *Star-crossed Orbits: Inside the U.S.-Russian Space Alliance* (New York: McGraw Hill, 2002), p. 325.

9. "Russia Lacks Cash to Pay Space Bills," memo to author on news report from Nadine Adreassen, NASA, March 26, 1996.

10. Warren Leary, "U.S. to Help Defray Russia's Expenses for the Space Station," *New York Times*, February 1, 1996, p. A14.

11. "Goldin Gives Russia Six Weeks to Get Station on Schedule," *Aerospace*, March 27, 1996.

12. Interview with Marcia Smith, December 6, 2001, Washington, D.C.

13. Oliveri, "Overruns Slash Heart of Station."

14. Marcia Smith of the Congressional Research Service has provided a series of reports over the years on the Space Station covering costs, schedules, and major decisions. A summary statement appears in her "NASA's Space Station Program: Evolution and Current Status," Testimony before the House Science Committee, April 4, 2001.

15. For a detailed account of the Shuttle-Mir Program, especially the mishaps, see Bryan Burrough, *Dragonfly: NASA and the Crisis Aboard Mir* (New York: HarperCollins, 1998).

16. *Report of the Cost Assessment and Validation Task Force on the International Space Station*, (Washington, DC: NASA, April 21, 1998).

17. Anne Eisele, "Goldin Rejects New Station Cost Estimate," *Space News*, April 27–May 3, 1998, pp. 4, 26.

18. Larry Wheeler, "Goldin Rips Russians, Promises New Station Schedule by June 15," *Florida Today*, May 7, 1998, p. A1. NASA: Russia has let us down, chief promises new report on space station costs in June.

19. Oliveri, "Overruns Slash Heart of Station."

20. Ibid.

21. Tamara Lytle, "NASA Loses Fight to Build Station Without Russia," *Orlando Sentinel*, August 6, 1998, p. A10.

22. Joseph Anselmo, "NASA Plans $660 Million Station Bailout for Russia," *Aviation Week and Space Technology*, September 21, 1998, pp. 26–27; William Broad, "To Buy Some Time, Russia to Sell U.S. Some Time in Space," *New York Times*, October 5, 1998, p. A1.

23. Joseph Anselmo, "Goldin: Fund Fixes or Kill Space Station," *Aviation Week and Space Technology*, October 12, 1998, pp. 24–25; Larry Wheeler, "No Cash, No Station, Goldin Says; NASA Boss Faces Hostile Legislators in Search of More Money for Russia," *Florida Today*, October 8, 1998, p. 1A.

24. James R. Asker, Ed., "The Way It Is, Walter," *Aviation Week and Space Technology,* November 2, 1998, p. 23.

25. Vladimir Isachenkov, "Yeltsin Gives Awards to Mir Crews," *Yahoo News,* April 12, 1999, http://dailynews.yahoo.com/headlines/ap/in . . . l/story.html?s=v/ ap/19990412/wl/mir_1.html.

26. Mark Prigg, "Russia 'Steals' Launches to Keep Mir Station Going," *Fox News Online,* May 4, 1999.

27. "Yeltsin Orders Officials to Concentrate on International Space Station," *Florida Today Space Online,* May 22, 1999, http://www.flatoday.com.80/space/ explore/stories/1999/052299a.htm.

28. Dan Goldin, "U.S. Should Learn from Russia," *Space News,* April 26, 1999, p. 21; F. James Sensenbrenner, "Be Realistic About Russia's Role in the Space Station," *Space News,* May 10, 1999, p. 24.

29. "What's Ahead in Aerospace; Koptev Puts Station First," *Aerospace Daily,* July 26, 1999, Vol. 191, No. 17; "Koptev: Russia Still Plans to Abandon Mir," *Florida Today Space Online,* September 16, 1999, http://www.flatoday.com. 80/space/today/09/699h.htm.

30. Yuri Koptev, letter to Dan Goldin, January 13, 2000, NASA History Office files.

31. Anatoly Zak, "Russia Responds to Goldin Attacks: Zvesda Will Fly By June," *Space.Com,* February 4, 2000, http://www.space.com/space/spacestation/ zvezda_update_000204.html. Paul Hoversten, "Goldin Rips Russia for Space Station Delays," *Space.Com,* February 3, 2000, http://www.space.com/space/ spacestation/goldin_rips_russia_000203.html.

32. Brian Berger, "NASA Pressured to Monitor Russia, *Space News,* March 6, 2000, p. 120; Alex Canizares, "Legislation Puts NASA between U.S. and Russia," *Space.Com,* March 3, 2000, http://www.space.com/space/spacestation/nasa_ legislation_000303.html.

33. Mark Carreau, "NASA Worries Revival of Mir Will Undermine Space Station," *Houston Chronicle,* April 20, 2000, p. 4; Alex Canizares, "NASA's Dan Goldin Angered over Mir," *Space.Com,* April 7, 2000, http://www.space.com/ space/business/goldin_congress_000407.html.

34. "Putin's Remarks Appear to Give Mir Priority over International Station," *Aerospace Daily,* April 14, 2000, Vol. 194, No. 10.

35. Brian Berger, "NASA Orders New Review of Station Propulsion Module," *Space News,* May 29, 2000, pp. 1, 19.

36. A Conversation with Daniel S. Goldin, Administrator, NASA, in Mark Abramson and Paul Lawrence, Eds., *Transforming Organizations* (Lanham, MD: Rowman and Littlefield, 2001), p. 135.

37. Craig Covault, "Zvesda Launches Amidst Russian Funding Problems," *Aviation Week and Space Technology,* July 17, 2000, pp. 33–36.

38. Todd Halvorson, "Destination: International Space Station," *Space.Com*, February 28, 2001, http://www.space.com/mission/launches/missions/exp_one_iss_001030.html.

39. *Report by the International Space Station Management and Cost Evaluation Task Force to the NASA Advisory Council* (NASA: Washington, DC, 2001).

40. Lon Rains, "Daniel Goldin Proud of NASA Tenure," *Space.Com*, October 17, 2001, http://www.space.com/news/goldin_resignation_011017.html. Frank Morring, Jr., "Goldin Changed NASA Forever, But Successor Must Pay Costs," *Aviation Week and Space Technology*, November 12, 2001, pp. 60–62.

Chapter 14

Worse Than an Infection: DOD's Struggle with the Anthrax Vaccination

JOHN ROBINSON

Until recently, Captain Clifton Volpe was a model pilot for the Air Force. A 1995 graduate of the Air Force Academy, Volpe consistently received high marks from his commanders. That all changed when he refused a direct order to take a vaccination against anthrax in preparation for a deployment to the Persian Gulf. "You're taught not to just blindly follow orders," Volpe recalled from his days at the Academy. "And this order [for the shot] was just wrong."[1] Although Volpe is only the second active duty pilot to be discharged from service for refusing the shot, his case represents an important flashpoint in a lingering problem for DOD leaders.

The Department of Defense has an anthrax problem. Because not a single service member has been infected with the deadly biological agent, many DOD leaders would acknowledge they face a challenge in the need for making the vaccine a servicewide requirement. DOD estimates only 350 personnel have been discharged for refusing to take the vaccine compared to the 511,000 that have lined up to take it. However, some of those discharged, like Volpe, are pilots—a community that is a precious commodity these days of far-flung deployments—so it would be misleading to look at the numbers alone. The topic has received wide attention in the media and is a hot topic on military-related Web sites.

This case study highlights some unique challenges confronting the Department of Defense for carrying out the policy. The main one involves carrying out an effective plan to protect its forces against the threat of biological warfare without diminishing readiness. An unfortunate byproduct of the anthrax vaccination plan is that it has sparked an active resistance movement in the ranks, raising larger questions about the Pentagon leadership. The Pentagon is grappling with how to quell the resistance to the program without creating even more problems.

In many ways, such a vaccine controversy is unusual but not unprecedented. For centuries the military has vaccinated its troops against naturally occurring diseases or biological warfare agents.[2] Resistance to the vaccines by service members has varied over the years—mirroring larger society's mixed emotions over vaccinations. Vaccinations are also fairly routine in the military. During the course of a military career, personnel receive anywhere from four to eleven vaccinations depending on assignment and occupation.

As much as the Pentagon defends its policy, it acknowledges on its official anthrax vaccination Web site that the current vaccine, developed in the 1950s and 1960s, is not "ideal."[3] Meanwhile, it continues to pursue a new vaccine that would reduce the number of shots in the series and cause fewer side effects. But that process will take years, so the Pentagon believes the best course is to go ahead with what is available—no matter how unpopular it might be.

"We are unwilling to leave Service Members vulnerable to the threat while waiting for the next-generation vaccine to work its way through the research-and-development pipeline and FDA review," DOD said.[4]

The anthrax controversy raises some important questions about the mistrust of the military leadership by rank-and-file personnel, a problem that could have far-reaching consequences for military preparedness. Much broader social pressures, which throughout history have tested the strength of military institutions, also come into play. The overriding concern, and much deeper challenge, for policymakers is the open questioning of military orders—something that tears at the fabric of the institution. If the military is at the point at which soldiers will only carry out orders they find justified—a claim made by many of the anthrax protestors—it is falling into a dangerous state. Military personnel are charged to follow orders, not question them. Once that very basic element of trust, which compels troops to do extremely dangerous things like fight wars, breaks down, so does the entire system.

The importance of solid military leadership in enforcing controversial military policies like the anthrax vaccination has become even more evident since the September 11 terrorist attacks. Such leadership needs to be equally strong in the reserve and guard because those elements are so closely integrated with the active forces. For example, the Air Force, which relies heavily on pilots in its reserve or guard component, has mobilized more than 35,000 personnel since the attacks.

Public resignations like Volpe's over a policy issue are actually quite rare in the military. They can also have a much broader impact, reaching deep into the military ranks. "The thing that really turned me around was talking to the people who testified to Congress about their reactions [to the shot]," Volpe said.[5] When officers like Volpe resign, disgruntled enlisted personnel, who look to officers for leadership, are not far behind.

OPPOSITION MOVEMENT

The first signs of trouble for the Pentagon's anthrax vaccine policy surfaced at state guard units gearing up for rotations in the Middle East. Since the units were heading to what DOD viewed as the highest anthrax threat area, they were required to receive the anthrax vaccination before deployment. Some pilots became skeptical of the policy after leadership in their units had difficulty answering questions about the vaccine's safety and possible side effects. The reserve pilots were especially interested because of such side effects disqualifying them from keeping their jobs flying commerical aircraft.

In January, 1999, eight pilots from the Connecticut Air National Guard resigned instead of taking the anthrax vaccine and the story started to get its first attention in the media. Word of the pilot exodus in Connecticut was circulating through the pilot community when the 163rd Fighter Squadron in Fort Wayne, Indiana, was notified in March that it faced an August deadline for members to receive the vaccination.[6]

With some squadron members becoming uneasy about the safety of the anthrax vaccine, Lieutenant Colonel Tom Heemstra, the commander of the 163rd, traveled to Maine to visit Dr. Meryl Nass, a self-described expert on the vaccination who actively opposes the Pentagon policy.[7] He believed such a step was important to get answers to questions members of his unit had about the vaccine.

Resistance to the vaccine is not limited to the military. After the anthrax attacks in the fall of 2001, exposing scores of congressional staffers and postal workers to the deadly bacteria, federal health officials offered the anthrax vaccine as a supplement to antibiotic treaments. Only 130 out of thousands offered the vaccination accepted it.[8] However, in the height of the anthrax scare, when the extent of the attacks was unknown, it is important to note that there were also reports of people who wanted the vaccine but could not get it because the limited supplies were reserved for the military.

In opposing the policy even before the anthrax attacks in the mail, some pilots expressed concern that the vaccine could produce some side effects that could prevent them from flying commercial airplanes and directly impact their livelihood. Though side effects from taking the vaccine cover a wide range according to media accounts, the most common ones involve joint and muscle pain and fatigue. The Pentagon claims the side effects are within the normal range for any vaccination.[9] "[The shot] was too much of a risk to my health," said Daniel Marohn, a member of the 163rd who resigned over the policy.[10] "As a commercial pilot, my livelihood depended on my medical certificate. If anything should medically disqualify me, that would be the end of a very good career, not to mention that it would be devastating to my family."

After his visit to Maine, Heemstra invited Dr. Nass to visit Fort Wayne and "educate" the rest of the squadron on the vaccine. In his role as commanding officer, he believed such steps were required to "go to bat" for his people who had questions about the vaccine. An order signed by the wing commander prevented her from appearing on base, but she traveled to Fort Wayne anyway and held a presentation off the base. After a five-hour meeting during a drill weekend attended by twenty pilots and thirty enlisted personnel, all those in attendance "were convinced by the facts to avoid the shot, and convinced that DOD had been less than truthful," Heemstra said. "Clearly this sort of situation puts you in a hole when you arrive," Major General Randy West, a special assistant to the Secretary of Defense for chemical and biological warfare, said.[11]

By the time Defense Department doctors arrived in Fort Wayne it was too late. DOD's vaccine expert faced a round of hostile questions from members of the guard unit and their families. "We knew more about anthrax than he did," Heemstra said of the visit from the DOD vaccine expert. "It was pure propaganda."

With Heemstra unable to find any sympathy for his opposition to the policy in his chain of command, the battle moved to a new front: Washington. In the spirit of "going to bat for his people," he personally contacted several members of Congress to "inform them of the severe potential impact of [the] shot on the health and safety, retention and readiness, and negative impact on morale." Dressed in civilian attire, Heemstra lobbied Congress in an "unofficial role" and did not officially represent his unit. Congress has been receptive to the concerns of the opponents to the vaccine and has held several hearings on the topic. Although lawmakers opposed to the vaccine have amplified the media coverage, in the end, they been unable to slow or overturn the Pentagon policy.

Such aggressive opposition to a DOD policy by a member of the Guard or Reserve would be unthinkable for an active duty service member. Heemstra, a graduate of the Air Force Academy, believes his actions as a "citizen-soldier" were justified. For refusing the shot, he said that he ultimately was removed from command and forced to retire.

Before he was forced to retire, Heemstra said that he warned Congress that half of his F-16 fighter pilots would resign instead of taking the shot. Indiana Guard officials said that the vaccination program has gone smoothly and the issue boils down to obeying military orders, not anthrax. "The military is not Burger King, you know, it's not 'Have it your way,' " said Colonel J. Stewart Goodwin, a Guard spokesman.[12] "The order was given for us, as military people, to take the shot. Those who decided to do something else disobeyed an order. It's very fundamental." Heemstra claims as many as fifteen pilots left over the vaccine. The Guard claims only one pilot blamed the shot for his departure and suggested other reasons, mostly related to the stress involved with flying F-16s, may be a greater factor.

IMPLEMENTING THE POLICY: ONE COMMANDER'S STORY

The anthrax policy was put to an immediate test among the active forces. As the USS *Abraham Lincoln* carrier battle group steamed toward the Persian Gulf in June 1998, its skipper, Captain J. J. Quinn, had a hunch the new policy could pose some problems. Since the *Lincoln* was entering the Central Command area of responsibility, its 5,500 sailors were required to get the anthrax shot. "In my opinion, DOD hadn't thought this thing through," he said.[13] "Any time you have that many people [objecting], you're going to have some problems."

Quinn put together a plan to educate sailors about the importance of the shot. In the spirit of leading by example, Quinn and the battle group commander, Rear Admiral Bill Putnam, were the first two to get it. The vaccinations of the top brass were photographed and put in the ship's newspaper. The ship also carried highly visible efforts to educate the sailors about the threat.

Nevertheless, the first signs of problems flared up when twenty-five sailors, all enlisted, refused to take the shot. In this case, the opposition was traced to a sailor who had collected adverse information about the shot from his wife, who had pulled it down from an anti-vaccination Web site. The sailor had shared the information with the others, whose opposition to the shot hardened. Quinn, the ship's executive officer, and the command master chief, the senior enlisted person on the ship, realized they had a potential problem on their hands. After a counseling session from the command master chief, the list of refusers shrank from twenty-five to three.

Quinn took the three holdouts to captain's mast, a disciplinary proceeding. The Pentagon has not issued a forcewide guideline to discipline any military member for refusing to take the shot, leaving unit commanders some flexibility to deal with the policy. Local military commanders apply the principles of the Uniform Code of Military Justice that apply to other cases involving the refusal of a lawful order. "My philosophy was that they [the sailors] had directly disobeyed an order," Quinn said. The three sailors were placed on restricted duty and penalized in pay. But just two days into the punishment, two of the sailors relented and took the shot. That left a single holdout, who dug in for the long haul. Eventually, as Quinn was preparing to punish the sailor again after fifty-nine days, he was getting pressure from his boss, Admiral Archie Clemins, Commander in Chief of U.S. Naval Forces in the Pacific, to send the sailor off the ship. Quinn resisted. "My intention was to keep him on the ship for the rest of the deployment, then throw him out of the Navy." Quinn feared that refusing to take the shot would result in a "get out of jail free card," perhaps spurring other refusals.

For every carrier deployment, there are 250 to 300 people who don't want to be on the ship, he said. Quinn realized that how he dealt with the sailor could have a big impact on the morale on his ship. With the ship steaming for the Persian Gulf, where its planes would be conducting dangerous missions enforcing the no-fly zone in Iraq, its skipper could not permit dozens of sailors using their refusal to take the shot as a free ticket home.

The lone holdout to the shot had created a stir in the local media where the aircraft carrier is homeported in Washington state. The issue began to draw attention from the local civil liberties groups and the congressional delegation. Quinn figured that Clemins was reacting to the bad publicity the sailor's wife had stirred up and was trying to head off a much larger problem. The sailor was sent home and discharged from the Navy. "Clemins just folded," Quinn said. "He sold me out as CO [commanding officer]. He just didn't want to take the heat. I just thought it was the wrong thing to do."

Not long after the incident, which failed to trigger additional refusals on *Lincoln*, Clemins sent a personal message to fleet commanders outlining some guidelines for commanders in dealing with the policy. He defended his approach to resolving the incident on *Lincoln*. Like Quinn, Clemins thought the Defense Department had done a poor job in explaining the policy. Even though he was one of two Navy four-star fleet commanders, responsible for 250,000 sailors and marines and 200 ships, Clemins recalled that he first learned about the mandatory vaccination policy by reading a newspaper. "They [Defense Department] had a strategy without a tactical implementation plan," he said.[14] "There was never any guidance from Washington that answered the problems people had."

With regard to the dissident sailor on the *Lincoln*, Clemins said that he did not support Quinn's decision to put him on consecutive restrictions. Such an approach amounted to "trying him twice for the same crime. . . . There was no end to it [the continual restrictions]," he said. "I knew that wasn't the right answer." Clemins also said that he was not under any pressure from "outside sources" to deal with the incident. But, he did see a need to address a problem emerging directly in his area of responsibility.

With ships under his command like the *Lincoln* continuing to struggle with the anthrax policy, Clemins thought the commanders needed better guidance. The personal message on anthrax he ulitmately sent out did not order skippers to automatically dismiss sailors for refusing the shot. Instead, it emphasized the importance of first educating sailors about the policy and, when disciplining those who refuse, to make sure the punishment fits the crime. The message gave commanders wide lattitude to implement the policy. "Good leadership can always prevail," he said. "But if you can't convince yourself that the policy is the right thing, then you won't be able to convince others it is right," he said.

LINING UP BEHIND THE ORDER

There had been some internal debates leading up to the final decision to go ahead with the vaccine. This reluctance would foreshadow some of the concerns ultimately raised by opponents of the vaccine. Several forces came together to reject the vaccination plan in 1996, when it was first considered, according to former Deputy Secretary of Defense John Hamre.[15] Although the military initially resisted the inoculation program, its senior leaders eventually became the most vocal advocate for it in discussions with the top civilian leadership. "We noticed a change in the military," Hamre said.[16] "By 1997, they all were saying we need to do this." The military chiefs were unanimously in favor of it. The Pentagon believed that it had "hard evidence" that Iraq was trying to weaponize anthrax. According to intelligence reports, Iraq had started to set up mobile production lines for anthrax and new, more lethal, ways of delivering it.

Retired Air Force General Ronald Fogleman, the Air Force chief of staff at the time the policy was approved, didn't recall much of a controversy about the decision when the chiefs reviewed it in the "tank." "I didn't see it as a big deal," he said.[17] "I saw it as a force protection issue." Even though it wasn't a big deal for him personally, he realized the implementation of a mass vaccination policy would not be easy with questions still swirling about the role vaccinations may have played in the Gulf War Syndrome, a variety of maladies reported by troops after the war. Some media accounts suggest that the anthrax vaccination is linked to one of the possible causes of the syndrome, a linkage the Pentagon strongly denies.[18]

"To me, it was an initiative that required bold leadership," he said. After the decision was made to go ahead with the shots, Fogleman immediately started the series of shots. "I wanted to know that if it became an issue, I could say 'Hey, I've done this.' "[19] Fogleman resigned in 1997, before the initial wave of refusals of the vaccination began to rock the Pentagon.

Perhaps anticipating some resistance to the total force vaccination policy, the Pentagon took additional measures before finally endorsing the policy. Deciding to go forward with the policy hinged on four conditions: additional testing of anthrax vaccine lots in the stockpile; approval of the services' implementation plan for administering the vaccine; setting up of a system for fully tracking the anthrax vaccine; and review of the health and medical aspects of the program by an independent expert.

The Joint Chiefs supported the policy, but not all of them led by example. According to Hamre, the failure of Chief of Naval Operations Admiral Jay Johnson to take the shot, as the other chiefs had, became a source of irritation between him and Defense Secretary William Cohen. Ultimately, Cohen sent Johnson a message, urging him to take it. Opponents of the vaccine naturally seized on the CNO's refusal, once it became public in news accounts, as a double standard. Johnson, through a spokesman, said that he didn't want to skip his turn in line for the shot.

With mixed signals from the top, it is not surprising that enthusiasm for the shot never filtered very far down the ranks, leaving commanders with the difficult challenge of implementing a controversial policy. Not long after military medical staff began administering the first shots in 1998, signs of resistance started to pop up. Even though DOD had gone to "special pains" to prepare for a smooth implementation, in the end the efforts were "insufficient" and "inadequate," Hamre said.[20] The resistance to the policy became a hook for "other agendas," he added.

In hindsight, Hamre believes that the warfighters simply turned the implementation of the policy over to the medical personnel. It sent a mixed message to the troops. "I thought we failed in securing a real commitment from the military leadership," Hamre said. "They never made it a priority. The biggest problem is that the services did not do a good job of getting command leadership for the program." Hamre said that if he had to do it over again, he would make it clear to the chiefs, in a face-to-face meeting, that the vaccination was a top priority for the civilian leadership. "I think that's the one thing we should've done and we didn't do that," he said. "Everything else we did was necessary and important, but we did not do this one thing."[21]

DILEMMAS OF DEALING WITH MILITARY DISSENT

The refusals presented another dilemma for the military: how to deal with the opposition groups and individuals refusing the shot.

With the Universal Code of Military Justice as a guide, commanders in the field were given wide latitude in disciplining those who opposed the shot.

Opposition varied from extreme cases of outright refusal to mild concerns from other military personnel. The Pentagon began to face tough questions from lawmakers on the policy. Despite the good intentions of the policy, was it actually decreasing, rather than increasing, military readiness by influencing people to leave the military? Given the health concerns, why not make the shot voluntary, as it is for the British military, for example?

The concentration of the resistance in the pilot community highlighted a special readiness challenge. Even before the anthrax controversy surfaced, the Air Force pilot community was in a state of turmoil. Pilot discontent, which was reflected in a growing number of resignations from the service, proved to be fertile ground for the opposition movement. According to a comprehensive RAND study, the Air Force was losing "unprecedented numbers of experienced pilots," who were departing after the conclusion of their active duty commitment and their initial bonus payback period.[22] The RAND report blamed the flourishing market for commercial pilots and the degraded quality of life from the high operations tempo to support far-flung contingencies. It made no mention of the role of the anthrax vaccination in pilot defection.

The study projected that by the end of 2001 the pilot shortage would rise to about 15 percent of the overall pilot requirement. In the fighter community, the problem is particularly acute—the pilot shortage could rise to about 20 percent. The pilot shortage, the study says, is projected to become over twice what it was during the "Hollow Force" period of the late 1970s.

Faced with these sobering observations, the Pentagon got blindsided in October 2000 by another survey, from the General Accounting Office, blaming the vaccine for huge personnel losses.[23] The GAO survey found that 25 percent of pilots and maintenance crew members who have left service since September 1998 did so because of opposition to the anthrax vaccine. On top of those who had already left, an additional 18 percent still in the Guard or Reserve said they planned to leave within the next six months. In that group, 61 percent said the biggest reason for deciding to leave was the anthrax program, the study concluded.

West, the Pentagon special assistant on chemical/biological warfare who is also a pilot, suspects that the chronic fear of any pilot getting grounded for adverse reactions to the shot are playing into the resistance of the re-servists and guardsmen, who already rely on flying commercially for a living. Pilots don't "want to miss a single hop," West said.[24] Potential side effects from any shot could be a factor in this regard. With pilots one of the precious commodities in today's military, the loss of any pilot, one could argue, results in a loss of readiness. If there was a direct relation-ship between the vaccination and loss of readiness, why not switch course and drop the mandatory policy?

DOD had walked away from at least one little-known vaccine in the past for cost reasons. In 1995, it stoppped purchasing the adenovirus vac-cine, which prevents respiratory illness, given to recruits in boot camp. A recent study said that the vaccine could have likely prevented two recent deaths at the Navy's boot camp in Great Lakes, Illinois. The way DOD has dealt with anthrax vaccine dissenters also presents some future dilemmas. Now that shortages in the vaccine have limited vaccinations to a small number of special mission units, it is not clear, when, if ever, the rest of the military will have to go through the full battery of shots. As a result, the opposition and refusals have quieted. Nobody has been physically forced to take the shot.

Nevertheless, the requirement to take the shot is being treated as an order. Regardless of the merit, if any, to the arguments of the groups op-posed to the vaccine, the Pentagon has been reluctant to back off the mandatory vaccination policy. Caving in to the opponents in this case could set a bad precedent for other unpleasant military orders that might need to be given. For this reason, the Pentagon has vigorously defended the policy.

In many cases, those active duty members who have refused the shot have been court-martialed; others have been administratively discharged. In the Guard and Reserves, it has been a trickier administrative disciplinary process, even though they are equally bound to military orders imposed on active duty forces. The trials and tribulations of many military members who have rejected the shot, which in many cases illustrate an inconsistent disciplinary policy, have been well documented in the media.

Another frustrating characteristic of the vaccine opposition movement for the DOD leadership is that it is centered in the Reserve and Guard pilot communities, which are in high demand for military missions around the world. Because Guard/Reserve forces typically only drill two days a month, they are relatively detached compared to the active force from the day-in, day-out rigors of military life. For this reason, it should not be such a surprise that the "weekend warriors" were fertile ground for opposition. But Hamre believes the "mini-revolts" to the vaccine did not reveal a divide between the active duty and Guard and Reserve. "When this [anthrax] issue came up it became a lightning rod, but it was a command climate issue," he said. "That's what really showed up."[25]

Ironically, Air Force Guard members can oppose the policy and still stay in the military by transferring to units not scheduled to receive the shot soon or to the Air Force Reserve, which is not slated to receive the shot until even later. Anthrax has not been as much of a controversial issue in the reserve components of the other services because they never had high enough priority to receive it. Air Force Guard units, however, frequently, deploy to high-threat anthrax areas. Limited supplies of the vaccine have also prevented much of the active force from receiving the vaccination, which has been spared for personnel in high-threat areas. Other service members have received some, but not all of the six-shot series, before the most recent slowdown order limiting the vaccination to special mission units.

Majors Tom Rempher and Russ Dingle, two former pilots in Connecticut Guard, the same unit where the anti-vaccination movement started in 1999, transferred to the Air Force Reserves after refusing the shot. The two have become leaders in the vaccination opposition movement. Rempher wrote a widely read opinion piece in *The Washington Post* in which he argued that military disobedience is justified when soldiers are ordered to blindly follow "questionable orders," like the anthrax shot, which has raised legitimate safety concerns.[26] The pilots have authored several other opinion pieces and letters to the editor outlining their opposition to the policy. Because of the latest shortage in the vaccine, the Connecticut Guard deployed to the Persian Gulf in the fall without taking the shot. The commander of the Guard unit refused the requests of Rempher and Dingle to be reinstated.[27]

In another case, the Air Force also court-martialed an active-duty physician, Captain John Buck, for refusing to take the shot for a deployment to the Middle East. Buck, whose case received a lot of publicity, was found guilty of disobeying an order and fined $21,000, but he is still serving on active duty.

Faced with manpower shortages, DOD leaders have been asked to consider amnesty for those in the Guard and Reserve, perhaps even special cases in the active duty force like Captain Buck, who avoided the shot. After all, if avoiding the shot were not a serious enough offense to throw out the service member, in the case of Buck, then why not let others back in who were thrown out for refusing it?

FIGHTING BACK

While the vaccine's supporters and opponents disagree over how many personnel have left over the policy, the Pentagon believes it has the problem under control. Nevertheless, it still goes to great pains to better explain the policy. The long reach of the opposition groups clearly left a lasting impression. The Pentagon has dedicated an elaborate Web site, (http://www.anthrax.osd.mil) with all sorts of information for commanders, including a "toolkit" for carrying out the policy. The Web site receives weekly updates concerning the threat, adverse reactions, and other information. A power-point briefing is also available for commanders from the Web site, and a hotline has also been set up. West, the Pentagon Special Assistant, believes that if the educational infrastructure in place now had been ready at the outset, the problem could have been taken care of early on.

Still, the Pentagon refuses to acknowledge any negative impact the vaccine policy may have had on military readiness. Trying to get a handle on retention problems in the Reserve, the Pentagon recently sent out an extensive questionnaire to reservists about why they left the Reserve. The survey did not contain a single question on anthrax.

One conclusion DOD leaders across the board seemed to have gained from the whole experience is that where leadership in the field was strongest, implementation of the policy was smoothest. But, even in the best of circumstances, the problems "never got to zero" because "there is somebody out there working against our purposes," West said.[28]

Notes

1. Rod Hafemeister, "Pilot: Others Told Him They Became Ill," *Belleville News-Democrat*, April 24, 2000, p. A1.

2. Ernest T. Takafuji and Philip K. Russell, "Military Immunizations: Past, Present, and Future Prospects," *Infectious Diseases Clinics of North America*, Vol. 4, No. 1, March 1990, pp. 149–50.

3. http://www.anthrax.osd.mil/.

4. Ibid.

5. Hafemeister, "Pilot: Others Told Him They Became Ill."

6. The testimony of pilots in the squadron was given to the House Government Reform and Oversight Committee in a public hearing on October 11, 2000.

7. Heemstra's entire account is provided in testimony to the House Committee on Government Reform on October 11, 2000.

8. Eliot Marshall, "Anthrax Vaccine Begins a New Round of Tests," *Science*, January 18, 2002, pp. 427–8.

9. See http://www.anthrax.osd.mil for more details on side effects of the shot, and frequency of the side effects, for DOD troops who have had the shot.

10. Marohn's remarks were made in testimony to the House Committee on Government Reform on October 11, 2000.

11. Interview with the author, August 22, 2000.

12. Amy Forliti, *Associated Press*, October 11, 2000.

13. Quinn explained the entire episode in an August 18, 2000, interview with the author. After his stint on the *Lincoln*, he was promoted to rear admiral and put in charge of a carrier battle group based in Norfolk, VA. Quinn has since retired from the Navy and currently works for Northrop Grumman, a defense contractor.

14. Clemins discussed his views of the incident in a September 5, 2001, interview with the author. He retired from the Navy in 1999.

15. Interview with the author, August 16, 2000.

16. Ibid.

17. Interview with the author, September 20, 2000.

18. Colonel Richard A. Hersack, USAF, "The Anthrax Vaccine Debate: A Medical Review For Commanders," *The Counterproliferation Papers*, Future Warfare Series No. 10, USAF Counterproliferation Center, Air War College, Air War College, Air University, Maxwell Air Force Base, AL.

19. Fogleman interview.

20. Hamre interview.

21. Ibid.

22. William W. Taylor, S. Craig Moore, C. Robert Roll, Jr. "The Air Force Pilot Shortage: A Crisis for Operational Units?" Santa Monica, CA: RAND, 2000.

23. Kwaj-Cheun Chan, "Anthrax Vaccine: Preliminary Results of GAO's Survey of Guard Reserve Pilots and Aircrew Members," *General Accounting Office*, October 11, 2000.

24. West interview.

25. Hamre interview.

26. Thomas L. Rempher, "Why Am I Resisting the Vaccine? The Military Trained Me To," *Washington Post*, January 30, 2000, p. B1.

27. Thomas D. Williams, "Departing National Guard Troops Won't Receive Anthrax Vaccination," *Hartford Courant*, June 13, 2001.

28. West interview.

Homeland Security

JAMES BLANDIN

This case is divided into two parts. In part I, the class will be divided into three subgroups representing federal, state, and local government interests. These subgroups will prepare a coordinated response to the questions in Memo I posed by the National Security Advisor to the President dealing with Homeland Security *objectives, threats, and strategy.*

In part II of the case, the same three subgroups will develop an integrated federal, state, and local *organization plan* in response to the tasking provided in Memo II by the Director of the Office of Management and Budget (OMB). In order to develop this organization plan, the three subgroups will use the results that they generate in response to Memo I.

PART I: HOMELAND SECURITY OBJECTIVES, THREATS, AND STRATEGY

> *"... the security of the American homeland from the threats of the new century should be the primary national security mission of the U.S. government...*"[1]

It was 8:30 PM September 15, 2001. Margaret Claire, the Deputy to the National Security Advisor, sat at her desk looking out the window in the Old Executive Office Building. Her life and the lives of her fellow citizens had changed forever as a result of the events of September 11.

A new wave of terrorism, involving new weapons, posed a security challenge unlike any ever faced by our nation. Since September 11, two truths were emerging from a series of seemingly unending meetings she had been attending. First, the very characteristics of American life that we so value—our freedom and openness—made us vulnerable to terrorism of catastrophic proportions. Second, the technological ability to launch attacks against civilian and military populations and infrastructure were increasing over time and were correlated with our economic growth and increasing interdependence both nationally and internationally.

It was clear that the need for homeland security was not tied to any specific terrorist threat. Instead, this need was part of our underlying vulnerability as a society and the uncertainty posed by our limited ability to be sure when or where the next terrorist act would occur. Not since World War II had our values and way of life been so threatened. This fact made securing the homeland a national priority.

Her boss had tasked Margaret Claire to coordinate the development of a combined federal, state, and local briefing for the president that would outline a plan to fight terrorism and secure the nation from future terrorist threats and attacks. Ultimately, she knew that this effort would involve major new programs as well as significant reforms by all levels of government. The plan would need to define what roles federal, state and local governments, industry, nongovernmental organizations and citizens should play to make our nation more secure. She began by outlining a tasking memorandum that would serve to focus the thinking of the best minds in the nation and lay the foundation for this integrated plan.

Memorandum I

From: National Security Advisor to the President

To: Combined Federal, State and Local Governmental Task Force on Homeland Security Objectives, Threats and Strategy

1. The president's most important job is to protect and defend the American people. Since September 11, all levels of government have cooperated like never before to strengthen aviation and border security, improve information sharing among our intelligence agencies, and deploy more resources and personnel to protect our critical infrastructure.

2. While the changing nature of the threats facing America will no doubt require major organizational change at all levels of government, we first need to think through a number of important strategic questions prior to turning our attention to the question of

organization. Government organizations are far too often guilty of starting to reorganize before fully understanding what should be done and, as a result, wind up doing the wrong things very efficiently.

3. As members of the Homeland Security Intergovernmental Working Group, I need your thinking on the following issues:

What do we want to achieve? How should we define the scope of Homeland Security in terms of security objectives? Are all objectives equally important or can priorities be established (e.g., borders, transportation, critical infrastructure, public health, intelligence information, detection, emergency response, etc.)?

What threats must we deal with? How can we define/characterize/classify the various threats that create risk for or threaten our homeland security? Are these threats equally problematic (e.g., weapons of mass destruction, cyber weapons, use of conventional weapons, etc.)?

What strategy should we adopt? Our strategy should help guide us in allocating our scarce resources among the many (abundant) alternative uses (programs). The strategy should be comprehensive in that it probably will contain offensive (e.g., prevention) as well as defensive (e.g., detection) elements.

4. Finally, let me thank each one of you for your willingness to serve on this working group. By having input from senior representatives from federal, state, and local government organizations, the president will receive the most comprehensive advice on these vital issues.

PART II: ORGANIZING FOR HOMELAND SECURITY

> We trained hard, but it seemed that every time we were beginning to
> form up into teams, we would be reorganized. I learned later in life
> that we tend to meet any new situation by reorganization, and a
> wonderful method it can be for creating the illusion of progress while
> producing confusion, inefficiency and demoralization.
>
> —Petronius Arbiter, 210 B.C.

At the Office of Management and Budget (OMB)

Kathryn was about ready to blow her stack. She closed her eyes for a moment and opened them again only to find the pages of press clippings were still on her desk. Her blood pressure must be at least 160/95 and headed up . . . a little biofeedback was in order but she had no time for that now. She scanned through the clippings[2] again . . .

"I think this idea of a Homeland Security Department is going to be very difficult to do. There's jurisdictional rivalry that goes on at every level, at every committee."

"I don't think you can do anything effectively without a starting point and that starting point is the threat. Assessing vulnerabilities is important but an effective strategy must be connected to the threat."

"The administration, which is full of business executives, might do well to borrow private sector techniques. They need to have a coherent assessment of risk versus security-value added."

"Just because you move all of these agencies and functions into one department doesn't mean that you are going to be any more effective . . ."

"He needs to have authority to approve the budgets of all agency counterterrorism programs. If he ends up with a small staff and simply generates ideas, he will be nothing but a speakers' bureau on terrorism."

"The issues here are so complex and the threat is so difficult to anticipate, nobody really wants to be responsible for the big picture. Instead, you have a very fragmented system with different people taking bite-size pieces of the problem. What are we preparing for? That's the real problem—nobody knows for sure. I can promise you nobody in this business anticipated the events of September 11."

"There is a natural tendency in each agency to protect their jurisdiction. While loyalty is an important quality necessary to the esprit of any organization, it can often inhibit cooperation necessary to any team effort. The first loyalty should be to the President but absent specific authority to enforce that control, that principle is often forgotten."

"The issue is whether we follow the National Security Council model, or the drug czar model."

"It is impossible to establish a clear mission and set of objectives without a strong leader having authority from the President and Congress."

"You know and I know there is a strong instinct to protect information relating to national security and the result is often times poor communication of vital information."

"Money is the lifeblood of each department. Unless there is a single individual with authority and responsibility for funding and budgets, departments will go after their own money whether or not it fits the overall strategy of homeland security."

"This is the biggest federal reorganization since 1947, the year Truman combined the armed services into the Defense Department. Before Truman's effort had any effect on military coordination, it spawned the mother of all turf wars. Not only did defense reorganization fail to end inter-service rivalry, it did almost nothing to improve joint military operations."

"Look, one thing that we have learned from past large-scale reorganizations is that they work best when they are directed by the agencies that will have to live with them."

"This will revolutionize the decades-old divisions of labor between the various parts of American government: between federal and local, intelligence and law enforcement, military and civilian, and above all foreign and domestic. There is no clear "at home" or "abroad" anymore."

Kathryn needed to pull together the guidance for the first in a series of meetings with the Combined Federal, State and Local Governmental Task Force on Homeland Security Organization. She found it both amusing and annoying that everyone inside and outside the Beltway seemed to want to voice his or her expert opinion on how "the cow should eat the corn" as her boss put it. This had been going on for the past week, ever since word leaked out that the administration was working on the most extensive reorganization in fifty years. What an exciting time to be in government service!

Memorandum II

From: Director, Office of Management and Budget

To: Combined Federal, State and Local Governmental Task Force on Homeland Security Organization.[3]

As you know, I have been tasked by the president to pull together a series of recommendations on how best to organize the national Homeland Security effort. We will use your previous efforts in response to Memo I for this current effort.

I want to thank you again for your willingness to serve in this historic effort to define a reorganized government capable of delivering homeland security to the American people. Our goal is to develop an organization structure that will be able to effectively and efficiently accomplish the critical homeland security objectives by creating a unified sense of purpose and action between the levels and agencies of government involved with this major undertaking.

As you know, American democracy is rooted in the precepts of federalism—a system of government in which our state governments share power with federal institutions. Our structure of overlapping federal, state, and local governance, some 87,000 different jurisdictions, provides unique opportunities and challenges for our homeland security efforts.

The challenge before us is to develop interconnected and complimentary systems that are reinforcing rather than duplicative and that ensure essential requirements are met. A national strategy requires a national effort.

State and local governments have critical roles to play in homeland security. They have primary responsibility for funding, preparing, and operating emergency services that would respond in the event of a terrorist attack. All disasters are ultimately local events.

The private sector, owner of 85 percent of our infrastructure, is also a key homeland security partner. Its creative genius will develop the information systems, vaccines, detection devices, and other technologies and innovations that will secure our homeland.

The president looks forward to receiving your recommendations on how best to organize, consolidate, coordinate, and integrate our federal, state, and local efforts as well as how we should allocate authority and responsibility for the vital tasks ahead.

Notes

1. "Roadmap for National Security: Imperative for Change," *U.S. Commission on National Security/21st Century Phase III Report*, February 15, 2001, p. 10.

2. Quotes taken from the following sources: Budget and Program Newsletter, 6/7/02; http://www.nationaljournal.com, 8/10/02; 2/09/02; 10/20/01; Government Executive 11/2001; 9/2002; http://www.nationaljournal.com/members/markups/2002/07/200220612.htm; http://www.montereyherald.com, 5/12/02.

3. For further detail consult John R. Brinkerhoff, "Reorganizing Is *Not* the Solution for Homeland Security," at http://www.homelandsecurity.org/journal/Articles/BrinkerhoffReorg.html.

Index

About the Contributors

ANDREW J. BACEVICH is professor of international relations at Boston University where he also serves as director of the University's Center for International Relations.

WILLIAM C. BANKS is a member of the faculty of the Syracuse University College of Law and Professor of Public Administration in the Maxwell School of Citizenship and Public Affairs. He has published numerous articles, book chapters, and books including *National Security Law and the Power of the Purse* (Oxford University Press, 1994); *Constitutional Law: Structure and Rights in Our Federal System,* 4th Ed. (Matthew Bender, 2000); *National Security Law,* 2d Ed. (Little Brown, 1997). Professor Banks' current research interests include the creation and implementation of administrative law reforms in China, domestic and international terrorism, emergency powers, war powers, and appropriations powers.

JAMES BLANDIN is Professor of Management, Naval Postgraduate School. Dr. Blandin has been a consultant to the Under Secretary of Defense (Comptroller), the Center for Naval Analysis, the Defense Security Assistance Agency, and the Joint Staff (J-5). During his career at the Naval Postgraduate School, he has held a number of management positions including Executive Director, DRMI (1983–92); Director, Center for Civil-Military Relations (1992–96); and Dean of Management and Security Studies (1995–97). He is currently a Fellow at Syracuse University's Maxwell Center for Advanced Public Management where he additionally serves on the Board of Advisors for the National Security Studies Program.

ARTHUR C. BROOKS is an Associate Professor of Public Administration at Syracuse University's Maxwell School of Citizenship and Public Affairs, where he teaches courses in economics and nonprofit management. His research focuses on nonprofit organizations, philanthropy, and national security.

ELIOT A. COHEN is Professor of Strategic Studies at the Paul H. Nitze School of Advanced International Studies, Johns Hopkins University. Dr. Cohen taught in the Department of Government at Harvard University for several years and has also taught in the Strategy Department of the U.S. Naval War College. He is the author and co-author of numerous books and articles, including *Military Misfortunes* (with John Gooch, Anchor Books, 1991), and directed the U.S. Air Force's official study of the 1991 Gulf War.

SCOTT DOUGLAS is a graduate of the Paul H. Nitze School of Advanced International Studies, Johns Hopkins University, and is currently completing his doctoral studies on a faculty fellowship with Columbia University's Department of Political Science. His particular interests are the post–Cold War use of coercive air power and the states of the former Yugoslavia.

VOLKER C. FRANKE is Associate Professor of Political Science and International Studies at McDaniel College in Westminster, Maryland. Dr. Franke also serves as Director and Managing Editor of the Maxwell/SAIS National Security Studies Case Studies Program. He is the author of *Preparing for Peace: Military Identity, Value-Orientations, and Professional Military Education* (Praeger, 1999) and numerous journal articles on social identity, peace and security studies and military socialization. He is also the editor of *Security in a Changing World: Case Studies in U.S. National Security Management* (Praeger, 2002).

THOMAS A. KEANEY is the Executive Director of the Foreign Policy Institute and Senior Adjunct Professor of Strategic Studies at the Paul H. Nitze School of Advanced International Studies, Johns Hopkins University, Washington, DC. He has previously written on the effects of air power in the Gulf War.

W. HENRY LAMBRIGHT is Professor of Political Science and Public Administration and Director of the Center for Environmental Policy and Administration at the Maxwell School, Syracuse University, where he teaches courses on environmental policy and science and technology policy. His writings include numerous books, articles, and reports. His most recent book is *Powering Apollo: James E. Webb of NASA* (Johns Hopkins, 1995). His current research projects include analyzing results from a National Science Foundation/American Association for the Advancement of Science grant to study research competitiveness in universities and states within the United States and a project for NASA looking at "Space Policy in the 21st Century."

LAURENCE POPE is a 31-year veteran of the U.S. Foreign Service. He was involved with Iraq policy as the State Department's office director for Iran and Iraq from 1987–90, and as Associate Coordinator for Counter-Terrorism (1991–93). He has also served as Ambassador to Chad, and as political advisor to CENTCOM. Since retiring from the Foreign Service, Ambassador Pope has worked as Staff Director for the International Fact-Finding Committee on the Middle East headed by former Senator George Mitchell, and as a senior advisor at the U.S. Mission to the UN.

JUSTIN REED is a recent graduate of McDaniel College where he served as research assistant in the Department of Political Science and International Studies.

JOHN ROBINSON is the managing editor of *Defense Daily*. He has been at the publication for over fourteen years, during which he has covered all the military services, the Missile Defense Agency and Congress, as well as military operations in Somalia, Bosnia, and Jordan. Mr. Robinson holds an M.A. from the Johns Hopkins University School of Advanced International Studies (SAIS) and a B.A. in Government from the University of Notre Dame. Robinson is also a lieutenant in the Navy Reserves.

JEFFREY D. STRAUSSMAN is Associate Dean and Chair of the Department of Public Administration at the Maxwell School of Citizenship and Public Affairs, Syracuse University. He specializes in government budgeting and public management and has published widely in a variety of professional journals. Professor Straussman was a Fulbright Scholar in Budapest, Hungary in 1992 and is very active internationally on behalf of the Maxwell School.

THEODORE S. WILKINSON joined the U.S. Foreign Service in 1961 and served at a number of American embassies in Europe and Latin America, at NATO, and at the UN. He was President of the American Foreign Service Association from 1989 through 1991, then Minister Counselor for Political Affairs in Mexico and in Brazil. From 1996 until 1998 he was the U.S. member of the Guarantors' Commission in Brasilia supporting peace negotiations between Peru and Ecuador.